HARD HATS, REDNECKS, AND MACHO MEN

HARD HATS, REDNECKS, AND MACHO MEN

Class in 1970s American Cinema

DEREK NYSTROM

OXFORD
UNIVERSITY PRESS

2009

OXFORD
UNIVERSITY PRESS

Oxford University Press, Inc., publishes works that further
Oxford University's objective of excellence
in research, scholarship, and education.

Oxford New York
Auckland   Cape Town   Dar es Salaam   Hong Kong   Karachi
Kuala Lumpur   Madrid   Melbourne   Mexico City   Nairobi
New Delhi   Shanghai   Taipei   Toronto

With offices in
Argentina   Austria   Brazil   Chile   Czech Republic   France   Greece
Guatemala   Hungary   Italy   Japan   Poland   Portugal   Singapore
South Korea   Switzerland   Thailand   Turkey   Ukraine   Vietnam

Published by Oxford University Press, Inc.
198 Madison Avenue, New York, New York 10016

www.oup.com

Oxford is a registered trademark of Oxford University Press.

Library of Congress Cataloging-in-Publication Data
Nystrom, Derek.
Hard hats, rednecks, and macho men : class in 1970s American cinema / Derek Nystrom.
    p.   cm.
Includes bibliographical references and index.
ISBN 978-0-19-533676-4; 978-0-19-533677-1 (pbk.)
1. Working class in motion pictures.   2. Rednecks in motion pictures.
3. Men, White in motion pictures.   4. Masculinity in motion pictures.
5. Motion pictures—United States—History—20th century.   I. Title.
PN1995.9.L28N97 2009
791.45'6352623097309047—dc22   2008048396

Printed in the United States of America
on acid-free paper

ACKNOWLEDGMENTS

This project first came to life as a dissertation and benefited immeasurably from the generous attention I received from my dissertation committee. Rita Felski offered me not only her expert and discerning grasp of cultural theory but also an immense amount of support and encouragement for this project from its earliest stages to its transformation into a book manuscript. Eric Lott combined his deep knowledge of American cultures of class with his persistent good humor and enthusiasm, expanding my understanding of class consciousness (and the class unconscious) while spurring me toward a more engaging and direct prose style. Sara Blair kept forcing me to address questions that I often hoped would go away if I just ignored them, questions that ended up reshaping this project very much for the better. In addition, Johanna Drucker, Richard Maltby, Fred Maus, Richard Handler, Scott Saul, and Jennifer Wicke all offered valuable advice along the way. This book was also vastly improved by the feedback of many of my fellow graduate students at the University of Virginia, including Bill Albertini, Scott Cohen, Karlyn Crowley, Eric Duryea, Brady Earnhart, Daylanne English, Mike Furlough, Tom Kane, Ben Lee, Heather Love, Mike Millner, Ana Mitric, Brenna Munro, Danielle Pelfrey, Kent Puckett, Megan Raymond, Kim Roberts, Lisi Schoenbach, Danny Siegel, Mason Stokes, Bryan Wagner, Rod Waterman, and Dona Yarbrough. They also provided a model of intellectual community and comradely spirit that I feel incredibly lucky to have experienced.

I am equally lucky to have found wonderful colleagues at McGill University. Erin Hurley and Ned Schantz have now read multiple versions of this book, and their comments and advice have been crucial in helping me to reframe, rewrite, and refine the manuscript. Their tireless collegial support—and Ned's endlessly ingenious responses to the films in question—made this process a deeply pleasurable one as well. Jenny Burman, Carrie Rentschler, and Janine Wiles offered careful readings of different chapters that enabled me to sharpen and clarify my arguments. Wes Folkerth cheerfully lent his computer expertise in corralling the illustrations. This book was also enriched by the great conversations I had at McGill with the amazing students in my courses on 1970s American cinema and on class and labor in post–World War II U.S. film and literature. One of these students, Pascal Emmer, also served as my research assistant in the summer of 2004; his work greatly aided my redrafting of the book's final chapters.

I am grateful to the anonymous readers at Oxford University Press, who posed a series of important questions about this book's argument and as a result made it stronger. Working with Shannon McLachlan, meanwhile, has been a delight, especially since she played such a formative role in this project's inception. I am glad to call Shannon not just my editor but also my dear friend. I also very much appreciate Brendan O'Neill and Gwen Colvin's patience with me as I fussed over various last-minute details.

Around the time I started work on this project, I took part in the formation of the Labor Action Group, an activist organization made up of students, faculty, and staff at the University of Virginia dedicated to creating the political space for university workers to assert their voices and their rights in the University's otherwise hostile, antilabor environment. I am intensely proud of the achievements of this group, which included the establishment of living wage laws in the City of Charlottesville and their near equivalent at the University, and the affiliation of groups of university workers and graduate students with the Communication Workers of America. Through my involvement with this group, I learned a great deal about the difficulties of establishing alliances between the working and professional-managerial classes. More than that, though, I learned of the absolute necessity of such alliances. It is my hope that this book can contribute to the essential political task of imagining cross-class solidarity.

Finally, I want to thank Manon Desrosiers, my favorite person to watch movies with.

This book is dedicated to my parents, Karen and Richard Nystrom, for their support, their wisdom, and their love.

A shorter version of chapter 1 appeared in *Cinema Journal* 43.3 (Spring 2004) under the title "Hard Hats and Movie Brats: Auteurism and the Class Politics of the New Hollywood." I thank them for their permission to reprint it here.

It is something of a commonplace in both popular and scholarly film histories that the American cinema of the 1970s is especially revealing of its social and political context. According to these accounts, an industry in disarray that threw open its doors to a new generation of filmmakers produced, almost in spite of itself, a cinema that addressed and grappled with the controversies of its time in a manner that has few precedents in the history of American film. Indeed, as the title of David Cook's *History of the American Cinema* volume[1] on the decade suggests, these films frequently evoked the lost illusions wrought by the Vietnam War and the Watergate scandal, speaking not only to the debacles of U.S. foreign and domestic policy but also to the failure of liberal-left dissent and countercultural resistance to prevent them. This dark, pessimistic vision can be traced through such works as *Little Big Man's* (1970) anti-Western, *The French Connection's* (1971) drama of urban decay, *Chinatown's* (1974) neo-noir about civic and personal corruption, *The Parallax View's* (1974) paranoid thriller, *Nashville's* (1975) cynical commentary on the American culture industry, and *The Deer Hunter's* (1978) melodrama of lost national manhood. To tell these kinds of stories, American films of the 1970s took advantage of the new freedoms unleashed both inside and outside of the film industry, as the scrapping of the Production Code and concomitant liberation of public discourse enabled a cinema that could render more directly and viscerally the tumult of the period. Even the eventual collapse of the "Hollywood Renaissance" of 1967–1976 can be read as an indicator of the political reaction and retrenchment that marked the close of the 1970s: the displacement of the often politically adventurous, art cinema-inspired, character-driven personal films of early 1970s auteurs by the consensus-oriented, spectacle-heavy corporate cinema of the later 1970s blockbusters (*Jaws* [1975], *Star Wars* [1977]) comes to appear as a kind of allegory for the Reaganite foreclosing on any hopes for 1960s-inspired social change.[2]

Martin Scorsese's *Taxi Driver* (1976), surely one of the most canonical films of the period, can be read as an exemplar of these dynamics. The film's protagonist, Travis Bickle (Robert De Niro), is a damaged Vietnam vet whose alienation and eventual descent into violence suggests a return of the war's horrors onto native soil. Travis's first love interest, Betsy (Cybill Shepherd), works on a presidential campaign that traffics in a sense of democracy thwarted by war and corruption, yet the candidate himself, Charles Palantine (Leonard Harris), is merely a hollow suit whose progressive populism is depicted as opportunistic at best. Iris (Jodie Foster), the drug-addled twelve-year-old prostitute that Travis decides to "save," appears as a nightmare vision of countercultural excess gone wrong, while Scorsese's virtuoso expressionist sequences depicting nighttime New York as a kind of hell on earth signify a more widespread breakdown in the social order. *Taxi Driver* tested the limits of the decade's new cinematic freedoms with its hyperviolent climax, during which Travis storms Iris's brothel and massacres everyone in his path. The perverse resurgence of what Reagan's political descendants would call "family values," meanwhile, is suggested by the film's ironic denouement, as Travis's psychotic rampage is celebrated by the press and praised by Iris's middle-American parents, who thank Travis in a letter asserting that they have "taken steps" to ensure that Iris never again strays from the family. This grim acknowledgment of the era's conservative backlash is echoed in the narrative of Scorsese's career. Despite the widespread critical and modest commercial success of *Taxi Driver*, Scorsese's status in Hollywood began to decline with his next film, *New York, New York* (1977), overshadowed as it was by another movie that opened on the same weekend, *Star Wars*. Although he went on to make a number of brilliant films in the next decade—such as *Raging Bull* (1980), a critical landmark but a commercial failure—Scorsese's challenging interrogations of the American obsession with masculinity and violence spent much of the 1980s consigned to the margins of the U.S. film industry.[3]

There is much that is persuasive in accounts like these that trace the connections between the era's cinema and its larger political dynamics. But they also seem to miss something important. For there is another narrative of social conflict that has gone largely unrecognized here: a narrative about class. Consider, for example, the relationship of Travis's working-class character to Betsy and to the campaign for which she works. Betsy's professional milieu is depicted in a way that emphasizes its difference from Travis's working conditions—the bright colors of her office are in marked contrast to the dark underworld in which Travis labors, while the witty, knowing banter between Betsy and her fellow campaign worker Tom (Albert Brooks) underlines the muddled, inarticulate dialogues Travis has with the other cabbies. (In fact, the scenes between Betsy and Tom seem to hail from a screwball comedy rather than the seething urban drama of Travis's gritty blue-collar struggles.) In this context, Travis and Betsy's brief mutual attraction turns on the class difference that each represents for the other—Betsy is the "angel" in a white dress who transcends the filth of the city, while Travis is the earthy "walking contradiction" that puzzles and fascinates her.

The presidential campaign for which Betsy works, moreover, claims to speak for working people and others ignored by the political process: "We are the people. We suffered. We were there. We the people suffered in Vietnam," Palantine declares, paraphrasing Walt Whitman in his stump speech. When Palantine meets Travis, who actually did suffer in Vietnam, he tries to cross the class boundaries that separate them by claiming, "I have learned more about America from riding in taxi cabs than in all the limos in the country." Yet Palantine is made visibly uncomfortable by Travis's vulgar rage when he tells Palantine that the president should clean up the "mess" of the city by "flush[ing] it right down the fucking toilet." (Betsy is similarly unsettled when Travis takes her to a pornographic film for their date.) Soon, Travis begins stalking Palantine's campaign events, and he comes close to assassinating him, before his violence is redirected toward Iris's pimp and customers. What *Taxi Driver* offers, then, is a complicated dance of desire, misrecognition, fear, and antagonism between its middle-class characters and its working-class protagonist; as the film's political professionals speak for and imagine an identification with the working masses ("We *are* the people," Palantine's slogan emphasizes), a member of those spoken-for masses engages in vigilante fantasies that target these same professionals.

Taxi Driver is not alone among American films of the 1970s in envisioning such a complex and vexed relationship between the professional middle class and the working class. *Hard Hats, Rednecks, and Macho Men* contends that a fundamental feature of the decade's cinema is its revelation of the crucial yet largely unacknowledged role class played in the major social, political, and cultural developments of the period. For example, while *Easy Rider* (1969) is frequently treated as a central cinematic rendering of the counterculture, this book maintains that in order to understand that film completely, one must pay special attention to the fact that its antiheroes are murdered by working-class men, who are depicted as the central enemies of the counterculture. Similarly, in order to grasp the rise of the New Right in U.S. political life during the 1970s—especially its consolidation of an economic and electoral power base in the South—one could do worse than screen the surprise hit of 1973, *Walking Tall*. But to appreciate fully *Walking Tall*'s tale of vigilante justice in a small southern town, one must note how the film's melodramatic appeal depends upon its vivid depictions of a working-class man's physical resistance to institutional authority. Finally, in order to get a handle on the massive upheavals in public and private life engendered by the women's and gay liberation movements, a good place to start might be the controversial films *Looking for Mr. Goodbar* (1977) and *Cruising* (1980). Something important about these films is missed, though, if one does not recognize that *Goodbar's* protagonist attempts to realize her protofeminist freedom by oscillating between a middle-class suitor and a working-class lover, while *Cruising's* powerful yet inscrutable affect derives largely from the iconography of working-class delinquency that characterizes its gay sado-masochistic setting. In other words, the American cinema of the 1970s tells us just how profoundly events like the fall of the counterculture and the rise of feminism were imagined *via* the rhetoric of class. To understand fully the period's central social and political developments, we must examine how this rhetoric of class operated in it.

This is not to say, of course, that American films of the 1970s are to be understood as mere reflections of the larger political landscape. Indeed, no one can look at the desaturated colors of the blood that is shed in *Taxi Driver's* hallucinatory orgy of violence and suppose that what is being presented is objective reality; the film—like all cultural productions—works over and reimagines the social materials that it confronts. What this book examines is the way that the films of the 1970s continually returned to the figure of the white, working-class male in order to articulate their cinematic rendering of the social world. And while I will argue that these depictions of white, blue-collar men were in many ways influenced by the contemporaneous activities of the actual working class, the characters are best understood as products of middle-class fantasy about that class. *Taxi Driver* may criticize Betsy and Senator Palantine for having a fantasized relationship to the working men they speak of and for, but the filmmakers—screenwriter Paul Schrader as well as Scorsese—were clearly operating under their own fantasies about an alleged working-class propensity for antisocial violence. Such cinematic fantasies prompt us to ask, what were the cultural investments behind this fascination with white, working-class men? What do the decade's films reveal about the class unconscious of the middle-class filmmakers who invented these characters, as well as the middle-class critics who evaluated and interpreted them for their (intended) middle-class audiences? In short, why was the middle class so transfixed by *this* figure at this time? In order to answer these questions—and thus gain a better understanding of the dramatic social changes of the period—we must look to the hard hats, rednecks, and macho men who filled the screens of the decade.

CONTENTS

HARD HATS, REDNECKS, AND MACHO MEN

INTRODUCTION

Making Class Visible in Film and Cultural Studies

The hard hats, rednecks, and macho men that became the objects of fascination for middle-class filmmakers, critics, and audiences in the 1970s appeared on the cinematic landscape during a pivotal period for Hollywood. Whether one focuses on industrial issues, such as capital investment, corporate ownership, and the organization of production, or textual questions on the development of postclassical film style and the shifting relationship between spectacle and narrative form, the 1970s mark a turning point in the history of American cinema. It was in the 1970s, for example, that Hollywood, after roughly a quarter century of corporate dis- and reorganization following the breakup of the old studio system, made the now-reigning regime of "flexible specialization" the standard model for film production.[1] The mid-1970s also gave birth to the New Hollywood, which established what Thomas Schatz calls the "blockbuster syndrome," in which high-budget, high-concept, saturation-booked, multimedia-marketed, spectacle-oriented films (such as *Jaws* [1975] and *Star Wars* [1977]) provided, as they continue to provide, the U.S. film industry with at least some of the economic stability it lost after the end of the old studio system.[2] Other critics, of course, emphasize an earlier, different New Hollywood, the so-called Hollywood Renaissance of Francis Ford Coppola, Martin Scorsese, Robert Altman, and others. For these critics, the years between 1967 and 1976 marked a brief but glorious time during which Hollywood produced a body of work as narratively, visually, and politically adventurous as that of the European art cinema—an aesthetic flowering that was cut down by the industry's shift to blockbuster filmmaking.[3] Interestingly, theorists of both New Hollywoods argue that the decade inaugurated the development of a "postclassical" mode of film style. Thomas Elsaesser suggested that the newly "experimental" (but still commercial) American films of the early 1970s were characterized by the displacement of classical Hollywood's goal-oriented hero, causally motivated narrative, and "invisible" cinematic style, while other critics focused on how later 1970s blockbusters diverged from classical Hollywood's focus on storytelling with what Warren Buckland describes as their "loosely-linked, self-sustaining action sequences" in which "narration is geared solely to the effective presentation of expensive effects."[4] In short, the 1970s was a time when Hollywood's method of producing motion pictures, and the very stories told by these pictures, underwent substantive changes.

One could offer an analogous story about the importance of the 1970s to the balance of class power in recent U.S. political economy. The worldwide economic slump that began in 1973, which ended what Eric Hobsbawm calls the "Golden Age" of the post–World War II boom years and inaugurated the ensuing "Crisis Decades," marked a watershed moment in U.S. class politics.[5] As labor historian and activist Kim Moody puts it, the 1970s was the decade during which "business organize[d] as a class." Largely setting aside their competitive interests vis-à-vis each other, U.S. businesses responded to the slump (and to increasing competition from foreign companies) by working together to thwart pro-labor legislation while promoting corporate-friendly changes in tax, regulatory, and antitrust law.[6] This concerted effort on the political front was matched by a shared economic strategy. Barry Bluestone and Bennett Harrison have described how "American corporate managers in the 1970s went to extraordinary lengths to shift capital as rapidly as possible, from one activity, one region, and one nation to another. In the process, the industrial base of the American economy began to come apart at the seams."[7] These strategies had the (intended) effect of disciplining the working class, a process that helped cause union membership to drop to only 16 percent of the private sector workforce by the end of the decade (compared to the postwar high of nearly 35 percent in 1953).[8] Mike Davis points out that these developments led to what he calls "the apparent hypertrophy of occupational positions in the United States associated with the supervision of labor, the organization of capital and the implementation of the sales effort."[9] The current lopsided balance of power between a triumphant, mobile capital and a weakened working class, along with the disproportionate growth and concomitant strength of the professional middle class, find their roots in the economic transformations of the 1970s.

Despite this concurrence of structural change in both Hollywood cinema and national class politics, though, film studies and American cultural studies have not yet explored the potential intersections of these two events. This is all the more perplexing since various film cycles of the decade treat class identity as a central feature of their characters. In one of the few essays to address class in 1970s American film, Peter Biskind and Barbara Ehrenreich point out that working-class men, who had heretofore mainly appeared "as enlisted men in World War II films...zoomed to individual prominence as the heroes of *Saturday Night Fever* [1977], *Blue Collar* [1978], *Bloodbrothers* [1978], *Rocky I and II* [1976, 1979], *Paradise Alley* [1978], *F.I.S.T.* [1978], and a handful of others."[10] To this list of working-class subjects, we can add the rednecks and good ole boys that are to be found in the dozens of films set in the South during the decade, the hard hats that found their way into some of the key films of the post–*Easy Rider* "youth cult" cycle, and the macho men who haunt the nightlife scenes of films like *Looking for Mr. Goodbar* (1977) and *Cruising* (1980).

It is the argument of this book that the new visibility of working-class characters in the 1970s was generated by a series of *middle-class* concerns and dilemmas. Much as representations of homosexuality are often more concerned with stabilizing heterosexual identity (or, for that matter, as images of blackness are frequently produced by white anxiety), the decade's cinematic renderings of white working-class masculinity tell us a great deal about the crises within what I will call the professional-managerial class (PMC) during this period. Sometimes posing as a figure of identification, sometimes as a disconcerting threat, the white, blue-collar men of these films ultimately signified, in a displaced fashion, widespread middle-class anxieties about class identity and class conflict. Indeed, the American films of the 1970s—produced in the midst of profound shifts in the national political and economic terrain, and during a period of aesthetic and industrial change in Hollywood—often testify to a vivid sense of class difference not seen since the 1930s. The fact that this difference has not yet been adequately explored by scholars tells us a great deal about the gaps in the critical frameworks of both film studies and American cultural studies. Interestingly enough, the story behind these disciplinary gaps also begins in the 1970s.

CLASS, *SCREEN* THEORY, AND THE BIRMINGHAM SCHOOL

Many critics have traced the relative dearth of work on class in film studies to the dominance of what came to be known as *Screen* theory (named after the British film journal), whose methodologies were largely derived from psychoanalysis, and whose primary concern was the question of sexual difference.[11] Yet it is important to note that the practitioners of *Screen* theory often claimed an affiliation with Marxism. As Stephen Heath put it, the explosion of film theory that took place in *Screen* during the 1970s promised an understanding of film spectatorship that engaged "Marxism and psychoanalysis on the terrain of semiotics."[12] Following the work of Louis Althusser, who utilized the Lacanian categories of the Imaginary, Symbolic, and Real to offer a Marxist account of ideology that acknowledged the specificity and relative autonomy of various signifying practices (including film production), the film theorists associated with *Screen* often declared that their interrogations of "how systems of representation inscribe (ideological) positions" contributed to the Marxist project of deconstructing bourgeois ideology.[13] In practice, though, the class analysis of this work rarely moved beyond diagnosing the ways in which dominant cinema constructed for its spectator an allegedly bourgeois subject position of imaginary coherence, plenitude, and mastery.[14] By aligning the formal realism of Hollywood films with larger traditions of classical realism, the Brecht-influenced *Screen* theorists sought to demonstrate how dominant cinema engaged in "a mode of representation coterminous with bourgeois society, a mode working to sustain a position for the transcendental or Cartesian ego—the bourgeois ego therefore."[15] Yet, as even defenders of *Screen*'s contributions to Marxism admitted, such analysis only addressed "modes of representation...on an *epochal* scale,"[16] leaving questions of less epochal and more historically specific class dynamics unanswered.

The attraction of Lacanian psychoanalysis to film theorists is quite understandable given Lacan's emphasis on various specular relations—the mirror stage, the gaze, the look, and so on—which provide a tempting set of metaphors for film analysis. Furthermore, with its focus on the patriarchal family and the dynamics of gender and sexual identity formation, psychoanalytic thought proved much more generative for feminist as opposed to Marxist theory. It is not surprising, then, that its adoption by the *Screen* theorists and related practitioners catalyzed a virtual renaissance in feminist film theory that continued into the 1980s and 1990s, forming the dominant locus of theoretical activity in film studies. And, despite its tendency to ignore questions of class, it is hard to overestimate the achievements of feminist film theory as a form of ideological and cultural analysis. It is now de rigueur to disparage the rigidity of Laura Mulvey's formulation of the "male gaze" in her watershed 1975 essay "Visual Pleasure and Narrative Cinema," but the theoretical work that has built upon this polemical salvo has been, at its best, enormously productive in its insights and frequently self-reflexive about its own critical assumptions. The investigations of this theoretical tradition into the processes of spectatorial identification, the interactions between narrative and visual form, the production of pleasure and its political consequences, and the relationship between textual modes of address and social contexts of reception all provide a wealth of tools for non-gender-based film analysis. Yet despite the later efforts of film theory to move beyond both the paradigms of psychoanalysis[17] and the parameters of gender and sexuality,[18] the mechanisms of class difference—quite unanalogous to those of sexual difference—have remained largely unexplored.

Still, the achievements and philosophical sophistication of feminist film theory might explain why this mode of analysis took precedence over other, contemporaneous efforts to construct a class-oriented film theory—efforts which, in the United States, took place in journals such as *Jump Cut* and *Cineaste*. While there is, to be sure, some genuinely compelling work in this body of writing, the predominant form of inquiry in these journals tended to be of the "images of…" school of analysis. Cinematic representations of workers were evaluated based on the "realism" (or lack thereof) of the portrayal, and the ideological work of such representations was understood to be more or less instrumental, the corporate-guided inculcation of false consciousness.[19] In other words, during the 1970s and 1980s, there was no theoretical revolution in class-based theory in film studies to match what was happening in gender-oriented film theory. For exciting developments in Marxist cultural theory, one needed to look outside film studies, and toward Birmingham, to the rise of British cultural studies.

The story of the formation of British cultural studies has been told many times, and I will not attempt to offer a synopsis here.[20] What I will empha- size is its early concern with developing a nonreductionist account of class formation and identity, and the ways in which this concern dissipated as the cultural studies model was adopted in the U.S. academy. Following upon the groundbreaking works on British working-class culture and politics by Richard Hoggart, Raymond Williams, and E. P. Thompson, col- lective projects from the Birmingham Center, such as *Resistance Through Rituals* and *Working-Class Culture*, as well as individually authored books like Paul Willis's *Learning to Labour*, all attempted to theorize contemporary articulations of class identity (particularly working-class identity) in light of the shifting material circumstances of class formation in postwar Great Britain. Take, for example, Phil Cohen's analysis of the mods, a subculture of working-class adolescent males who fetishized Italian suits, American R&B, and Vespa scooters. A reductive Marxist account might characterize this consumerist practice as an example of false consciousness, in which working-class youth are distracted from their "true" class identity by the commodity culture in which they have been interpellated. Cohen instead describes how this deployment of affluent style by the mods can be under- stood not only as a response to their complicated class location—as chil- dren of working-class parents who are situated in a reorganized educational system that encourages middle-class aspiration—but also as a gesture of rebellion against both the working-class culture of their parents' generation as well as the "proper" use of these commodities as ordained by dominant culture.[21] Such an account refuses to ascribe a necessary or authentic rela- tionship between economic class location and cultural practices by recog- nizing the productive (and relatively autonomous) role of these practices in articulating class identity. Furthermore, this sort of analysis highlights the complexity of class formation: its multiple sites of determination (school, family, and marketplace, in addition to the site of production) and the many ways in which class identity is constituted with and through other identity categories, especially generation, gender, and race.[22] In short, British cultural studies from the 1970s and early 1980s provided a theoretically sophisticated and methodologically attentive approach to understanding both the complex processes by which class subjects are formed and the cultural practices through which these subjects respond to, signify, and contest their class positioning.

This careful attention to the intricacies of class formation and identity, however, largely did not survive the trip over the Atlantic. I should acknowledge here the difficulty of discussing the American adaptation of cultural studies, since the term now frequently refers to a wide range of academic practices, and more often than not, as Rita Felski observes, is used "simply [as] shorthand for political approaches to literature"[23] (and, I would add, any study of popular culture, whatever its methodology). Yet one can specify an initial wave of U.S. cultural studies, dating from roughly the mid-1980s, that claimed an affiliation with British cultural studies, and that was often practiced by actual Brits (such as John Fiske and Andrew Ross) and Americans who had studied in Birmingham (like Lawrence Grossberg)—all of whose work would be influential in defining the field for American audiences. At the risk of overgeneralizing the diverse (and often illuminating) writings of these and other early U.S. cultural studies practitioners, it is fair to say that their analyses tended to emphasize the active and productive nature of the interpretive work engaged in by consumers of popular culture without specifying the class positions from which this engagement occurred. To take just one example, note the vagueness of social referent for "the people" in Fiske's claim that "hegemonic force can be exercised only if the people choose to read the texts that embody it, and they will choose only those texts that offer opportunities to resist, evade, or scandalize it."[24] As Meaghan Morris noted, in the work of Fiske and others, "'the people' have no necessary defining characteristics—except an indomitable capacity to 'negotiate' readings, generate new interpretations, and remake the materials of culture."[25] Furthermore, even in scholarship more carefully attuned to the complexity of class position and identity, such as Ross's *No Respect: Intellectuals and Popular Culture*, the class antagonisms investigated were primarily those articulated in expressions of taste. As a result, the ensuing discussions of such antagonisms too often reproduced the more reductive moments of Pierre Bourdieu's work in positing a dominant, "bourgeois" regime of taste, against which is opposed an insolent, disrespectful (and hence resistive) working-class culture. In other words, the first wave of

U.S. cultural studies either eschewed class analysis entirely—preferring to describe cultural struggle along the vaguely defined lines of "the people" vs. "the power bloc"[26]—or, when it did discuss class cultures, utilized a simplistic, binary understanding of class structure and posited a direct, one-to-one relationship between class position and its cultural expression.

UNDERSTANDING THE "NEW" MIDDLE CLASS

This reductive form of class analysis, or the wholesale evasion of the topic, is particularly disconcerting given the profusion of insightful work on the complexities of class formation undertaken by U.S. and British sociologists in the 1970s and 1980s—that is, at about the same time as the renaissance of psychoanalytic theory in film studies. (Indeed, the relative inattention of cultural studies to neo-Marxist sociological work on class is a telling blind spot in its ostensibly inter- and transdisciplinary vision.) The "resurgence of Marxist theorizing on the problem of class" undertaken by these sociologists, Erik Olin Wright explains, had as its impetus "what might be termed the 'embarrassment' of the middle class" (which is to say, the embarrassment of their continued existence).[27] This social grouping, which, according to traditional Marxism, was supposed to disappear with the polarization of class structure under capitalism, had not only persisted but actually grown, changed shape, and taken on what seem to be central roles in the functioning of advanced capitalist societies. In an effort to explain these developments while still acknowledging the fundamental contradiction between capital and labor, Marxist theorists such as Nicos Poulantzas, Adam Przeworski, Guglielmo Cardechi, Erik Olin Wright, and Barbara and John Ehrenreich offered complex maps of class position, which suggested how people can find themselves situated in these positions in multiple, even contradictory ways. Again, I will not attempt to summarize here the extensive, sometimes arcane debates that this theoretical conversation engendered. However, since my project is fundamentally concerned with diagnosing the middle-class anxieties and dilemmas that shaped American cinema in the 1970s, I do want to note two key conceptualizations from these debates that will be central to this book's understanding of the middle class. As I will note in a moment, these two formulations of the middle class are in tension with each other; however, I will suggest that this tension is indicative of the difficulties in theorizing middle-class formation and identification.

The first conceptualization is best described through the Ehrenreichs' definition of the middle class as the professional-managerial class (or PMC), which consists of "salaried mental workers who do not own the means of production and whose major function in the social division of labor may be described broadly as the reproduction of capitalist culture and capitalist class relations."[28] Situated "between labor and capital," members of this class engineer, administer, and supervise the workplace as well as produce and sustain the ideological superstructures—such as the legal and educational systems, the mass media, and various state apparatuses—which help ensure (in a highly mediated way) popular consent to capitalist relations of production. As such, the PMC has an "objectively antagonistic" relationship to the working class, the Ehrenreichs argue, in that its role is one of directing and controlling labor in order to benefit the interests of capital. Yet the PMC also often finds itself at odds with the capitalist class, especially over issues of occupational autonomy and technocratic reform. As a result, the PMC has developed over its short history certain strains of anticapitalist thought and action, although the relationship between these currents and other, more familiar working-class-based forms of socialism has been a vexed one.

The second, related theorization of the middle class that informs this book is Wright's description of the middle class as a set of "contradictory class locations."[29] Wright argues that class relations can be defined along two axes, those of "property or ownership relations and possession or control relations"—more concisely, axes of "exploitation" and "domination."[30] Managers, therefore, can be described as occupying a capitalist-class position by virtue of their domination of the working class, even as they are located in a working-class position due to the fact that they do not own and control the means of production. Similarly, professionals can be said to be petty bourgeois in their control over their labor process, while also a part of the proletariat because they must sell their labor to capital. In general, then, the middle class is conceived by Wright as a series of contradictory locations whose political affiliations and allegiances may be—and often are—oriented and mobilized in a number of different directions.

Both models of the middle class open up the binary oppositions of the (generally implicit) class theory of most U.S. cultural studies. For example, the Ehrenreichs' attention to the middle class's occasional antagonisms to capital, despite its structural role in serving its interests, illuminates the ways in which this class's deployment of cultural capital not only serves to distinguish it from the working class but also frequently functions to establish its prerogatives against those of capital. Furthermore, Wright's analysis of the ways in which managers and professionals may find themselves, in different moments, aligned with either capital or labor indicates the "multiple possible coalitions" that may coalesce around various middle class positions.[31] More importantly, both models point to how middle-class identity is frequently understood and articulated through the signifiers of its class others, as the middle class's shifting antagonisms and alliances encourage various imagined connections with other classes and class fractions. These theoretical accounts deeply inform my analysis of the professional middle class's efforts to read its class situation through filmic representations of the working class—a class that sometimes offers a site of identification for the middle class, while in other moments signals a threat to its authority.

While not uncontroversial, both Wright's and the Ehrenreichs' models have been influential in shaping subsequent understandings of the middle class. However, it does bear noting that they also present some conflicting claims: the Ehrenreichs argue that the PMC is a separate class—one whose functions and interests cannot be reduced to those of either capital or labor—while Wright insists that the middle class is better understood as a contradictory mix of capital and labor positions. Of course, Wright's description of the contradictory roles of the middle class is not inherently opposed to the Ehrenreichs' theorization of the PMC; in fact, the Ehrenreichs' position is in large part motivated by an interest in the ways in which the middle class may find itself allied, at different moments, with capital or labor. The differences between these two ways of describing the middle class hinge largely on the question of how to describe its role in capitalist relations of production, but whether this role constitutes a fundamental reorganization of these relations or merely a modification of the original capital-labor dialectic is a question that is not central to this book's argument. Nevertheless, I am foregrounding these issues because they point to the ways in which the middle class, as John Frow argues, "constitute[s] a more or less coherent class in some respects but not in others; the new middle class...is an entity that doesn't respond well...to the question: is this a fully formed class?"[32] For example, due to their different functions and roles, some fractions of the middle class (such as social workers) are more likely to be antagonistic to capital than others (like chemical engineers). Similarly, these middle-class fractions operate according to differently inflected notions of occupational autonomy, endogenously determined workplace standards and ethics, and other key markers of professional and managerial authority. Thus, Frow contends that the modern middle class is best understood as *"weakly formed as a class."*[33]

It is for this and other reasons that will soon become clear that I will most often utilize the Ehrenreichs' appellation: the professional-managerial class. The hyphen between "professional" and "managerial" signals the multiple orientations of this class, as its different members find themselves located (and locate themselves) in various relations to capital and labor. But the hyphen also serves to remind us of the *connections* between these various middle-class occupations: social workers' labor may be guided by their disempowered clients' needs, yet their activities also serve to manage the population in the interests of a capitalist economy; chemical engineers may feel more at home with the bottom-line concerns of capital, yet their professionally inculcated standards will militate against cutting certain corners in order to sweeten the profit margin. Finally, the denomination PMC also highlights the occupational modalities that serve to distinguish the class from any easy assimilation into either capital or labor. To work in a profession is to claim a specialized knowledge that distinguishes one from other laborers. This specialized knowledge, though, cannot be handed down to one's offspring like other forms of capital; instead, it must be reearned by each generation. To work as a manager, meanwhile, is to claim authority over labor. Yet managers are managers *for* someone else, whose interests they must serve just as labor must. While these positions can be diagnosed, as Wright argues, for their capital- or labor-located instances, PMC members do not inhabit these instances in a sufficiently consistent fashion to take up any stable residence in them.

Given the PMC's structurally complex roles that place it between capital and labor, and the concomitant difficulty in drawing clear, sharp boundaries between the PMC and other classes, an account like Frow's that sees class identification as an ongoing process of class formation is all the more salient for my purposes. Following on the work of Nicos Poulantzas and Adam Przeworski, Frow argues that class is better understood not as "defined on the terrain of the economic but on each of the levels of economic, political, and ideological structure," for "ideological and political struggles constitute a process, not of class-*representation* (that is, representation of pre-given interests) but of class-*formation* (including the formation of class interests)."[34] Therefore, the practice of class analysis for cultural studies should not be one of first isolating an economically defined social group—a difficult task with respect to the PMC's variously oriented fractions—and then outlining its cultural practices as expressions of these economic interests. Instead, classes are to be grasped as defining themselves through their struggles in relation to other class groupings (class others that are themselves identified by their location in such struggles). These struggles are waged on the terrain of culture as often as they are at the site of economic production; in other words, while these processes of class formation are not "merely" discursive, they are also not solely the product of the economic sphere. Thus, the processes of class formation, as Frow suggests, are to be understood as "without absolute origin or telos" as they are "played out through particular institutional forms and balances of power, through calculations and miscalculations, through desires, and fears, and fantasies."[35]

In the same spirit, this book will treat various cinematic moments of the 1970s as instances of PMC class formation, which unfold as discursive struggles with a working class that is imagined through the desires, fears, and fantasies of the middle class. Through a consideration of the "youth-cult" film, the neo-Western "Southern," and the "new nightlife" film, I examine how these processes of class formation were shaped and informed by three key social and political developments of the decade (developments for which these film cycles[36] can be understood to be the cinematic analogues): (1) the cultural aftermath of the New Left and the counterculture; (2) the reconstruction of the post–civil rights South as the modernizing, industrializing Sunbelt; and (3) the women's and gay liberation movements. In other words, we can see the PMC as a social grouping whose identity—sometimes as a class in itself, sometimes as a class for itself—was reconstituted (and reconstituted itself) in response to these crucial events, largely through its collective imaginings of a working class and *its* (fantasized) relation to these events. In mapping these cinematic acts of class formation, I pay particular attention to the various collective actions of the working class during the decade—such as the so-called "hard hat riots" of May 1970 and the crippling nationwide trucker shutdowns of 1973 and 1974—which raised the specter of class division and antagonism that the professional middle class then needed to negotiate. These actions, of course, also draw our attention to the larger shifts in global political economy that established the terrain on which these class confrontations were played out. These film cycles, then, can be understood as cinematic responses to the various dilemmas for PMC authority and legitimacy posed by the social, political, and economic upheavals of the decade.

RACE, GENDER, AND THE MULTIPLE MOMENTS OF CINEMATIC CLASS FORMATION

These films of PMC class formation and articulation most often turn on the figure of the white, working-class male. There were, to be sure, films during the decade that featured nonwhite and/or female working-class protagonists. In the conclusion, I discuss three such films—*Blue Collar* (1978), *Norma Rae* (1979), and *9 to 5* (1980)—and examine how their visions of class diverge from that of the majority of 1970s films as a result of these differently positioned protagonists. For the most part, though, when American culture thinks of class—when it allows itself to imagine the possibility of class difference and class antagonism—it tends to be an affair between (white) men. In fact, Biskind and Ehrenreich argue that Hollywood's fascination with the working class in the 1970s was actually a fascination with a certain kind of masculinity—a defiant form of white ethnic *machismo* resistant to the challenges of the black, women's, and gay civil rights movements. What these films offer the middle-class viewer, Biskind and Ehrenreich suggest, is a form of male identity whose unreconstructed nature is to be surreptitiously enjoyed even as it is depicted to be ultimately untenable. That most of these working-class white men are also "ethnic"—that is, tied to a community of Irish, Italian, Polish, or other "Old World" nationalities—serves both to underline the outdated nature of their masculinity and to mark their whiteness as a particularized racial identity, one that differs from the supposedly unmarked norm of dominant whiteness. In doing so, the class position of these men is both naturalized—it appears as a quasi-racial identity—and transformed into a brand of masculine feeling, rather than a category of political economy. The decade's cinematic projections of an imagined working class, on this argument, are best understood as primarily dramas of masculinity and whiteness; they are films in which class, to invert Stuart Hall's maxim, is the modality in which race and gender are lived.[37]

In many ways, Biskind and Ehrenreich are correct. The class conflicts figured in the Southern cycle I examine in part II are deeply informed by the recent racial past of the South and the subsequent need to reconstruct both regional and white identity. Furthermore, the PMC fascination with working-class masculinity, which is a leitmotif of this book, comes into sharp focus in chapters 4 and 5, in which I discuss the importance of the working-class male body to a series of films that responded to the women's and gay liberation movements. However, if we attend to these representations as signs only of masculinity and/or whiteness in crisis, we will also miss the important cultural work being performed on the level of class identity. The tectonic shifts in the global economy and the corresponding battles over the balance of class power in the United States meant that class identities were being revised just as profoundly as those of gender, race, and sexuality during the 1970s. For example, while the good ole boys of Southern films like *Walking Tall* clearly served to reimagine southern white masculinity after the civil rights movement, they also helped invent a new, hybrid class identity that took root in the industrializing Sunbelt, which would serve as a key vehicle of the New Right's political appeal. This book examines how the PMC responded to the political and economic developments of the decade by (mis)recognizing itself in cinematic representations of the working class: they saw in the white, blue-collar male, whom they took as a synecdoche for the entire class, a figure that inspired both attraction and antipathy—an ambivalent structure of feeling that spoke to both the PMC's then current anxieties and the more long-standing and more fundamental contradictions of its own class position.

I trace this structure of feeling through not only the films themselves but also the contexts of their reception. As many critics have noted, one of the key developments in film studies after the theory explosion of the 1970s was the encounter between text-focused, psychoanalytically derived models of spectatorship and the reception-oriented, ethnographically based understandings of actual audiences undertaken by television studies (the latter of which, Jackie Stacey notes, was closely affiliated with British cultural studies).[38] The television studies-influenced model argued that a viewer's response to a film or television program was not simply the product of the text alone but also of the social conditions in which the viewer was situated as well as the circumstances of the act of viewing itself. Rather than treat the spectator as a mere effect of the text—one who passively accedes to the position allocated for him or her in the textual system—reception-oriented studies emphasized how spectators were active producers of a text's cultural meaning. As Barbara Klinger puts it, "ideology is not, then, a thing a text *has*; such meanings are *produced* for it. And while a text's formal features may set into motion certain procedures of decipherment for the spectator, these features alone cannot explain the range of meanings a text can have in different contexts of reception."[39] The project of the critic on this model is to study these different contexts of reception and to analyze the ways films are interpreted and utilized by their spectators.

Klinger has outlined elsewhere the multiple factors that a film scholar should examine in order to get a full understanding of the "discursive sur-round" that shapes how a viewer might respond to a film.[40] In the first place, the film industry's own efforts to market and promote a film—as well as its strategies of distributing and exhibiting it—privilege certain meanings of a film over others and suggest a set of preferred readings that the audience is encouraged to pursue. A film that is initially released in drive-ins in the South, as were many Southerns, will prompt a different mode of popular and critical response than a film previewed for national film critics and initially released in major urban areas before being slowly "rolled out" to theatri-cal outlets across the country. Similarly, the critical reception of a film—as well as other journalistic coverage of the film industry—also serves an "agenda-setting" function, as Robert C. Allen and Douglas Gomery explain, in that such journalistic accounts do not tell "audiences what to think so much as it [tells] them what to think *about*" when evaluating a film.[41] The critical focus on the youth of the initial New Hollywood's filmmakers and audiences, for example, undoubtedly led audiences to interpret these films through the lens of "generation," instead of, say, "class." The various mean-ings offered by a film also inevitably intersect with the emergent, dominant, and residual ideological discourses of its historical moment—the "larger social processes which, in concert with cinematic practices and intertextual zones, help produce meanings for films," in Klinger's description.[42] As we will see, the bewildered responses to *Cruising* (1980) were a product not only of the film's often oblique narrational method but also the heightened confusions around the category of working-class masculinity that beset the period. In keeping with Klinger's persuasively articulated agenda for historical film research, this book will make frequent reference to the distribution, exhibition, and promotional strategies of the films discussed as well as to the larger discourses about class (and other social questions) that subtend the representations of class dynamics found onscreen, in order to investigate the multiple moments of class formation activated by these films.

I pay especially close attention to the reception these films received from journalistic reviewers, for this context is especially revealing of how these films were positioned and seen in relation to class. Film critics for national publications are, by the very nature of their occupation, members of the professional-managerial class. Furthermore, their reviews frequently imply a middle-class reader, an implication testified to by their structure of address—which often makes distinctions between the knowing spectator and less sophisticated, tacitly lower-class viewers—as well as by the simple economic fact that these publications appeal to such readers in order to attract advertisers.[43] While film reviewers of course differ in their orientation to various sorts of middle-class readers (i.e., cinema lovers who read *Film Comment* versus readers of general interest magazines such as *Time* and *Newsweek*), these reviews can provide a suggestive sampling of the class assumptions that PMC spectators brought to these films and, in turn, show us how an implicitly middle-class readership was encouraged to interpret them. In this way, the reviews serve as an index of how the cinematic representations of class identity in the 1970s were made to function for PMC audiences.

My attention to these contexts of reception, and the cultural meanings that these contexts enabled, will be coupled with an interrogation of the potential meanings that are *not* recognized by these receptions. The films I am discussing, after all, turn on issues of class difference, and often on class antagonism. Given the official U.S. ideology of classlessness, these differences and antagonisms are often present in repressed or displaced form. By examining the political unconscious of a given film, and then comparing it to the PMC critical reception of it, we can get a better sense of how these films worked to offer their middle-class viewers various imaginary resolutions to the class contradictions they mediated. In other films, such as *Deliverance* (1972), depictions of class conflict are surprisingly open to view as part of the film's manifest content. In these cases, an examination of the ways in which the reviews handled such depictions (or, in some cases, labored to ignore them) can be equally telling about the larger cultural anxieties these films speak to. In short, by combining textual analysis, which can illuminate the various meanings that a given film makes possible, with the tools of reception studies, which tell us which interpretations were taken up by a distinct group of viewers (and which were disregarded), we can create an informed profile of how these films were mobilized by and for their PMC audiences to shape and articulate their sense of class identity.

Finally, I will relate these discussions of textual structure and contextual reception to the conditions of film production. Hollywood cinema of the 1970s has been a favored site of critical work on the political economy of the film industry and its influence on the films produced. As Tino Balio observes, the late 1960s "ushered the American film industry into the age of conglomerates," as film companies were either taken over in corporate mergers, or became conglomerates themselves, in an effort to "stabilize operations by creating numerous 'profit centers' as a hedge against a business downturn in any one area."[44] Yvonne Tasker explains that "to some extent...the newness of new Hollywood stems from its existence within a changing media market-place in which diversification and conglomeration are essential to survival."[45] Critics such as Timothy Corrigan and Thomas Schatz have connected this new corporate order to the film aesthetics of the period, particularly the emergence of postclassical style.[46] They argue that the blockbuster film's rejection of classical Hollywood's devotion to character development for "ruthlessly linear chase-film plotting," genre syncretism, and special effects-driven spectacle generates a "purposeful incoherence" that serves to offer "multiple interpretive strategies" in order to attract disparate audiences.[47] In addition, these incoherencies point to the importance of ancillary markets—"secondary" sources of profits such as soundtrack albums, action figures and toys, and television and video sales (all of which often generate more income than a film's original theatrical run)—as the postclassical text is assembled with an eye toward its "shareability" with other divisions of a corporation's various operations.[48]

While I agree with critics who argue that claims for a full-blown postclassical era in cinema are ultimately overstated—as they tend to overestimate the homogeneity of classical cinema and underestimate the continuities between current textual strategies and those of the studio era[49]—these accounts, with their attention to the relationship between the industrial processes of film production and textual structure, present a compelling model for a materialist film studies. Following this kind of approach, I argue for the importance of investigating a relatively underexplored aspect of the film industry—its labor relations. Steven J. Ross argues that in order to understand and explain the class ideologies put on offer by a given period's cinema, one must examine "the nature of internal labor relations" as well as other, more familiar factors (such as audience profiles and the broader political climate).[50] There have been a few good examples of this kind of analysis—Ross's own book on the "capital-labor" films of the silent era is one—but the histories of Hollywood labor relations tend to taper off in the 1950s, after the major film unions had been established and the Red Scare had cemented the defeat of progressive unionism initiated by the dismantling of the Popular Front-affiliated Conference of Studio Unions (CSU).[51] While developments in Hollywood labor relations during the late 1960s and 1970s are less dramatic than, say, those of the tumultuous 1930s and 1940s, these poststudio-era decades saw a marked diminution in the power of organized labor within the industry and a concomitant increase of PMC authority, as the reorganization of film production undercut the old sources of union strength and placed more control in the hands of professional and managerial personnel.[52] This more or less ignored story not only expands and complicates our understanding of Hollywood's modes of production, but, as I will demonstrate, it also provides some important insights into the representations of class identity (especially working-class identity) found in the films of the period. To grasp fully the ways in which American films of the 1970s encode and enact moments of PMC class formation in relation to an imagined working class, one must inquire into the material struggles—between Hollywood's own PMC and working class(es)—that attended their production.

By tracing the class relations that inform the various moments of industrial production, textual form, and audience reception in 1970s American cinema, I aim to make class visible to film and cultural studies. In doing so, I also seek to contribute to a critical history of the visual and narrative repertoire of class that has informed, and continues to inform, the U.S. political imaginary. American film of the 1970s proves to be a particularly rich archive for such a history. The closer one examines the class dynamics of the period's films, the clearer it becomes that some of the central social and political upheavals of recent U.S. history are driven by and envisioned through that musty old character—the class struggle (accounts of whose demise have been greatly exaggerated). The "youth-cult" cycle, the subject of part I, helps us see that the dilemmas of the counterculture were, among other things, anxieties over class reproduction. The spectacle of southern working-class violence and reaction that makes up a central feature of the "Southern" cycle, discussed in part II, comes to appear as a middle-class nightmare of the class antagonisms that subtended the Sunbelt's political and industrial modernization. The panicked responses to feminism and gay liberation found in the "new nightlife films" examined in part III unexpectedly disclose a nostalgia and mourning for the working-class male body of the Fordist manufacturing regime. Throughout all of these films, one sees how the professional-managerial class sought to reassert and reimagine its cultural, political, and economic hegemony in relation to a working class that was sometimes envisioned as a benevolent ally, and sometimes as a sinister threat. In other words, during the 1970s, class became the screen onto which the dramas of the period were projected, even as it generated some significant dramas of its own.

PART I

HARD HATS AND MOVIE BRATS

1

CLASS AND THE YOUTH-CULT CYCLE

The late 1960s and early 1970s were marked by two seemingly unrelated developments: what Barbara Ehrenreich has called the "discovery of the working class"[1]—a discovery violently induced by, among other things, the May 1970 "hard hat riots" against antiwar protesters—and the establishment of a "New Hollywood" of film school-trained, European art cinema-inspired "movie brats." The quasi-sociological fascination of the middle class with what appeared to be a conservative backlash of blue-collar Americans would seem, at first glance, to have nothing to do with a youngish group of nascent auteurs[2] intent on creating a personal cinema that spoke to their generational experiences. Yet some of the signal films of the New Hollywood turn out to be surprisingly dependent on this new understanding of the working class. Consider, for example, 1969's *Easy Rider*, a film that, following upon the unexpected success (especially among young audiences) of *Bonnie and Clyde* and *The Graduate* (both 1967), appeared to announce a new kind of American film. In a prescient foreshadowing of the hard hats' violence against peace activists, *Easy Rider* ends when its two countercultural protagonists, Billy (Dennis Hopper) and Wyatt (Peter Fonda), are senselessly murdered by a pair of men whose status as "rednecks" is signified by not only their Deep South accents but also their working-class appearance. Co-screenwriter Terry Southern described the significance of this ending as "an indictment of blue-collar America, the people I thought were responsible for the Vietnam War."[3] An earlier campfire scene spells out the film's sense of the psychology of "blue-collar America." George (Jack Nicholson), the civil libertarian lawyer who Billy and Wyatt have befriended, describes the hostile rednecks the trio had come across earlier as men who were "bought and sold in the marketplace." Yet he also cautions that these men refuse to acknowledge their lack of freedom, that they will "get real busy killin' and maimin' to prove to you that they are free"—a sensibility that makes them "dangerous." This observation is confirmed when George is beaten to death by a few of these same men, and Billy and Wyatt are later shot and killed by another pair of rednecks. Some of the New Hollywood's first antiheroes, then, meet their politically resonant ends at the hands of the class just being discovered by the national media.

If, as Peter Biskind puts it, *Easy Rider* can be understood as "the automatic handwriting of the counterculture,"[4] then we might link this representation of a murderously reactionary working class, mired in false consciousness, to the New Left's belief that the working class had been incorporated into the cultural, political, and economic systems against which the counterculture was rebelling. Certainly such a representation is of a piece with the roughly contemporaneous arguments of critics like C. Wright Mills, Herbert Marcuse, and William A. Williams, who had claimed that the working class had been "bought off" by postwar affluence, and now stood as a kind of rearguard defense of the status quo. In this light, the film's guiding assertion that its countercultural protagonists are the genuine representatives of American freedom—a claim reproduced in the famous tagline from its marketing campaign: "A man went looking for America and couldn't find it anywhere"—could be read as an expression of the similarly New Leftist contention that youth itself should be considered a new revolutionary class.

Yet this understanding of the film's implicitly suggested antagonism—youth vs. the working class—poses as many questions as it answers. Given the wide range of social groups opposed to the counterculture, why was it that "blue-collar America" served as the face of the forces arrayed against it? In what ways was the category of "countercultural youth" articulated differently when it was opposed to the working class rather than its other social antagonists? Perhaps most importantly, how did the particularly class-specific nature of the one side of this opposition function to obscure and/or mediate the class identity of its other, seemingly nonclassed component?

The questions raised by *Easy Rider*'s articulations of (and silences around) class extend to the larger cultural formation of the New Hollywood. The film's opposition between a disaffiliating, rebellious youth and an apparently reactionary and often violent working class makes up a recurrent feature of some key New Hollywood films. In order to understand better this connection—to map its features and its consequences—this chapter will explore the ways in which the productions of the New Hollywood were shaped, in part, by the discovery of the working class, and how the discovery of the working class was shaped, in part, by the productions of the New Hollywood. For these two events were ultimately the product of a crisis within the *middle* class over its central institutions and its very reproduction. Building upon Ehrenreich's suggestion that the discovery of the working class "was the imaginative product of middle-class anxiety," I will show how the New Hollywood's first significant cycle of films—the youth-culture or "youth-cult" cycle—addresses and stages this anxiety for the younger cohort of the middle class.[5] By tracing the different formal strategies and thematic concerns of two youth-cult films, *Joe* and *Five Easy Pieces* (both 1970), I will demonstrate how the films' imagining of the newly discovered working class comes to offer a kind of imaginary resolution to the crisis within the middle class. Moreover, *Joe* and *Five Easy Pieces* were the product of new filmmaking practices that were exemplary of those created by the New Hollywood—practices that strengthened the hand of the industry's professional and managerial members at the expense of its working class. Through its films and its industrial practices, the New Hollywood served as a key institution in the articulation and negotiation of the crisis within the PMC—and, as a result, a central influence on the constructions of the working class that marked its "discovery."

This way of understanding the New Hollywood also offers a new perspective on the debates over the development during the period of a "postclassical" film style.[6] For example, rather than rehearse the arguments over whether the formal and thematic characteristics of New Hollywood films achieve a significant break from classical Hollywood style,[7] I explore how these potentially postclassical elements were read and theorized by contemporary film critics and journalists. These contemporary debates over the ostensibly "new" elements of the New Hollywood films were often discussed in ways that influenced the implied middle-class audience's understanding of the films' class dynamics. This focus on class dynamics also casts new light on the political economy of the New Hollywood. Instead of pursuing the question of whether the changes in studio ownership, film financing, production, marketing, and exhibition during this period can be understood as a shift from a Fordist to a post-Fordist mode of production,[8] I examine the ways in which these restructurings and reorganizations affected the balance of class forces within the industry and suggest how these shifts may have shaped the representations of class in the films themselves. By addressing questions of class struggle and class consciousness in the production and reception of the New Hollywood, I hope to reframe the terms of these debates within film studies by highlighting the cultural and political work that these terms performed in their historical moment.

THE NEW MOVIES AND THE NEW CLASS

The young filmmakers of the late 1960s and early 1970s were described—and described themselves—as a new cultural force developing in opposition to the established practices and leaders of what would be called the Old Hollywood. This emergence was described in a number of ways—as a generational changing of the guard, the product of shifts in economic and institutional contexts, and/or an aesthetic and political renaissance. However, it is important to note how these developments also signified, mostly implicitly but sometimes explicitly, telling shifts in class orientation.

The first wave of younger filmmakers to gain entry into Hollywood during the 1970s did so in the midst of the industry's infamous slump of 1969–71. A crisis in overproduction, combined with the high interest rates that attended the Vietnam War, caused five of the seven major studios to begin the decade in the red. Worse still, the revenue-generating strategy the studios followed during the 1960s—that is, to produce big-budget extravaganzas, such as *The Sound of Music* (1965), in the hopes of even bigger returns—led to increasingly expensive flops like *Dr. Dolittle* (1967), *Star!* (1968), and *Goodbye, Mr. Chips* (1969). As film historian Robert Sklar describes it, "it was as if the rules of baseball had been changed so that the only hit that mattered was a home run. The studios became interested only in the motion-picture equivalent of a home run."[9]

In light of these difficulties, the success of such films as *Bonnie and Clyde*, *The Graduate*, and especially *Easy Rider* seemed to offer a way out of this crisis. Not only did the films' low budgets yield an astronomical return on investment (*Easy Rider* is estimated to have grossed over twenty-five times its cost in its initial run) but the youth-cult film cycle these pictures helped launch also promised a way of securing younger audiences. For the film industry's crisis was also one of diminishing audiences. Motion picture attendance, which had been declining since 1946, reached an all-time low by 1971. The largest segment of this dwindling audience, though, consisted of younger viewers: 62 percent of the filmgoing audience in 1970 was between the ages of twelve and thirty. As a result, many of the contemporary accounts of the New Hollywood characterized the changes in the industry as driven by a need to connect with this younger audience. As *Newsweek* put it in their December 1970 cover story on the "New Movies," "it is the needs, tastes and temperaments of this new audience that have given birth to a new kind of American movie."[10]

Yet *Newsweek* also noted that this audience was "drastically smaller than the mass audience that supported the old Hollywood system." As a 1971 study commissioned by the Motion Picture Association of America demonstrated, the young viewers who accounted for nearly two-thirds of the moviegoing audience made up less than a third of the general population. These audience demographics caused *Life* film critic Richard Schickel to worry that film had become, as he put it, "Something Less than a Mass Medium." Schickel, like many other contemporary observers, noted that the new audience to which the New Hollywood pitched itself was not only younger but also more educated and affluent. Indeed, there was an almost direct relationship between education and film attendance: about a third of

college-educated viewers were regular (more than once a month) moviegoers, while 65 percent of those with less than a high school education claimed
never to go to the theater at all. Schickel reasoned that this shift in audience
composition would mean that movies "will soon be more or less exclusively
directed" toward "an elite," a "New Class...who are custodians (or, perhaps,
prisoners) of the technostructure." As a result, Schickel argued, film could
no longer be considered the "art of the masses" it once was (television, he
noted, had usurped that position). Instead, movies would now be understood to be "the playthings of The New Class."[11]

While this conclusion is surely overstated, it is also not without productive insights. In the first place, the audience fragmentation Schickel bemoans
had indeed occurred, as the combined events of the *Paramount* divorcement
decrees, the rise of television, and the shift toward suburban living patterns
had diminished and splintered the almost universal audience of Hollywood's
classical era.[12] In fact, Richard Maltby proposes that the introduction of
the MPAA ratings code in late 1968 should be seen as Hollywood's "formal acknowledgement that the industry was no longer attempting to appeal
to an undifferentiated audience." Yet it is important to emphasize that this
audience fragmentation did not necessarily imply a wholesale abandonment of other, older audiences. As *Look* magazine observed in its late 1970
cover story on the New Hollywood, only a few youth-cult films managed to
become notable successes, while old fashioned "family" films were still finding their way into *Variety*'s Top Ten Box Office Champs. Thus, the youth-
oriented filmmakers who were seen (and saw themselves) as constitutive of
the New Hollywood should not be taken to represent all of Hollywood (an
elision implied by Schickel's account). Instead, they made up only an emergent fraction of the film industry.[13]

That said, Schickel's attention to the class orientation of this emergent
fraction is quite salient. His characterization of the "New Class" as the "custodians of the technostructure" is derived from John Kenneth Galbraith's
then current *The New Industrial State*. Galbraith described the technostructure as the part of the corporation that is not strictly speaking head management but instead "extends from the most senior officials of the corporation
to where it meets, at the outer perimeter, the white- and blue-collar workers
whose function is to conform more or less mechanically to instruction or
routine. It embraces all who bring specialized knowledge, talent or experience to group-decision making."[14] It is a group, in other words, that later
theorists would describe as the professional-managerial class.

As Ehrenreich points out, the PMC is made up of "all those people
whose economic and social status is based on education, rather than on
the ownership of capital or property." Suggestively, many New Hollywood
figures, while describing their audience in generational terms, focused on

the education levels of this audience. *Two-Lane Blacktop* (1971) producer Michael Laughlin explained to *Business Week* that "our generation has gone beyond mere entertainment. We are too well educated, too intelligent to be just entertained." Similarly, *The Graduate* screenwriter Buck Henry described how, in the New Hollywood, "heroes can now be intellectuals, which they never were in American films. Perhaps it's because, until recently, the audience was so profoundly anti-intellectual itself. But the younger generation identifies with the melodrama of ideas." Paul Williams, who directed *Out of It* (1969) and *The Revolutionary* (1970), made the connection between New Hollywood's appeal to "educated" audiences and its class affiliations explicit:

> I can now go to Columbia or Universal or United Artists and talk to men of taste. This change is a class thing. Harry Cohn and Louis B. Mayer were lower-middle-class and made their films for the mass of people who belonged to that class. But now the film audience has grown more educated and so have the studio people. Directors don't have to deal with aborigines any more.[15]

What is important here is not the question of whether this younger audience was actually as sophisticated and intellectual as this rhetoric claims, but rather that such an audience was assumed by many New Hollywood practitioners, and as such was a determining factor in shaping their cultural production. In other words, by imagining an audience whose salient features were their youth and their high level of education, the New Hollywood filmmakers presupposed a specific set of ideal readers: the younger members of (and aspirants to) the PMC.

THE CRISIS WITHIN THE PMC

The younger members of the PMC came of age during a growing critique of the class and its institutions. Barbara and John Ehrenreich, for example, note that the New Left's[16] initial formations were made up largely of activists born and bred within the middle class, and as such tended at first toward a political program that was "an attempt to reassert the autonomy which the PMC had long since ceded to the capitalist class." However, as the movement expanded both its membership and its political reach, and as the complicity of many PMC institutions (especially the university) in the Vietnam War became more evident, this younger cohort began to direct their critique—and their protests—against their own class. When antiwar protests turned against the universities, though, many otherwise left-leaning faculty members repudiated the New Left campaigns—a repudiation the Ehrenreichs see as motivated in part by the class location of these older members of the PMC. As Barbara Ehrenreich explains elsewhere, "the university is, after all, the core institution of the professional middle class—employer of its intellectual elite and producer of the next generation of middle-class, professional personnel. Attack the university and you attack the heart—and surely the womb—of the class itself."[17]

This generational dispute over the legitimacy of middle-class institutions constitutes the dominant thematic template for the youth-cult cycle of films that introduced the New Hollywood to mainstream America. In fact, many films in this cycle, such as *The Strawberry Statement*, *R.P.M.*, and *Getting Straight* (all 1970), focus directly upon student attacks on the universities. For example, *Getting Straight* centers on Harry (Elliott Gould), who seems unsure whether to join New Left protests or assume a professional occupation. A wizened activist (he marched in Selma), Harry spends the film doing his best to avoid becoming involved in the current campus unrest as he tries to finish his master's degree in order to become a teacher, despite the fact that he balks at the outdated and oppressive pedagogy taught to him by the older generation of education professors. Other youth films, of course, represent this generational split in less political terms, as in one of the cycle's founding works, *The Graduate*. In that film, the protagonist's (Ben, played by Dustin Hoffman) alienation from the older members of his class seems to be characterized more by a dilatory hesitation than anything else. Yet the class specificity of his generational dilemma is nevertheless underlined. Ben's sole explicit articulation of his "confusion" occurs during a brief conversation with Elaine (Katharine Ross) in a drive-in burger joint. As he explains his dissatisfaction with the middle-class life for which he has been thoroughly trained, he is interrupted by the loud music of the car next to them, which is filled with more bohemian-appearing youth. He and Elaine roll up the windows of his Alfa Romeo, insulating their genteel disaffection from a more raucous, downwardly mobile form of youth culture.

Joe and *Five Easy Pieces* also adhere to this thematic requirement of the youth-cult cycle: *Joe*'s story begins with the estrangement of an advertising executive from his hippie daughter, while *Five Easy Pieces* traces a son's alienation from his professional musician/conductor father. *Joe* and *Five Easy Pieces* also represent the two aesthetic and institutional poles of the New Hollywood. While the New Hollywood of the late 1960s and early 1970s is often (and not inaccurately) characterized as the development of an American art cinema influenced by the various European New Waves,[18] the movement also had its roots in exploitation film companies such as American International Pictures (AIP). Not only did many of the New Hollywood auteurs (such as Martin Scorsese, Francis Ford Coppola, and Peter Bogdanovich) get their first working experience with AIP, especially with producer Roger Corman, but many of the production, distribution, and marketing techniques that the New Hollywood would eventually adopt were originally developed by exploitation film companies (which had, in many ways, "discovered" the youth market in the first place).[19] *Joe* has its roots firmly in this tradition, both institutionally—it was produced by the Cannon Group, a company that started out by distributing a number of Swedish "sexploitation" films—and aesthetically, in its sensationalist screenplay and crudely lurid cinematography.[20] *Five Easy Pieces*, however, was made under the auspices of a major studio (Columbia Pictures, which bankrolled BBS Productions) and utilized narrative and visual strategies that were clearly indebted to those of the European art cinema. By examining both of these films we can understand how the New Hollywood articulated the class concerns of the PMC on different registers of cultural value.

Joe and *Five Easy Pieces* were also among the few post–*Easy Rider* youth-cult films to succeed at the box office. While most films of the cycle were resisted by their intended viewers (that is, the younger members of the PMC) and failed to attract a more general audience, *Joe* and *Five Easy Pieces* placed tenth and thirteenth among the top rentals for 1970, respectively.[21] It is striking that one of the main features that distinguishes these two films from most of the period's other youth-cult productions is that their meditations on professional identity are explored through an engagement with *working-class* subjectivity. That is, while the narratives are ostensibly concerned with generational conflicts within the PMC, these conflicts become triangulated through working-class characters and settings. *Joe*'s advertising executive is befriended by a welder, and the two find common cause in their opposition to the counterculture, while the protagonist of *Five Easy Pieces* disaffiliates from his middle-class origins by dropping out to become a manual laborer on an oil rig. Why do these films utilize working-class elements to complicate their generationally oriented story lines? How does this encounter with working-class subjectivities reorient the intra-PMC disputes over their class's position? The answers to these questions help illuminate why this particular rearticulation of PMC identity—and its concomitant imagination of the working class—gained for these films a cultural currency and popularity that other youth-cult films failed to generate.

THE DISCOVERY OF THE WORKING CLASS

On or about August 1968, the working class was (re)discovered in the United States. After the violent disorder of the 1968 Democratic Convention, media professionals, many of whom had been attacked and beaten alongside the antiwar protesters by the Chicago police, were surprised to find that a majority of the public had sided with the police. Terrified at the possibility that they had lost touch with the majority, the national media began to explore this unknown population of apparently conservative, traditionalist "Middle Americans" to whom Richard Nixon appealed to a little more than a year later as "the great silent majority." However, during the first moments of their discovery, these Middle Americans were an ill-defined social grouping. The category was delimited largely *via* exclusion: a Middle American turned out to be anyone who was not a student protestor, black power advocate, or media or education professional. When it named the Middle Americans as its "Man and Woman of the Year" for 1969, *Time* admitted that it was difficult to describe the group's identity (whose number, they estimated, "probably approaches 100 million, or half of the U.S. population"), since the Middle Americans were "defined as much by what they are not as by what they are." The magazine clarified this point by observing that "few blacks march in the ranks of Middle America. Nor do the nation's intellectuals, its liberals, its professors, its surgeons," and that "Middle America offers no haven to the New Left." *Newsweek* offered an even more capacious definition: the only groups excluded from the Gallup Poll commissioned for their "Special Report" on the "Troubled American" were nonwhites.[22]

However, these accounts returned repeatedly to the proposition that the working class was "the cutting edge" of Middle American "disgruntlement," as *Newsweek* put it. Barbara Ehrenreich has offered a few reasons for this attention to the blue-collar segment of the Middle Americans: she cites the dubious notion of "working-class authoritarianism" inherited from sociologists as well as the relative novelty offered by the "exotic" appearance and speech of the blue-collar interviewees that gave the articles on Middle America an attention-grabbing hook. Finally, she suggests, for a media uneasy about its status as a certain kind of "elite," the apparent hostility of the working class to the PMC seemed to guarantee that *this* was the group they needed to pay attention to in order to ensure that they did not lose touch with "the majority" again.

All of these suggestions are plausible, but they seem insufficient to explain fully why this amorphous, negatively defined category of reaction and retrenchment would come to be represented by the working class. That is, the hegemonic force that the discourse of blue-collar conservatism would take on for the rest of the decade (and beyond) seems underdetermined by the ideological elements Ehrenreich identifies. To understand how this representation of the working class consolidated its hold in the middle class imaginary, we must turn to a seminal moment in the blue-collarization of the Middle Americans: the hard hat riots of May 1970.

These events (ultimately, there were several demonstrations) began on May 8 in Manhattan, when roughly two hundred construction workers, almost all wearing hard hats and some brandishing their tools as weapons, crashed a peaceful antiwar rally near Wall Street and began beating the mostly college-aged protesters and a few passersby. They later proceeded to City Hall, where they turned their anger on the liberal Mayor John Lindsay, and managed to raise the City Hall flag, which was flying at half-mast in honor of the four students killed at Kent State earlier that week, to full-mast. In the following week, similar (although more peaceful) demonstrations of antiprotester, anti-Lindsay, and pro-patriotic sentiment were held in the Wall Street area, again by construction workers, which culminated in what *Time* referred to as "a kind of workers' Woodstock"—a rally organized by the Building and Trades Council of Greater New York in support of President Nixon's Indochina policies and attended by sixty thousand to one hundred thousand apparently blue-collar supporters.[23]

While these events were largely reported as essentially spontaneous out-pourings of a pro-war, pro-Establishment sentiment—the release of Middle America's long-pent-up feelings of disgust and anger with the antiwar, countercultural left—the demonstrations were, as a few critics then and now have pointed out, a bit more complicated than that. In the first place, they were not spontaneous: reporters noted the presence of gray-suited men directing the original May 8 attacks, and a few construction workers had in fact called City Hall the evening before to warn that the union's hawkish leaders (the construction unions being historically among the most conservative of the labor movement) had been disseminating plans among the rank and file for just such a confrontation. It was later revealed that many workers were promised that the time they spent rallying at these counterdemonstrations would not be docked from their pay—and in some cases workers were even offered cash bonuses.[24] Secondly, as many construction workers were at pains to explain in the numerous newspaper and magazine articles about them that appeared after the counterdemonstrations, while they were infuriated by the more deliberately shocking and theatrically provocative aspects of radical street protest (especially any act of flag desecration), they did not necessarily support the war. As one worker who participated in the demonstrations told *Time*, "I'm not against the students. They have a right to dissent....But we just can't let them burn down buildings the way they do....Don't get me wrong. Don't think we're for the war. No one is....But we elected Nixon and we have to back him."[25] This is a deeply conflicted and ambivalent statement, of course, but it is important to recognize it as just that: conflicted and ambivalent, not univocally reactionary.

Finally, and perhaps most puzzling, was the fact that the initial, brutal May 8 rampage had more than just construction workers as participants.

In fact, as the *New York Times* reported the next day, "there did not seem to be more than 200 construction workers, but they were reinforced by *hundreds of persons* who had been drawn into the march by chants of 'All the way, U.S.A.' and 'Love it or leave it.'"[26] A later *New York Times Magazine* feature titled "Joe Kelly Has Reached His Boiling Point," about a construction worker who had participated in the counterdemonstrations, explained that the unnamed, yet not-so-silent majority of the counterprotesters were in fact office workers from Wall Street area. As Joe Kelly himself put it:

> I will say this: there was as many of these anti-war demonstrators whacked by Wall Street and Broadway office workers as there were by construction workers. The feeling seemed to be that the white-collar-and-tie-man, he was actually getting in there and taking as much play on this thing as the construction worker was....
>
> I'd never witnessed anything like this in my life before, and it kinda caught me in awe that you had to stop and see what was going on around you. It was almost unbelievable. This was the financial district of New York City, probably the financial district of the world, and here was this mass clash of opposite factions, right on Wall Street and Broad, and you could hardly move, there were so many people taking part in this aside from the five hundred construction workers. It was just something that you had to stand back and blink your eyes and actually look a second or third time, and you couldn't believe that this was actually taking place in that particular area.[27]

I will return to Joe Kelly's evocative account of this historic moment later. What I want to note here is that, despite the evidently heterogeneous, cross-class identity of the counterprotesters, the events of May 1970 were (and still are) described almost without exception as the emergence of the "hard hat" as the new figure of conservative reaction.[28] As in the initial descriptions of the Middle Americans, a cross-class backlash against dissent is represented synecdochically by the working class—in this case, the white, working-class male.

JOE'S WORKING-CLASS THREAT

Joe, the tale of a "white-collar-and-tie man" and a hard hat uniting in acts of reactionary violence, illustrates the political use-value of the hard hat to the PMC in this cultural moment. *Joe* tells the story of Bill Compton (Dennis Patrick), an advertising executive whose hippie-ish daughter, Melissa (Susan Sarandon), lives with her drug dealer boyfriend, Frank. When she overdoses and ends up in the hospital, Bill goes to her apartment to gather her belongings. There, he runs into the boyfriend, they fight, and Bill accidentally kills him. Bill goes to a bar to collect himself, and he sits next to Joe Curran (Peter Boyle), a welder from Queens, who is in the midst of an extended monologue about "niggers," "hippies," "liberals," "queers," and so on. Joe mentions that he would like to kill a hippie, and Bill mutters to himself, "I just did." Joe overhears him and tracks him down a few days later. Yet rather than blackmail Bill, Joe explains that he would just like to get to know him, since he admires what he did. The film then follows the two men through a series of encounters in which they engage in a kind of cross-class male bonding, until the two end up searching Greenwich Village for Bill's runaway daughter. They find themselves at a hippie party, where they smoke pot and engage in an orgy (which Joe pronounces with a hard "g") with the hippie women. However, the other men steal their wallets and head up north toward their commune. Bill and Joe follow them and end up shooting all of the hippies at the commune, including, in an ironic yet predictable conclusion, Bill's daughter.

Joe was originally to be called *The Gap*, referring to the generational split which is the film's narrative frame. In fact, the title character does not even appear until we are almost an entire half hour into the film. During this first half hour, the film evokes the generational divide on several registers, especially in the brief confrontation between Bill and Frank, where the opposition of age vs. youth is overlaid with those of adman vs. artist, materialist vs. bohemian, and sexually repressed rectitude vs. libertinous vulgarity. When Bill kills Frank and flees the apartment, the film cuts abruptly to Joe—his first appearance in the film. This jarring introduction suggests that the violent generational conflict has in some way engendered the working-class character. To put it another way, "the gap" produces, and is thus filled with, Joe.[29] This unexpected appearance of a hard hat serves to realign the available subject positions of social conflict with which the film began, rearticulating the terms of debate away from those of the generational split, with all of its political and cultural antagonisms, and toward those of a different kind of opposition, and a different set of adversarial identities.

But why insert *this* new identity? Why triangulate the generational split with the hard hat? On a fairly obvious level, the film's crudely Freudian gestures (the abrupt cut from a postmurderous Bill to Joe and the fact that the bar where Bill meets Joe is underground) ask us to think of Joe as Bill's violent, reactionary id—thus invoking the familiar association of a lower-class character with the lower drives.[30] Indeed, Bill's friendship with Joe seems to derive, at least in part, from the fact that he can tell Joe about the "pleasure" he felt as he killed his daughter's boyfriend. As Bill later explains to his wife, "The crazy thing about Joe is that it's as if he shared in it. As if he killed that boy, too." But this id also functions as a superego. A moment later in the same scene, Bill says that "there's something else about Joe. Sometimes with him I almost feel that what I did was a humanitarian act. I saved the world from another lousy junkie."

This oscillating psychoanalytic metaphor seems to be fairly intentional on the part of the filmmakers—screenwriter Norman Wexler and director John G. Avildsen. Both of these men later in the 1970s produced two central filmic representations of the working class: *Saturday Night Fever* and *Rocky*, respectively. But before they got involved in filmmaking, Wexler and Avildsen were admen—that is, they were younger versions of Bill Compton.[31] This is important to keep in mind as we consider the following exchange between Bill and Joe:

> Bill: Now you see those buildings, Joe? Those beautiful monuments of concrete and glass. I work in one of them. And do you know what they do in those buildings, Joe? They move paper. That's right—they pick it up in one place, and they move it to another place. They pass it all around their offices. And the more paper you move, the more important you are, the more they pay you. And if you want to really show how important you are, what you can get away with, you make little paper airplanes, and you sail them right up somebody else's ass.
>
> Joe: You ever get the feeling that everything you do, your whole life, is one big crock of shit?
>
> Bill: Yeah.

In keeping with the aforementioned psychoanalytic metaphor, Joe's lower-class presence seems to engender an alimentary and scatological rhetoric. But Joe's status as Bill's class other apparently also prompts Bill to account for his class position. In doing so, Bill derides the emptiness of his profession with a kind of bitter, sarcastic glee, and in terms that could describe the occupational duties of much of the professional-managerial class. In short, the character of Joe provides Bill—and, one imagines, the two former admen who created Joe—with a working-class (and, not incidentally, hyper-masculine) perspective from which to ventriloquize a sense of the apparent bankruptcy of his (Bill's) class's labor, and to admit that, as Joe puts it, middle-class existence is "one big crock of shit."

But isn't this what the counterculture was saying? In fact, in the film's bloody denouement, Joe convinces Bill to join him in killing the hippies in the commune by reminding him that "these kids—they shit on you. They shit on your life. They shit on everything you believe in." So why is Bill able to take pleasure in the denigration of his professional status made possible by his friendship with Joe?

There are perhaps two answers to this question. In the first place, Joe does not shit on *everything* Bill believes in. In addition to their hatred of hippies, both men share a love of money. When Bill admits that his salary is $60,000 a year, Joe's eyes light up in a kind of awe: "You gotta be kidding! Only movie stars make that kind of money! The fuckin' president of my union pays himself that kind of money!" In other words, when Joe realizes the level of material comfort Bill has attained, his response is not to sneer, as Frank does earlier in the film, "How are your toasters doin'?" Instead, he looks upon Bill with a sense of increased admiration.

Second, while Joe's friendship with Bill provides the occasion for the latter's critiques of professional labor, it is almost always *only* Bill who makes these critiques. For example, when Bill takes Joe to an executive-filled bar, Joe remarks that the other men at the bar "gotta be smart" to have reached this level of achievement—a statement that Bill quickly undercuts by demonstrating just how stupid and obsequious his fellow professionals are. Were Joe to articulate these attacks on the qualifications and skills of Bill's fellow professionals, Bill might find himself in a position similar to the one he occupied in his confrontation with Frank—that is, put on the defensive about his class status. Yet by taking on Joe's working-class perspective as his own, Bill is able to ironize this status and acknowledge the ways in which it is upheld by a set of ideological fictions. Importantly, though, Bill's unmasking of class privilege does not require him to renounce this privilege. Joe may inspire him to look askance at his class identity, but Bill also can rely on Joe to respect and envy his material success—in sharp contrast to the counterculture's response to the perceived bankruptcy of the PMC, which is to spurn its materialistic pursuits and to critique its role in perpetuating unjust social relations. Joe's social location offers only a site of imaginary identification for Bill—a fantasized space that allows for a foul-mouthed, masculinist derogation of his profession—rather than an opposing voice (which might, incidentally, offer a working-class critique of the PMC). As a result, the precarious and perhaps even defenseless nature of class distinction is admitted, yet in such a way as to preserve one of the engines—material acquisitiveness—of this distinction.

This imaginary identification reaches a kind of apotheosis in the film's final moments. When *Joe* was first released, several reviewers noted incidents of young audience members shouting back at the screen after the final scene's shooting spree, "We'll get you, Joe!"[32] This response is fascinating in any number of ways, but notice that the cry was not, "We'll get you, *Bill!*" Even though both Bill and Joe participate in the shooting, this act of reactionary violence is perceived to be entirely the responsibility of the working-class character—a perception shared by virtually all of the critics who reviewed the film at the time. It would seem that Bill's willed association with Joe's class location becomes so complete as to subsume his actions into Joe's. Just as the class identity of the white-collar Wall Streeters who participated in the May 8 counterdemonstration somehow disappeared into that of the construction workers, so does Bill's class position undergo a kind of erasure through his alliance with Joe.

As this occurs, the site of social conflict is transformed. No longer is the antagonism between an older PMC generation, associated with a series of dominant political and cultural institutions, and a younger generation disaffiliating from those institutions. Instead, the disaffiliating youth are now counterposed to a working class resentful of the privileges being disavowed by this social group. As the class locations and interests of men such as Bill are assimilated into the populist figure of the hard hat, the challenge posed by radical dissent to the PMC's collaboration in capitalist and imperialist power relations is now transfigured into a battle between students and workers—that is, the principally named combatants of the May 1970 Wall Street demonstrations.

A SPECTER IS HAUNTING WALL STREET

It could be objected that what I have said here does not take into account the fact that Joe is, well, a monster. While we are asked to take pleasure in his character's vulgarian disregard for middle-class pieties—this is part of what Bill finds so appealing in him as well—we are also supposed to view Joe's perspectives and actions as largely sociopathic. For Joe—and the hard hats with whom he is identified in nearly every contemporary review of the film—serves as both as a representative for an earthy, authentic brand of traditional values *and* a figure of monstrous excess. If the terrain of social conflict is being rearticulated here, it is being re-formed in such a way that neither side may be unambiguously valorized. Rather than endorse its image of conservative populist revolt, *Joe* seems to suggest that such a cross-class alliance would be something of a Faustian bargain for the PMC.

The contradictory nature of Joe's character, and the instability it implies, can be unpacked by recalling Joe Kelly's awestruck description of the Wall Street demonstrations. One of the most uncanny aspects of these events for him was that they occurred on the doorstep of "the financial district of the world." This was a fact not lost on journalistic observers of the scene: as *Newsweek* put it, the police stationed around Wall Street during May 1970 "look[ed] for all the world as if they were about to defend the palaces of capitalism and the Establishment from the ravages of some proletarian mob." The *New Yorker* described how the streets in the City Hall and Wall Street areas "at midday lately have often resembled union shape-up centers." And the May 9, 1970, *New York Times* editorial denouncing the counterprotesters chose to characterize the participants as "rampaging unionists."[33]

The persistent association of the anti-antiwar demonstrations with other signifiers of organized labor (anticapitalist "proletarian mobs," "shape-up centers") is puzzling, especially since, as I have already noted, the mainstream media by and large regarded the protests as unorganized and spontaneous (rather than directed by the construction unions). The fact that the union membership of the rioters was the salient demographic detail in these accounts—rather than, say, their age, race, or gender—starts to make sense, though, when one recalls that 1970 marked the high point of the strike wave that rose and crested through the late 1960s and early 1970s. As labor activist Kim Moody notes, more than sixty-six million workdays were lost to strikes during that year; during the post war era, only 1946 and 1959 saw more strike activity. Workers were indeed in the streets throughout the late 1960s and early 1970s, but it was most often not in conjunction with any supposed support of Nixon's foreign policy. Instead, it was part of the rank-and-file militancy that was challenging not only the automation and production speedups that had been and would continue to ravage the labor market for the rest of the decade but also the often complacent and conservative leadership of the workers' own unions.[34]

Such challenges, Moody explains, were often over issues of "shop-floor jurisprudence"—that is, conflicts concerning workplace conditions. However, the postwar consensus between labor and capital had been one in which the unions had largely ceded control over the organization of production to management.[35] Unable to challenge working conditions on the shopfloor, workers were typically forced to defer such battles to the grievance procedures, where they "were either arbitrated if they were regarded as important by higher levels of the union or bargained away at contract time." In other words, the terms of conflict were set not on the physical site of working-class labor but instead on the legal-bureaucratic terrain of the PMC. Seen in this light, the explosion in wildcat strikes (1969 saw twice as many strikes not authorized by union officials as 1960) and contract rejections (which "soared to over 1,000 in 1967") can be understood as a forceful attempt on the part of the organized working class to challenge the prerogative and scope of PMC power.[36]

Curiously, though, this surge in labor militancy was often lumped in with scattered "backlash" events like the Wall Street demonstrations as expressions of the same "blue-collar blues." For example, in their cover story on the topic, *Time* magazine explained that "blue collar anger has burst out this year in the worst epidemic of strikes since just after World War II, and in the form of hardhat riots in New York City, St. Louis and elsewhere." Similarly,

Louise Kapp Howe, in her introduction to the 1970 collection *The White Majority*, noted that the average "air-conditioned city apartment dweller" knows "next to nothing…[about] what it was like to live on the wages of a mailman…Only the recent mail strike has begun to bring that home." Yet she describes the essays in the book as attempts "to learn more about the people who comprise the majority of the country, how they live, [and] what forces are pushing them to the right," seemingly ignoring the fact that the aforementioned strike, one of the most daring and successful wildcat rebellions of the period, could not in any way be construed as an expression of a rightward shift. In short, in many popular accounts of the period's various forms of working-class collective action, the political valence of these activities was insistently blurred, as racist backlash and rank-and-file radicalism were equated as like expressions of working-class "anger and bewilderment" at rapid social change.[37]

Yet such ideological confusion can cut both ways. If Louise Kapp Howe can see a rightward shift in actions like the postal workers' wildcat strike, others might see harbingers of worker rebellion implicit in events like the hard hat riots. This might be the case especially in a period when *Time* quotes a "top industrialist" comparing the wage raises won by the building trades—that is, the same workers who participated in the Wall Street demonstrations—to "a kid in class with a case of the measles. You've got to isolate it before they all catch it." Despite the fact that the hard hats' antiprotester actions were chosen to represent "the great silent majority," the headline for an October 1970 *Fortune* magazine feature story, denouncing the high labor costs of construction work, made clear where these hard hats stood *qua* workers: "The Building Trades Versus the People."[38] While the anti-antiwar protestors offered an appealing portrait of a traditionalist, conservative backlash, the presence of a "proletarian mob" on Wall Street—"the financial district of the world," as Joe Kelly put it—may have also suggested, in a displaced manner, a labor militancy that threatened to reorient the balance of class forces in the United States and to disrupt the global restructuring of capital that accelerated as the 1970s progressed.

I would argue that the volatility of Joe's character bears traces of this extratextual anxiety. After all, much of the film's tension turns on the fact that while Joe may offer Bill reassurance and even encouragement for his homicidal actions, his knowledge of the killing also serves as an implicit threat. Moreover, Bill's responses to Joe's outbursts of anger frequently turn from a sense of conspiratorial pleasure to profound unease. For example, after meeting Joe, Bill's wife, Joan, remarks that being with him "is like sitting on a powder keg." In these moments, Joe—like the Wall Street hard hats—seems to be more of a threat than a savior. So while the film offers the PMC a compelling rearticulation of the terms of social conflict—as the New

Left and the counterculture's class (auto)critiques are preempted by the fact that these groups find themselves pitted against the workers rather than the older generation of the PMC—it also implies that this new social terrain will be an inherently unstable one. As Joan implores her husband regarding his alliance with Joe, "You *have* to keep on the good side of him."

FIVE EASY PIECES: THE DIFFICULTY OF DROPPING OUT

In some ways, *Five Easy Pieces* offers a mirror image of *Joe*'s political geometry. The film posits another middle-class disappearance into working-class identity that is once again occasioned by a generational split—this one between the film's protagonist, Bobby Dupea (Jack Nicholson), and his concert musician father. Yet here the working-class position is aligned, at least initially, with the disaffiliating youth rather than with the (culturally) elite member of the older generation. In other words, if Bobby can be said to be the male counterpart to *Joe*'s Melissa, this time the disaffiliation takes the form of joining Joe on the factory floor. But does this alternate triangulation of the generational split offer a different class lesson than the one suggested by *Joe*? Does this reconfiguration ultimately work to offer a different mediation of PMC identity?

Of course, it could be objected that *Five Easy Pieces* is only tangentially about a generational conflict, and thus it does not address itself to the antagonisms of this conflict as directly (nor as luridly) as *Joe* does. Although I will suggest a bit later that the film does draw from a certain rhetoric of generational anxiety, it is true that comparatively little screen time is given to Bobby's Oedipal struggle with his father, and that the film eschews any explicit association of its protagonist with an identifiable counterculture.[39] But the context of the film's release—coming, as it did, during the main deluge of youth-cult films—made some of the connections between the conflicts played out by the film and those identified with generational disputes a bit more pronounced. Furthermore, since *Five Easy Pieces* was made by the same young production team (BBS) responsible for *Easy Rider*, and starred one of that film's breakout performers (Nicholson), reviewers of the film tended to read it as aligned with a youthful, countercultural ethos. For example, even though she acknowledges that Bobby is depicted "not as a generalized dropout saying no but as a particular and cultivated man of thirty-odd," Penelope Gilliatt still described his character as a type that is "contemporarily the bane of the United States government and of the United States complex of recruitment to industry." Similarly, *Time*'s Stefan Kanfer characterized Bobby as the "older brother of the easy riders of 1969," and

Five Easy Pieces as "an undrugged, mature version" of the aforementioned countercultural landmark.[40]

Despite these contextual and extratextual associations, the film does not initially appear to be a tale of youthful rebellion. In fact, *Five Easy Pieces* consists of two, almost wholly discrete parts: the first is a portrait of Bobby's working-class existence as an oil field worker, while the second follows him back to his family of music professionals after he hears of his father's failing health, where he then confronts the upper-middle-class life he has abandoned. This narrative structure is in some ways the inverse of *Joe's*: where the latter film begins with a depiction of the generational split, and later inserts a working-class character into this conflict, *Five Easy Pieces* begins with a depiction of working-class life, only to have that narrative turn into a story about the protagonist's alienation from his father's world. And just as Joe is not introduced until we are a half hour into that film, *Five Easy Pieces* does not begin to hint that Bobby is anything other than an oilfield worker for the first twenty minutes and reveals the extent of his family's musical legacy only gradually during the last two-thirds of the film.[41]

This shift in our understanding of Bobby begins in a famous scene in which he discovers a piano on the back of a truck trapped in the middle of a traffic jam and unexpectedly begins playing a Chopin piece (figure 1.1)—the first sign that he is, as Kanfer put it, "no average hardhat."[42] Yet rather than providing an adjoining, expository scene explaining this outburst of musical talent, the film proceeds to follow Bobby's aimless blue-collar life, and it is only much later that we learn he had been trained as a classical pianist.

Figure 1.1. From *Five Easy Pieces*. Bobby (Jack Nicholson) the hard hat plays Chopin in a traffic jam.

This withholding of Bobby's past—a diegetic inversion of cause and effect—characterizes the narrative strategy of the film as a whole.[43] This violation of classical Hollywood's linear, causally motivated narration—what Peter Wollen has called "narrative intransitivity"—is a key feature of the postclassical style that many film theorists and historians have argued is characteristic of New Hollywood filmmaking.[44] Furthermore, it was this narrative intransitivity that was consistently praised by the film's many enthusiastic reviewers. In a typically glowing review, *Esquire*'s Jacob Brackman cited this scene as "the first in a series of astonishing fake-outs" that help make *Five Easy Pieces* "the opposite of a genre film," in that the viewer is offered "what you least expected."[45] Similarly, Richard Schickel wrote in *Life* that the film "totally reverses our cinematic expectations":

> Typically, movies place their characters in some sort of emotional or physical peril, some forcing chamber which compels them to reveal themselves as archetypes. Here, however, there is no crisis. It occurred before the movie began. There is only a series of incidents—moments of anger, comedy, nostalgia, passing sadness—that reveal the central character...to be neither what we thought he was in the beginning nor anything like an archetype.[46]

What is important to note about this characteristically New Hollywood narrative strategy is that it reframes our original understanding of Bobby's supposed working-class identity. Up until the Chopin scene, the film trades in a kind of authenticity guaranteed by its working-class subject. The exuberant pleasure Bobby takes in drinking, card playing, and picking up women; his mixture of frustration with and affection for his waitress girlfriend; even his occasional existential alienation (suggested by his quiet melancholy when he is left alone for a brief moment in a bowling alley)—all are presented as emblematic of his blue-collar existence. Yet as the narrative reveals Bobby's classical musician past, all of these signifiers of Bobby's allegedly working-class identity are recast by the subsequent depictions of his PMC origins. We are now asked to see Bobby's pursuit of sensual pleasures as a response to the uptight, confined behavior of his family (personified by the paralysis of his father, as well as the awkward prissiness of his neck-brace-wearing brother, Carl [Ralph Waite]). Rayette (Karen Black), his waitress girlfriend, now represents a relief from the sort of "pompous celibate" that characterizes his family's social circles as well as an annoyance to a man who is thus presented as her intellectual and cultural superior. Even his alienation is now clearly shown to be a product of his educated disaffection. In short, the latter sections of the film ask us to view Bobby's experience of working-class life as negatively constituted, as a reaction formation to his middle-class identity. As in *Joe*, the working-class position operates less as a signifier of its own identity than as a perspective from which to analyze and critique middle-class existence. As if to underline this fact, the film largely abandons Bobby's blue-collar environment after the opening thirty minutes, retaining only Rayette, whose apparently class-specific tackiness and ignorance tend to function as embarrassments to Bobby.

The fact that the film chooses this particular mode of existence, this style of dropping out—rather than, say, having him join a countercultural commune—suggests that what is at issue in *Five Easy Pieces* is the transmission of cultural capital and its centrality to the professional middle class's reproduction. For what Bobby's adopted blue-collar status offers him is a way of disaffiliating from the cultural capital of his family's music professional heritage. The weight of this heritage is signified in a scene during which Bobby plays another Chopin piece, this time for Catherine (Susan Anspach), Carl's fiancée (and the woman he is trying to seduce). As he plays, the camera pans in tight close-up across a series of snapshots and portraits of the many generations of Dupea musicians, as if to emphasize both the depth of his family's musical history as well as its suffocating burden. The Chopin prelude comes to act as a score to this photographic montage. Thus, when he claims after he has finished that he felt nothing during his performance, it is as if he is also disavowing any connection to this history. By denying any "inner feeling" to his piano playing, Bobby seems to be literally disowning the musical skills which are the cultural capital that is the product of this lineage.

It is this refusal that caused critics like Gilliatt to refer to Bobby as representative of those who are "contemporarily the bane...of the United States complex of recruitment to industry," despite the fact that his resistance is to a fairly rarified form of professional labor. For such middle-class disaffiliation—specifically, a disaffiliation from the cultural capital that legitimates the PMC's role in the division of labor—strikes at the core of the class's self-identity. Cultural capital, after all, cannot be passively bequeathed to one's offspring; instead, it must be rearned with each generation through education and professional training. Therefore, the failure or refusal to acquire and embrace the fruits of this training reads as a kind of "class treason," as Ehrenreich has put it. One of the most overt articulations of this sense of treason was Midge Decter's 1975 jeremiad titled "A Letter to the Young," in which the author indicts the children of "America's professional, or enlightened, liberal middle class" for their "voluntary downward mobility," for not fulfilling their parents expectations of "manning a more than proportional share of the positions of power and prestige":

> you were to be its executives, its professionals, its artists and intellectuals, among its business and political leaders, you were to think its influential thoughts, tend its major institutions, and reap its highest rewards. It was at least

partly to this end that we brought you up, that we attended so assiduously to your education, that we saw to the cultivation of every last drop of your talents.

This kind of anxiety over class self-reproduction drives much of *Five Easy Pieces* as well. It is not a coincidence that Bobby's tearful attempt at rapprochement with his silent, nearly paralyzed father, in the film's emotional climax, is concluded by Bobby's acknowledgement of his failure to fulfill his father's professional expectations: "Anyway, we both know I was never that good at it."[47]

However, Bobby's disaffiliation is not as clean-cut as that. A scene from late in the second half of the film hints at some ambivalence on this issue. During Carl's party of intellectuals, Bobby explodes with furious rage at Samia, a woman who treats Rayette with a kind of self-satisfied condescension. His righteous anger at her snobbery is clearly another rejection of his family's world, and as such becomes another disavowal of his inherited class position. Yet the viewer cannot help but notice that Bobby frequently treats Rayette with a similar condescension; thus, his vituperative attack on Samia seems directed as much at himself as at her. His ensuing tantrum can be seen as a desperate attempt to escape the sterile intellectuality of his class of origin through a spontaneous outburst of proletarian physicality—he ends up picking a fight with the muscular Spicer, his father's male nurse, as if to transmute (and displace) the verbal sparring of Carl's party into a literal wrestling match. The almost pathetic impotence of this outburst—Bobby is roughly subdued by Spicer—suggests Bobby's failure to disassociate himself entirely from the cultural prerogatives of his family.

In fact, Bobby's often sneering attitude toward many of the elements of working-class existence (as they are represented by the film) demonstrates that his attempted disaffiliation from his inherited cultural capital does not entail an identification with his adopted class. Bobby may find classical music inauthentic, since it produces no feeling in him, yet he also disparages the country music to which Rayette is so attached.[48] Similarly, just as he is shown to be visibly uncomfortable during the dinners at his family's home—he drinks cheap beer, while everyone else drinks red wine—Bobby also squirms his way through an evening in the trailer of Elton (Billy "Green" Bush), his fellow oil rigger, as he mocks Elton's wife for her spellbound attention to the television. This class-bound disdain comes to a head when Elton tells Bobby that Rayette is pregnant and that the right thing to do is to marry her. Just as Bobby later resists being associated with his family's cultural capital, so here does he refuse the traditional role of blue-collar family man. When Elton remarks that he too was afraid of family life at first, but that he has come to like it, Bobby sneers, "It's ridiculous. I'm listening to some cracker asshole who lives in a trailer park compare his life to mine."

The events that follow, though, suggest that such a comparison is anything but ridiculous. Elton's apparently uncomplicated praise of the joys of family life is undermined almost immediately thereafter by his arrest for skipping bail on a robbery charge. It is a crucial moment in the film—the working-class life that had hitherto appeared to offer a space of coarse liberty for Bobby has begun to seem more like a prison, a feeling emphasized by the tight, almost claustrophobic close-ups utilized throughout the scene in Elton's trailer (which immediately precedes Bobby's rejection of Elton's advice). Therefore, when we realize that Elton too chafes under the limitations of "the good life" as he has described it, it serves as an implicit rebuke to Bobby's claim that their lives have nothing in common. As we watch Bobby fight with the men who have come to arrest Elton at the oil field, Elton appears as nothing less than a fellow blue-collar rebel—suggesting that Bobby's alienation is not solely the provenance of middle-class dropouts.

Yet, in another of its "astonishing fake-outs," the film cuts abruptly from this scene to Bobby, now outfitted with suit and tie, en route to visit his sister's recording session. This unexpected narrative shift sets in motion Bobby's return to his family and his class of origin, and his abandonment of Elton and the working-class environs of the California oil town, for the rest of the film. Why does the break between the film's two main sections occur at this point? Why is this narrative tangent—that is, Elton's resistance to the blue-collar traditionalism he had just been sanctioning—tantalizingly offered only to be ignored? Why, in other words, do we not see Bobby demonstrate his disaffiliation from his middle-class past by following up not on his father's health but instead on Elton's legal predicament?

As a way of answering these questions, let me compare this scene with a previously noted narrative "fake-out": Bobby's Chopin performance on the back of a truck. The traffic jam in which Bobby is trapped serves as a kind of objective correlative to the constraints of working-class life on his hedonistic impulses—especially since he and Elton are there because they had been sent home from work for being drunk. In the scene, Bobby leaps out of Elton's car and shouts that the other drivers are "crazy" for spending "the most beautiful part of the day" stuck in their cars. He then discovers the piano on the truck ahead of them and begins playing Chopin's Fantasy in F Minor. As the truck pulls onto an off-ramp, and thus out of the traffic jam, with Bobby still at the piano in back, the scene becomes a depiction of an almost lyrical transcendence—it is as if Bobby rises above it all through his classical musicianship.

Bobby's figurative means of escaping this literal trap, though, are precisely the musical skills—that is, the cultural capital—that he endeavors throughout the rest of the film to renounce. One cannot help but see the parallels with Bobby's response to the news of Rayette's pregnancy, where he returns to the family he has repudiated, and pursues a woman who is Rayette's class opposite. In short, when his negatively constituted, reactive association with the working class threatens to become too binding, too permanent, Bobby draws upon the middle-class resources he otherwise disdains in order to escape. Of course, it could be argued that this is merely part of the film's intended character study of a restless iconoclast uncomfortable with being limited to any one way of life. Yet in a film otherwise so dedicated to arguing "that intellectuality and culture are nothing but hollow shells inhabited by hollower shells" (as *Newsweek*'s Joseph Morgenstern put it), the protagonist's repeated recourse to precisely this realm of intellectuality and culture in order to avoid becoming trapped in a working-class identity appears as nothing less than a kind of bad faith.[49]

Elton's arrest, then, might serve as the film's acknowledgement—conscious or unconscious—of this bad faith. Elton's (rather significant) resistance to the limitations of family life could establish him as a fellow rebel. But its juxtaposition with Bobby's ineffective attempt to demonstrate his own alienation by quitting his job (his foreman responds dismissively: "I don't care what you do") seems to dramatize the ways in which these rebels, and their respective situations, also differ. For in many ways, Bobby's bad faith mirrors the film's—just as the protagonist adopts a working-class identity only in opposition to his class of origin, dropping it as soon as it becomes a hindrance, so does the film evacuate its working-class setting after it has served its function of signifying its protagonist's middle-class disaffiliation. While that setting provided a way to imbue its protagonist with an earthy, authentic (and, not incidentally, masculine) brand of alienation, the film, despite its opening self-presentation, has never been about an examination of this kind (that is, Elton's kind) of experience. Instead, it has been about a quasi-countercultural rejection of cultural capital (the "crisis" that occurred before the film began, as Schickel put it), and thus must return to the site of this cultural capital's transmission in order to carry out its narrative logic. Therefore, we can see the scene of Elton's arrest, and his subsequent disappearance from the film, as the moment in which the film runs up against its own contradictory investments in working-class experience. This contradiction is then circumvented through the film's reliance on a signal characteristic of its *own* cultural capital—that is, a self-consciously elliptical narrative strategy that refuses linear representations of character motivation.[50] In short, the film evades the difficult questions it raises concerning class identity and affiliation via the culturally privileged filmmaking strategies that would come to signify the New Hollywood.

In fact, for a film so ostensibly committed to critiquing the artistic pretensions of its protagonist's family, *Five Easy Pieces* frequently draws attention to its own. It does this through not only its moderately intransitive narrative structure but also its frequently conspicuous cinematography. Stanley Kauffman echoed many other reviewers when he commented that "the photography by Laszlo Kovacs is extraordinary in a time when extraordinary camerawork is becoming common."[51] Yet just as many other reviewers noted the excessively obtrusive nature of this cinematography, which caused "frame after frame [to look] like something destined for the covers of the photography annuals," as John Simon complained in the *New Leader*.[52] Indeed, Simon singles out the film's "grandiosely flashy shots...of the inactive machinery of the oil field looking, at nightfall, like a combination petrified forest and Calvary" as particularly egregious examples of this tendency.[53] Since the effect of such visual flourishes is, of course, to foreground the act of filmmaking itself—which has the corollary effect of calling attention to the cultural and material resources of the filmmakers—it is no coincidence that these moments of stylistic excess occur primarily in scenes depicting a site of working-class labor. For in presenting its blue-collar subject matter through the lens (literally) of its artful cinematography, the film seems to offer a gritty realism, yet also imposes a kind of aesthetic distance through its elegant compositions and meticulous attention to color. The effect is not unlike that achieved by Bobby as he played Chopin on the back of a truck in the middle of a traffic jam—an authentic working-class location is both inhabited and transcended. In this way, we might see the implicit contradiction between the film's formal embrace and thematic rejection of highbrow aesthetics as analogous to Bobby's own radically ambivalent relationship to his cultural capital.

Thus, *Five Easy Pieces* can be described as a film shot through with antinomial impulses regarding cultural capital and class identity. While the film utilizes working-class signifiers to express a downwardly mobile and vaguely countercultural disaffiliation from middle-class identity, its concomitant deployment of various forms of cultural capital serves to establish a sense of distinction from these signifiers—a deployment that, in turn, seems at odds with the film's implicit critique of the class privileges such resources provide. Just as *Joe* presents an ironizing of class distinction that still authorizes the ideologies of upward mobility and material acquisitiveness that help produce such distinctions, *Five Easy Pieces* offers an analogous critique, only to remain too invested in its own markers of cultural distinction to interrogate thoroughly the operations of taste that subtend the privileges it seeks to oppose.

But if *Joe* transfigures the dynamics of generational conflict toward an opposition between traditionalist workers and countercultural youth, *Five Easy Pieces* offers a somewhat different diagram of social alliances. For while both working- and middle-class experience are presented as barriers to the quasi-countercultural freedom sought by Bobby, in no way are these two forces imagined to be aligned as they are in *Joe*. Neither, however, is the initially suggested connection between Bobby's disaffiliation and his adopted working-class identity shown to be anything other than a marriage of convenience. In other words, we do not find in *Five Easy Pieces* an alternative triangulation of the generational split—one that aligns students and workers—to counterpose to *Joe's* political geometry. Where *Joe* enacts a kind of disappearance of middle-class conservatism into the figure of a resentful working class, the opposite process occurs in *Five Easy Pieces*. The latter film's narrative logic entails the gradual *emergence* of the disaffiliated protagonist's genuine identity—and thus, his distinction—from the working-class position in which he is initially situated. In this way, *Five Easy Pieces* becomes a document of generational nonalignment—a nonalignment ratified by the film's final image, which, in a typically ambivalent gesture, borrows from both countercultural ideology and American literary tradition: Bobby hitches a ride on a north-bound truck and lights out for the territories.

THE (UN)MAKING OF HOLLYWOOD'S WORKING CLASS

Five Easy Pieces's deeply conflicted relationship to cultural capital is not just a sign of the class anxieties that beset the period; it can also be understood as symptomatic of material conflicts within the New Hollywood, particularly those concerning the conditions of film production. We can therefore see the formal and thematic negotiations of cultural capital and class identity I have described above as textual traces of the struggles over the relations of production that marked the formation of the New Hollywood.

These struggles often pitted aspiring young filmmakers against the aging, conservative Hollywood unions. This conflict was directly addressed by *Variety* Hollywood correspondent A. D. Murphy in his August 18, 1968, editorial for the *New York Times* titled "Students: Stay Out of Hollywood." In this influential piece (it was soon reprinted in *Cineaste*), Murphy argued that the "inbred, protective unionism" of the Directors Guild of America (DGA) and the International Alliance of Theatrical and Stage Employees (IATSE, which represents technical and craft workers) had caused a "near-total freeze-out" of young people from most filmmaking positions. This "freeze-out" was abetted, Murphy asserted, by studio management "congenitally frightened at even the hint of labor trouble," and by other established filmmakers, almost all of whom, he claimed, "are afraid to speak out against the system." Even the newly established American Film Institute—charged, in part, with cultivating and developing a new generation of filmmakers—was characterized by Murphy as "approaching these unions in a supplicant's posture."[54]

While Murphy's portrayal of Hollywood unions may have been exceptional in its vituperative nature, his central contentions were decidedly unremarkable. As early as 1965, NYU film professor Robert Gessner had bemoaned in the pages of *Variety* the aging population of film industry workers—estimates put the average age at fifty-four—and he placed "unions [and] guilds" at the top of his list of forces keeping "American youth...locked out" of the studio gates. *Television* magazine's 1967 three-part series on television- and film-related unions confirmed this view of the unions' power, depicting the film crafts as "locked in something resembling a strangle hold" by IATSE; the union was then likened in a sidebar article to "a feudal landowner" that "rules its province with an apparent disdain for outsiders." *Newsweek* quoted one DGA member who described Hollywood as "a police state patrolled by the unions." [55]

These critics and others argued that this apparently autocratic control —over both film production in general, and the entry of newcomers into the industry in particular—stemmed from a few key union policies. First among these was the use of experience rosters, which required that, for any given job opening for a studio film, all qualified union members be employed before a nonunion member could be considered for the job. In addition, the nonunion member needed to have worked for at least thirty days, and sometimes as much as 120 days (depending upon the particular union), before being able to join the experience roster him/herself. Therefore, Murphy explained, for young filmmakers to enter the industry, "there must be full employment of current union members, plus a long-enough job" that ensures future union membership. Furthermore, if a young filmmaker wanted to make a film outside of the studio system, union requirements for a "minimum" crew often made the production of independent films prohibitively expensive. As a result, according to director Lew Clyde Stoumen, there was "a general feeling among independent film-makers that the unions stand between them and their art." [56]

Often, then, in an industry described by the *Monthly Labor Review* as the one with the "most highly unionized professional employees in the United States," the filmmakers who came to make up the New Hollywood got their first experience on nonunion sets. One of the main reasons that Roger Corman and AIP were so influential in helping many of these filmmakers get started is that none of their films had "orthodox" union contracts, and they could therefore employ workers without union cards—often at extremely low pay and under exploitative working conditions. Others, such as Brian De Palma, made their films "undercover," claiming that since "the unions say you can't make a non-union picture," he had to make his first films in "absolute secrecy." De Palma argued that such measures seemed necessary after the Screen Actors Guild forced nine SAG actors (including the lead) to withdraw from Robert Downey's *Putney Swope* (1969) because the film's producers had refused to contract with SAG. (Soon after this incident, letters were sent to SAG members warning them not to work in "experimental" or "underground" films that did not contract with the guild.) Finally, *Easy Rider*—produced by the same company (BBS) that made *Five Easy Pieces*—was filmed under a contract with the National Association of Broadcast Employees and Technicians (NABET), a largely television-based union and rival to IATSE. NABET had been engaged in several jurisdictional disputes with IATSE in the years preceding *Easy Rider*'s release but had been unsuccessful at making inroads into the film industry. With the film's success, though—*Variety* noted that *Easy Rider* was "the first box office hit filmed under other than an [IATSE] agreement"—NABET began to sign a number of contracts with other independent producers, including those of *Joe* (figure 1.2).[57]

The rise in nonunion and rival union filmmaking shook the already weak position of the film unions at the time. Combined with the continued practice of "runaway" production (studio-financed films made in foreign countries for cheaper costs) and the film industry's general slump during the period, these challenges to the film unions caused many locals to begin the decade with 40 to 50 percent of its members unemployed—a situation one IATSE spokesperson declared he had not witnessed since the Depression era. In response, the unions began making concessions in order to encourage production in the hopes of spurring greater employment for their members. SAG, for example, eventually allowed actors to work at half of the guild's scale pay for independent productions whose budget was under $50,000. Perhaps more profound, though, were the broad concessions granted by IATSE for productions budgeted at under a million dollars. IATSE president Richard F. Walsh told *Variety* that the agreements reached between his union and the Association of Motion Picture & Television Producers (AMPTP) allowed for both "a great reduction" in crew size for these Hollywood productions and the elimination of the requirement to hire additional, local IATSE workers on location shoots. Yet the effect these concessions had in spurring production was mixed at best, and dissatisfaction with them helped bring about, at IATSE's convention later that year, the strongest challenge to Walsh's presidency of his three-decade tenure.[58]

In short, the material interests of aspiring young filmmakers and those of film union workers were often fundamentally opposed. To many young New Hollywood filmmakers, the unions' policies represented a series of roadblocks, both financial and professional, to the realization of their visions. Over and over, the message they got from the film unions was the one recounted by a still photographer who had struggled for years to get into IATSE: "They said forget about this business, find another line of work."

From the crew* that
helped create you:

NABET 260 West Broadway
New York, N.Y.10013
(212) 226-2040

Figure 1.2. NABET ad in *Variety* (April 7, 1971, p. 21). An ad taken out by the
National Association of Broadcast Employees and Technicians celebrating—and
boasting of their inexpensive work on—*Joe*. (The fine print lists the costs involved
in the location shooting done in New York City.) Image used by permission of
NABET-CWA.

Yet to many unionized film workers, the filmmaking practices of the New Hollywood threatened to exacerbate an already dire unemployment situation. When Robert Altman, fresh from the success of *M'A'S'H* (1970), declared that the unemployment crisis among Hollywood unions might be a "healthy phenomenon," as it might reduce the "overdeveloped" rosters of union personnel, film workers could not help but imagine that the birth of a New Hollywood threatened the end of the job security for which they had organized unions in the first place.[59]

Furthermore, anecdotal evidence suggests that the two groups' clashing cultures of work added to the tensions produced by these material conflicts. A 1961 *Film Culture* roundtable discussion on unions and independent filmmaking provides a fascinating early example of the conflict between these differing cultures. Consider the following exchange between former film union local president James Degangi, director Shirley Clarke, and critic Gideon Bachmann, concerning union rules that restrict one craft worker from doing the job of another:

> DEGANGI: The answer is the same as it would be in automobile work: a man who designs the body of the automobile would not be permitted to perform some other functions—
> CLARKE: But there is a difference between an automobile and a movie.
> DEGANGI: There isn't any difference.
> BACHMANN: To put a bolt in an automobile is not a creative process.

This distinction between the creative labor of filmmakers and the routinized labor of unionized workers is underlined later in the roundtable by director Adolfas Mekas, as he described the New American Cinema Group (whose work influenced many in the New Hollywood) as "a new breed of people. They are not producers, not cameramen, not teamsters: you cannot split them into locals: they are film-makers."[60]

To be fair, the New American Cinema Group crafted an artisanal cinema that eschewed industrial modes of production. Yet this romantic conception of filmmaking often carried over into the industrialized contexts of the New Hollywood. During the production of *Hi, Mom!* (1970)—a film he described as dealing "with the obscenity of the white middle class"—Brian De Palma complained:

> We can't just hire technicians. Suppose I had a union crew here. All those guys are four hundred years old. I would probably have very little rapport with them on any level. You know, "We come, we do our job, we leave as soon as possible." There can't be that kind of feeling on a movie like this. Everybody's committed, politically, because they like the material, in all ways.

According to Deborah Fine, a former librarian at Francis Ford Coppola's American Zoetrope film company, Coppola demanded a similar kind of commitment—one which precluded unionization efforts among the company's employees: "The feeling from working for Francis is tough shit if you don't think you're getting paid enough or if you don't think your working conditions are good enough. There's a million people out there that would kiss the ground to work for him for nothing." In these scenarios, a working-class (or, more precisely, trade-unionist) conception of the workplace as a site to be regulated in order to ensure fair pay, decent hours, and other nonexploitative working conditions clashed with one that emphasizes the importance of the work itself over all other considerations—in other words, a conception of work that bespeaks a middle-class orientation toward the intrinsic rewards of one's professional labor.[61]

This assertion of PMC-derived workplace values may seem ironic in light of *Joe*'s critique of PMC labor and *Five Easy Pieces*'s attempted derogation of the cultural capital associated with this class position. Yet it suggests the ways in which much of the New Hollywood's practices and productions can be seen as a class-specific struggle for PMC occupational autonomy—an issue that constitutes one of this class's main sources of antagonism with capital. After all, what else is the auteur theory—the claim that the director must be the controlling author of the film, which was the New Hollywood's central legitimating discourse—but a declaration of independence from the interests of capital (that is, studio control of film production)? Yet this reclamation and revaluation of PMC control of the workplace came to be articulated in direct opposition to organized labor's interests as well.[62] In this light, Bobby's inability in *Five Easy Pieces* to align himself, in his rebellion from his PMC origins, with a working-class position—as well as the film's own ambivalent representations of working class experience—appear as allegories for the complicated class positioning of the New Hollywood itself.

Joe's figuration of a working class hostile to all things associated with the youthful counterculture takes on a similar significance in this context. Given the contradictory material interests of the young New Hollywood practitioners and the film unions as well as their opposed cultures of work, it is unsurprising that the working-class figures found in New Hollywood productions were so often depicted as antagonists to these films' younger characters. In other words, *Joe*'s hippie-hating title character may have been inspired as much by the aging members of the exclusionary film unions as by the working-class supporters of George Wallace. Hollywood electrician Michael Everett, who began working during the 1970s on nonunion film productions because he could not get an IATSE card, explains that "the film unions looked to us like the same people who wore hard hats and beat up hippies." And even though such non-blue-collar unions as SAG often accounted for the difficulties New Hollywood filmmakers experienced, the recalcitrance of the mostly manual labor-oriented IATSE came to stand in as the main figure for the film unions' obstructionist character. For example, though he included SAG and the Writers' Guild of America in his criticisms of the "myopic backwardness" of the film unions, *Sight & Sound* critic Axel Madsen still referred to them as the "Archie Bunker unions" (whose "slow fade-out…nobody is mourning").[63]

Ultimately, such sentiments meant that the relationship between youth and the working class shown in New Hollywood films was not the one taking shape on the picket lines outside Standard Oil, General Electric, General Motors, and other sites of the militant strike wave of 1969–1971. As historian Peter Levy has demonstrated, the willingness of many factions of the New Left to support the struggles of the Oil, Chemical, and Atomic Workers, the United Electrical Workers, the United Auto Workers, and the wildcatting postal workers (among others) "showed that segments of the New Left and labor were reconciling their differences." Yet, largely as a result of labor relations within the film industry itself, the idea of a student-worker alliance represented the unrepresentable to the New Hollywood. The face of the working class in New Hollywood films, instead, was that of a unionized craft worker—aging, politically and culturally reactionary, and, most importantly, hostile to the younger generation.[64]

This representation not only implied the impossibility of a student-worker alliance. The depiction of the working class as middle-aged—and the corresponding figuration of the young as middle class—also rendered the younger generation of the working class all but invisible. Joe frequently complains about his kids, suggesting that they are just as rebellious and wrapped up in the counterculture as Bill's, yet they never appear on screen. Although Bobby's blue-collar associates are roughly his age, the traditionalism of their social practices—underlined by the "Stand By Your Man"-isms of Tammy Wynette's country music score—locates their milieu in an earlier era (just as their more significant transgressions, as I have shown, are elided by the film's narrative strategy). Despite the growing affiliation of working-class youth with many elements of the leftist and/or countercultural insurgencies of the period—an affiliation that would soon be illustrated by the young worker-led rebellions of 1971–72 at the Lordstown GM plant—New Hollywood found the categories of "youth" and "worker" to be mutually exclusive.[65]

The persistent characterization of the working class as an aging, conservative social group offered undeniable benefits for the professional middle class. Consider how Axel Madsen's lamentation that "every advance" in New Hollywood filmmaking "has been a battle against vested labor interests" dovetails with *Time* magazine's description of workers as "the Americans most affected by rapid social disruption and technological change—and least prepared for it." By associating the working class with a fearful opposition to "change," the PMC is defined, by contrast, as more able to manage—in all senses of that term—this change. Note too how the New Hollywood's generational articulation of class identities works to naturalize this representation of each class's predilections, as it valorizes the allegedly youthful PMC's prerogatives against the supposedly aging and outmoded interests of the working class. This generational logic does not simply delegitimate working-class collective action; if one wanted to find a magical resolution to the crisis within the PMC over the proper role and function of the class itself, one could do worse than depict the reassertion of PMC power and control as an apparently inevitable generational changing of the guard.[66]

Of course, it is with just this sort of generational self-definition that the New Hollywood conceived of and presented its films—and itself. As they triangulated their narratives of youthful disaffiliation through working-class characters and experiences, the most visible New Hollywood youth-cult films helped encode these class identities with generational accents. Furthermore, the auteurist industrial strategies of the New Hollywood legitimized a PMC reclamation of workplace autonomy and control that, ultimately, was purchased against both capital and labor. Finally, through their often overheated declarations of generational exceptionalism (such as *Easy Rider* director Dennis Hopper's claim that "we may be the most creative generation in the last nineteen centuries"), New Hollywood practitioners argued for the dominance of their PMC-centered productions and production strategies through the naturalizing rhetoric of generational change. In these ways, the New Hollywood can be understood as a central force for— and representative figure of—the cultural reimagining of a resurgent and reinvigorated professional middle class.[67]

Yet, without downplaying the soon-to-be hegemonic power of this cultural reimagination, we should also note the (necessarily) incomplete nature of this project. Consider the ways in which the class politics I have traced in these New Hollywood films came into being only through the frequent and persistent representation of a deep suspicion of and hostility toward PMC authority. In other words, in order to manage the crisis within the PMC, the signs and symptoms of the crisis needed, inevitably, to be articulated. This anti-PMC suspicion and hostility appears in the middle-class self-hatred encouraged by the presence of *Joe*'s title character but finally voiced by Bill in his attacks on his own profession. It also shapes the undeniable attraction of the supposed liberties of working-class experience imagined by these films—pictured in Bobby's free-wheeling drinking and sexual exploits during the beginning of *Five Easy Pieces*, as well as the vulgar jokes Bill feels emboldened to utter during his budding friendship with Joe. Here the white working-class male performs, for the male members of the PMC, a sort of minstrel function, in which the pleasures that must be foregone in order to maintain one class identity are displaced and projected onto a denigrated other. As with blackface minstrelsy, of course, one cannot disregard the dominant function of this practice, which is to belittle and master the (here, class) other. Yet it would be equally misguided to ignore the class anxieties and antagonisms that generate the pleasures of these minstrel-like performances.[68]

This "minstrel in a hard hat" is perhaps the most lasting representation of the working class that the New Hollywood youth-cult films bequeathed to the larger culture in the 1970s, one that reappeared on the nation's television screens for the rest of the decade in the form of *All in the Family*'s Archie Bunker. And in fact we will see this kind of figure in many guises throughout the rest of this book. But this is not the only trace of anti-PMC sentiment to be found in these productions. For these sentiments also produced the figure of the "unmotivated hero"—a figure at the center of the debates over postclassical style in film studies, and one exemplified by Bobby in *Five Easy Pieces*. We can now see the "almost physical sense of inconsequential action, of pointlessness and uselessness, a radical skepticism, in short, about the American virtues of ambition, vision, drive" that Thomas Elsaesser identifies in these unmotivated heroes as the allegorical representation of the PMC's uncertainty over its legitimacy. The fact that this exploration of doubt over professional identity utilizes the very resources and privileges of this class perhaps accounts for the "transitional status" of these films for Elsaesser; the fact that their directors "seem a little unsure of how to objectify into narrative the mood of indifference [and] post-rebellious lassitude." Thus, the unmotivated hero can be recognized as the middle-class counterpart to the working-class hard hat—both emblems of a submerged, displaced resistance to or suspicious hesitation toward PMC values and power. Any account of this figure's role in the development of postclassical style must recognize him as the product of the New Hollywood's class struggles.[69]

PART II

Rednecks and Good Ole Boys

The Rise of the Southern

The 1970s were hard on the Western. Despite the fact that, as Thomas Schatz has observed, there was "something of an upsurge in western production" during the period, the genre, which had been a consistent feature of Hollywood filmmaking for roughly half a century, was in the midst of decline; the Western virtually disappeared from U.S. filmmaking after the decade's close. David A. Cook suggests that "the political violence of 1968, Vietnam, and Watergate" dealt the Western a "death blow" by making "the heroic utopian mythography of the American West...impossible to sustain." In fact, many of the Westerns produced during the period, such as *The Wild Bunch* (1969), *Little Big Man* (1970), and *McCabe and Mrs. Miller* (1971) engaged in a systematic deconstruction of the genre's ideological underpinnings, utilizing the form to critique its racialized narratives of national/ imperial Manifest Destiny. Furthermore, since the Western also served, as Schatz argues, "to enable the audience...to negotiate a transition from its rural-agrarian past and into its urban-industrial (and post-industrial) age," it makes sense that the form's attraction would wane as the dilemmas of this transition became increasingly distant from and irrelevant to large sections of the American public.[1]

However, at the end of the 1970s, many film critics observed that the decline of the Western was accompanied by the rise of a new kind of film that borrowed many of its elements. James Monaco described the emergence of a group of films that "celebrate small-town self-reliance, everyday working-class life, and the ongoing struggle with the Man"—films he designated as "'country' movies," for they are "most often shot in the South and earn most of [their] income there." Monaco argued that these films had "the same raw ethic of survival that used to characterize American westerns," a comparison he later sums up by defining country movies as "westerns on the road." This last quality prompted Monaco to claim that the "grandfather of the country movies is *Easy Rider*."

Monaco was not alone in his characterization of the legendary youth-cult film as a progenitor of this other cycle of films; Warren French also posited *Easy Rider* as part of what he called the rise of the "southern," which he similarly described as an adaptation of Western generic elements. French argues that *Easy Rider* both reverses the Western's geographical progression (the young men go east, via the South, not west) and updates it from a "horse opera" to a "gasoline opera." By thus displacing the rival genre of the Western, and relocating its elements to a modern, automobile-centric South, *Easy Rider* serves, for French, as the film that enabled the decade-long proliferation of movies preoccupied with "fast driving and disrespectful confrontations with malign forces of the law"—a cycle he sees as culminating in 1977's *Smokey and the Bandit*. *Film Comment's* Richard Thompson dubbed this emergent genre the "redneck movie" and noted that both it and the Western "contain oppositions of city and country," offer "individualist heroes [who] are pitted against the forces of authority," and "take place in wide open spaces through which the hero has special mobility (the horse, the stock car)."[2]

While it went under a few different names, the Southern (as I will call it here, for reasons that should soon become apparent) can be identified as a film set in a southern, most often rural landscape, in which automotive-based action is central as both narrative and spectacle, and whose villains are the various functionaries of a corrupt "System," embodied by racist, vindictive policemen and/or organized crime. As the accounts above suggest, the features of this film cycle may be best understood as adaptations of Western generic elements. And since the Western's popularity stemmed at least in part from the ideological work it performed for its audience, it is worth asking how this new adaptation of Western narrative strategies and visual iconography spoke to a new set of social concerns and dilemmas. In fact, Schatz's argument that the Western functioned to articulate and negotiate the nation's transition from rural to urban ways of life is also germane to the concerns of the Southern, for the cycle's popularity coincided with the widespread recognition of the rise of the Sunbelt—that is, the rapid industrialization and urbanization of the South and Southwest during the decades following World War II. In other words, the Western's interest in the tensions between rural and urban traditions and lifestyles did not necessarily end: it just migrated to the South.

In this light, Thompson's assertion that there is "one essential difference" between Westerns and Southerns seems especially salient: "the Western hero is located outside of class structures and so is relatively classless, exercising extreme social mobility; the redneck is specifically a working-class hero in his style, concerns, iconography, and limits." In the next two chapters, I argue that this cinematic foregrounding of class identity (and class conflict) indicates the important role that class played in the Sunbelt's emergence—and ensuing dominance. Spurred by postwar military spending, the mass relocation of industry from the largely unionized Northeast "rust belt" to the anti-union South, and the demographic transfers that attended these developments, the formation of the Sunbelt constituted what Mike Davis calls "the most rapid and large-scale shift in economic power in American history." This shift furnished the economic and political base for the "New Right," a movement of conservative politicians and organizations who took advantage of the Democrats' loss of the South (after the civil rights movement) and the breakdown of New Deal economic policy to transform the terrain of U.S. politics—a transformation that culminated in the election of Ronald Reagan in 1980. Many critics have noted how this transformation was accomplished through a "backlash" politics of gendered and racialized resentment. What the Southern cycle shows us is that it was also made possible through a rearticulation of traditional class identities. In other words, the Southern cycle was not just made possible by the Sunbelt's rise, but it also projected new ways of imagining class that the New Right would capitalize on in their realignment of class affiliation.[3]

One of the signs of this realignment was the shift in popular representations of white working-class masculinity. As the historian James C. Cobb has observed, the rise of the Sunbelt was accompanied by the discovery that "yesterday's repulsive redneck had suddenly developed rustic charms." This transvaluated figure, dubbed the "good ole boy" by various journalistic accounts of the Sunbelt, appeared as the most frequent protagonist of Southern films; Cobb himself noted the crucial part played by Burt Reynolds's various "'good ole boy' roles" in recasting "working-class white southerners" as "harmless, fun-loving, and well-intentioned." To grasp the success of this cinematic project, just consider how unthinkable it would have been in 1969 for a television show to have as its heroes two southern white working-class men who resist law enforcement, often while driving around dangerously in a Confederate-flag-bedecked car named after a southern Civil War general. Ten short years later, though, the success of *The Dukes of Hazzard* would apotheosize this reimagination of rednecks as, in the words of the *Dukes* theme song, "just the good ole boys."

I will trace this move from redneck to good ole boy by comparing the films of the Southern cycle to a crucial pre-Southern, 1972's *Deliverance*. Chapter 2 discusses John Boorman's adaptation of James Dickey's best-selling novel as offering something like an allegory of the Sunbelt's rise—one that illustrates the cultural and political stakes involved in the New South's attempted erasure of the redneck. The next chapter addresses the good ole boy heroes of the Southern films that followed, with particular attention to the minicycle of trucker films that offer some of the more overtly politicized films of the cycle. These trucker films, and their charged relationship to the 1973 and 1974 shutdowns of the nation's highways by wildcatting truckers, generated a telling form of class anxiety in their PMC viewers, while their good ole boy protagonists embodied a hybridized class position that spoke to the new class modalities made possible by the Sunbelt's political and cultural economy.[4]

At the same time, the good ole boys who populated these films can be seen as a product, in part, of the period's newly decentered and dispersed forms of film production. Hollywood's increased reliance on location shooting in the South shifted the balance of class power within the film industry, which in turn helps explain the films' changed representations of the southern white working class. For the relocation of film production to the "right-to-work"[5] South, where many crews were nonunion, not only undercut the ability of the film unions to defend the interests of its members but also influenced Hollywood's filmmakers in their understanding of and relationship to southern workers. Hollywood's anti-union labor strategy, furthermore, was homologous to that which helped produce the Sunbelt in the first place, as U.S. corporations decentralized production by moving their plants from the demographically concentrated, highly unionized sectors of the Northeast to the geographically scattered realms of the anti-union South. This shift in industrial organization generated crucial changes in class formation and affiliation—changes seized upon by the New Right in their discursive and electoral struggles to realign the political map of the United States. Such struggles, as we will see, found a crucial cultural resource in the figure of the good ole boy.

2

DELIVERANCE

An Allegory of the Sunbelt

It is not too much to say that *Deliverance*'s narrative is literally generated by the Sunbelt. The film opens with Lewis Medlock's (Burt Reynolds) harangue about how the Cahulawassee River that he and his friends are planning to canoe, "the last wild, untamed, unpolluted, unfucked-up river in the South," is soon to be dammed up to power "more air conditioners" for the "smug little suburb[s]." Lewis's speech is meant to trivialize what is being gained (air conditioning) by comparing it to what is being destroyed (hitherto untouched Nature). But the role air conditioning played in the rapid and disproportionate growth in economic and political power experienced by the South after World War II was far from trivial. More than one historian has described air conditioning as the "most critical technological innovation" in the Sunbelt's industrial and demographic boom.[1] When the 1970 census revealed that the 1960s was the first decade since the Civil War during which more people migrated to the South than emigrated from it, the *New York Times* dubbed it "the air-conditioned census."[2] Key Sunbelt political and business figures similarly emphasized the importance of air conditioning to this regional growth. Houston mayor Fred Hofheinz went so far as to proclaim that "without air conditioning, Houston would not have been built— it just wouldn't exist," while Frank Trippett argued that Sunbelt cities such as Atlanta—the urban area from which *Deliverance*'s canoers hail—"could never have mushroomed so prosperously without air conditioning."[3]

Since *Deliverance*'s narrative is also driven by air conditioning—the suburban men wish to experience the river before it is dammed up, and their conflict with the local residents seems linked to this impending hydroelectric project—it is necessary to inquire into the film's relationship to this momentous shift in the South's political economy. For while *Deliverance* has frequently been considered as another cinematic contribution to the

Southern Gothic, the film does not present us with a mythic, ahistorical South. Instead, as its opening shots of construction vehicles churning up the river valley indicate, the film discloses a materially determined and historically specific region—the Sunbelt—and, most importantly, the class dynamics that generated it.

Deliverance also serves as an exemplary demonstration of the ways in which generic elements from the Western were adapted to the Southern, which in turn highlight the importance of this shift to representations of the Sunbelt. As urbanist Carl Abbott has argued, "the discovery of the Sunbelt" envisioned a "South that [wa]s essentially an enlarged version of the West."[4] It is true that almost all definitions of the Sunbelt—from its earlier formulations in Kevin Phillips's *The Emerging Republican Majority* and Kirkpatrick Sale's *Power Shift* to the mid-decade deluge of magazine cover stories on the region—included both Southern California and the Southwest as well as the states of the old Confederacy. But the region was most often represented as a resurgent South: *Fortune* magazine's 1977 cover story on the region (titled "Business Loves the Sunbelt (And Vice Versa)") begins with the observation that "if Horace Greeley were dispensing trenchant advice today, he would surely counsel: 'Go south, young man.'"[5] Similarly, in the first of its six-part series on the Sunbelt, the *New York Times* description of this "new frontier" uses the rhetoric of the old West to define the New South:

> It has been the American experience that new frontiers, once they are open for settlement, are overrun and the environment battered. Then they are abandoned when greener pastures beckon.
>
> But this time, the continent is being exhausted by the movement; it is the last migration into relatively unused open space.[6]

The migration of Western generic elements into the Southern cycle would seem to follow this other "last migration."

Therefore, even though *Deliverance* is not, strictly speaking, of the Southern cycle—its literary and art-cinema associations, as well as its absence of fast-driving action sequences, have excluded it from most critical accounts of this low-brow group of films—it serves as a crucial antecedent to the cycle. *Deliverance* adapts Western generic elements in ways that would come to be familiar in the Southern, especially in its emphasis on class conflict. What is particularly striking is the way *Deliverance* draws our attention to the role that class antagonism played in the Sunbelt's rise. Yet the dominant interpretive lens put on offer by the journalistic and academic reviewers of the film tended to obscure these class politics by dehistoricizing the conflicts depicted in the film.[7] To counter these ahistorical readings, we must read *Deliverance* against the larger cultural narrative of the rise of the Sunbelt and note the ways in which the film recodes this narrative. Ultimately, *Deliverance*'s retelling of the story of the Sunbelt's rise highlights the ideological faultlines of this narrative, revealing the repressed history of class confrontation that has most often been overlooked in accounts of the region's ascendance.

One of my aims is not just to survey the cultural work *Deliverance* has performed during its initial reception but also to delineate the cultural work that it may still perform. The point of such an analysis is not to argue for some "true" meaning, hitherto obscured by previous, ideologically clouded writers. Instead, my critical review of the film's reception is an effort to understand why certain of the film's meanings were circulated and why others were ignored. My own reading of the film is meant to explore some of these excluded meanings and activate their more radical critiques of the film's historical moment. To do so is to argue not only that a text does not have its signifying potential exhausted by its reception; it is also to suggest that such inquiries into a text's repressed meanings can illuminate the larger cultural logics that structure its reception. In other words, while a film's reception generates its socio-cultural value at the time, a careful textual analysis of a film can also reveal the governing critical assumptions of that reception—and thereby provide us with a new understanding of the larger cultural moment of which they are both a part.[8]

With this in mind, I will argue that *Deliverance* illuminates the class narratives that were used to articulate the rise of the Sunbelt. The dominant accounts of the Sunbelt involved not just a redescription of regionality in the post–World War II United States—with its curious yoking of South and West—but also the imbrication of professional-managerial class identity with this redescription. *Deliverance* highlights the ways in which class was deployed in the production of regional (and, by extension, national) identity. The link between class and regional identity was studiously avoided in the film's reception, which indicates a larger repression of this connection in contemporary understandings of the Sunbelt. By teasing out the work that class identity performs in the film's allegorical structure, we can unearth the social history of this region's production. In order to do so, though, we must first grasp the ways in which the film adapted Western generic elements to this new political and economic frontier.

"AN EMPTILY RHETORICAL HORSE-OPERA PLAYED IN CANOES"

Questions concerning the film's relationship to the Western informed the response to *Deliverance* even before it became a film. Several critics commented upon what they saw as the negative influence of this genre on the original 1970 novel. In an influential critique in the *Saturday Review*, Benjamin DeMott argued that Dickey's novel, in the first fifty pages, "promise[s the reader] a genuine novelistic experience" in its treatment of the relationship between Ed Gentry, the self-deprecating narrator, who is an unadventurous, "get-through-the-day" adman, and Lewis, his fitness-obsessed, quasi-survivalist friend who persuades Ed and two other middle-class men (Bobby and Drew) to take a canoe trip down the Cahulawassee. Yet, DeMott claims, the novel fails to explore and interrogate the complex challenge that Ed and Lewis's ways of life pose to each other; for DeMott, this theme is derailed by the novel's ensuing action, in which the men are attacked by locals, Lewis becomes injured on a stretch of rapids, and Ed seems to take over his role as expert woodsman (and ruthless survivor). Thus, "in place of a novel, where qualities of character and understanding are set in full view, compared and assessed, the reader is offered an emptily rhetorical horse-opera played in canoes." In other words, the drama and sensation of the novel's quasi-Western events cause it to lose its capacity for exploring the interior life of its protagonists.[9]

Although many critics disagreed with DeMott's assessment of the novel, they often adopted the terms of his evaluation—terms that were then retained in the critical reception of the film. In these accounts, the film's merits were frequently understood to rise and fall according to how well it transcended its association with the Western. For example, in its mixed review of the film, *Variety* criticized the film's treatment of violence, complaining that "it's the stuff of which slapdash oaters and crime programmers are made these days, but the obvious ambitions of *Deliverance* are supposed to be on a higher plane."[10] Similarly, James Beaton faulted the film adaptation for not remaining faithful to the novel's exploration of Ed's inner life; without such an exploration, Beaton insists, the text "is little more than a sort of Southern Western."[11]

What is puzzling about these recurrent references to the Western generic elements of *Deliverance* is that, with the exception of *Variety*'s brief nod to the oater's predilection for violence, these accounts are largely silent as to what, precisely, these elements are. Carol Clover's discussion of *Deliverance*'s relationship to Western narrative traditions suggests some telling reasons for this silence. Describing the film as "the influential granddaddy" of "urbanoid horror" films, Clover remarks that it "resemble(s) nothing so much as thirties and forties westerns of the settlers-versus-Indians variety." These Westerns, she explains, "in one stroke admit the land theft and even the genocide" committed by settlers against the indigenous populations, "but in the next attribute to the Indians characteristics so vile and deeds so heinous that the white man's crimes pale in comparison." *Deliverance* adheres closely to this template. Long before the infamous rape sequence, in which Bobby (Ned Beatty) and Ed (Jon Voight) are attacked by two vicious mountain men, the film establishes an economic relationship between the four suburban men canoeing the Cahulawassee and the people who live in its valley—a relationship of dispossession. Lewis's opening tirade pointedly asserts that the residents of the region are being forced from their homes in order to increase the domestic comforts of the middle class. As Clover puts it, "it is as if the demonizing" of the hill people "must begin by acknowledging that which must be overridden"—that is, the middle-class expropriation of the valley.[12]

In fact, it is worth looking closely at both this opening sequence and other, later scenes that highlight the Western narrative logic of the film in order to examine how such scenes figured in the film's initial critical reception. The opening sequence is particularly important, not only because of its relevance to the narrative logic of the Western but also for its sharp divergence from both the novel and the screenplay (the latter, also written by Dickey, follows the novel quite faithfully). As I noted earlier, DeMott praises the opening passages in the novel and argues that the rest of the book fails to live up to their promise. Others have also emphasized the importance of these early passages in establishing and developing not only the text's main characters but also what these critics see as the central themes of Dickey's novel.[13] For Robert F. Willson Jr., the film's elimination of (among others) the scene of Ed at work in his advertising office "severely limits the moral dimension of the movie" by not making clear the ways in which Ed "desires proof that he is alive and not just a fixture of the ad man's plastic world; he wants deliverance from fears about impotence; and he searches for a means to demonstrate his courage by touching what he fears."[14] Similarly, Ernest Suarez maintains the importance of the screenplay's opening scenes, as they map out the "complex relationship between the characters and, particularly, *within* Ed," especially the "sensations of 'disgust, boredom, fed-upness' and 'simple ennui'" that Ed associates with his PMC profession.[15] In short, these critics praise the opening section of Dickey's novel and screenplay for its focus on Ed's psychological, affective relationship to his masculinity and class position.

This is not the focus of the film's opening sequence. In this sequence, we hear Ed, Lewis, Bobby, and Drew (Ronny Cox) discussing their trip in voice-over, as a tracking shot moves slowly along the still lake being created by the damming of the river (this lake, we are told, is soon to be the site of middle-class recreation). The film then cuts to a montage sequence of bulldozers and other construction vehicles churning up the landscape. Here, as elsewhere, *Deliverance* follows a central axiom of realist cinema, as defined by Colin MacCabe: "the camera shows us what happens—it tells the truth against which we can measure the discourses" of the characters.[16] The opening shots in fact provide a mordant counterpoint to the men's conversation. At the precise moment that Ed declares that dams are "a very clean way of making electric power," a bulldozer pushes and dumps a load of filthy-looking blasted earth directly into the camera. As the others chastise Lewis for insisting that "we're gonna rape this whole goddamned landscape"—they label his claim "an extreme point of view"—a siren initially heard in the background of the conversation gets progressively louder, as if to drown out the voices of the other men. This alarm, we soon learn, signals an impending blast—an explosion that the camera lingers over, as if to corroborate the earlier, "extremist" alarm sounded by Lewis (figure. 2.1).

After some more incidental voice-over conversation (accompanied by shots of their cars en route), the four characters arrive in Oree, the starting point of the canoe trip, where we see them for the first time. We do not see Ed at work, nor do we know much of anything about the four men's lives before the trip. Thus, the opening sequence of the film dwells on the social and economic relations that constitute the conditions of possibility for the proposed canoe trip, rather than the psychological roots of the characters' interest in such a trip. Instead of Ed's private, individual dilemma, we are presented with a social conflict generated by competing material interests— a shift that is highlighted by the fact that the initial conversation is conducted by disembodied voices. Rather than being individuated personalities, the middle-class men are, at this point in the film, identified only by their structural location on one side of an antagonistic class relationship. Finally, the film's opening sequence not only emphasizes the social conflict that forms the context of the suburban men's trip but also their refusal (with the exception of Lewis) to acknowledge this conflict. Indeed, Ed's sardonic defense of and identification with the middle-class recreation made possible by damming projects—he proudly (and drunkenly) announces "my

Figure 2.1. From *Deliverance.* "We're gonna rape this whole goddamned landscape."

father-in-law has a houseboat on Lake Bowie"—underlines his inability to grasp the effects of this development on the valley and its inhabitants.

The film also implies a connection between the canoers' inability to acknowledge the social conflict in which they are implicated and the attack on them later in the film. Clover describes the film's rape sequence, following the logic of the Western, as one in which the violence perpetrated by the (here, redneck) other both justifies the heroes' revenge and overrides the initial violence associated with the heroes' culture. Yet the actual attack in the scene seems motivated (albeit not sufficiently motivated) by Ed and Bobby's misrecognition of what their presence on the river signifies to the two mountain men they happen upon. When these men greet Ed and Bobby with hostility, the two canoers conclude that they must be protecting an illegal moonshine distillery. In a way, this misrecognition rhymes with the one that greeted the canoers themselves as they arrived in Oree. The first hill person they meet, a gas station attendant, immediately asks them, "You from the power company?" This assumption on the part of the local man is technically incorrect yet expresses a larger truth: these are company men, and the suburbs from which they hail represent the power that will be displacing the questioner from his home and business. Similarly, Ed and Bobby's misrecognition of the mountain men is, to invert a Lacanian axiom, also a recognition. If the men they meet on the river are not necessarily involved in an underground, locally controlled economy, their material welfare is indeed being endangered by the likes of Ed and Bobby. As a result, Ed and Bobby's protestations that they represent no threat to the mountain men cannot help but ring false. In this context, the pointed question put to Ed and Bobby by one of the hillbillies—"Boy, do you know what you're talking about?"— becomes an accusation of class-bound myopia. And even though Ed claims that the mountain men's activities are "none of our business," the hillbilly's angry reiteration of this assertion emphasizes that it is precisely the canoers' suburban "business" that is the source of the hill people's hostility.

Perhaps this is the best place to note that conflicts over land between suburban seekers of leisure and rural residents were not merely the invention of Dickey's novel. The significant expansion of public and private development that marked the South's rapid economic growth after World War II occasioned many such battles, a few of which have a suggestive resonance with that depicted in *Deliverance.* For example, the Appalachian residents of the Ashe and Alleghany counties in North Carolina spent much of the 1960s and early 1970s defeating the construction of two hydroelectric dams on the New River that would have drowned fifty thousand acres of local farmland and rendered another fifty thousand acres virtually unusable.[17] The residents of the Land Between the Lakes, located on the border of Tennessee and Kentucky, were not so successful. The Tennessee Valley Authority, which had earlier dammed the

Tennessee River (turning the Land Between the Rivers into the Land Between the Lakes), announced in 1964 their plans to appropriate one hundred thousand locally owned acres of the area—which would displace roughly three thousand residents—in order to build a public recreation center (and thus encourage private development nearby). For the next eight years, many local residents refused to sell their family homes and fought the planned annexation, without success, in court. In 1970, after one of the last residents was removed from his land by federal marshals, the TVA's chief solicitor, Thomas A. Pedersen, disavowed the political principles of the protesters by dismissing them as "troublemakers, thieves and moonshine makers." This last allegation, of course, highlights to the potential political meanings encoded in Ed's presumptive reading of the mountaineer's hostility.[18]

Despite this historical background of political conflict, and the film's efforts to undercut the middle-class canoers' professions of ignorance of this conflict, many reviewers of the film seemed to share in this ignorance. For example, *Newsweek*'s Paul D. Zimmerman praised the film for the way it retained the novel's "relentless suspense as *these innocents* battled a primitive hillbilly sniper."[19] Robert Armour took Zimmerman's claim of the canoers' innocence one step further by describing them, using R. W. B. Lewis's formulation, as "four variations of the American Adam," figures who are "innocent individual(s) who rel[y] only on [their] own resources during some adventure." In fact, Armour claimed that the film's opening sequence actually *enhances* their innocent status, since their background is eliminated, and thus they appear "happily bereft of ancestry."[20] In contrast, Stanley Kauffman did acknowledge the ways in which the opening sequence indicted "the despoilment of nature by technology," yet he tartly insists that "the two bestial mountaineers...would have been what they are if bulldozers had never been invented."[21]

Kauffman's remark, of course, illustrates Clover's contention that the seemingly unmotivated violence of the rural working-class other works to erase, or at least make irrelevant, the crimes committed in the name of middle-class comfort acknowledged in the beginning of the film. This perhaps explains why the accusations of the film's quasi-Western logic went unexplored by the film's contemporary critics. To outline the narrative affinities of *Deliverance* with that of the "settlers-versus-Indians" Western would be to acknowledge that the film turns on just such a social conflict, which would thus challenge the imagined innocence, asserted by these and other critics, of the film's PMC protagonists. Indeed, given the period's unease with the imperialist subtext of the Western, any recognition of *Deliverance*'s analogous political undercurrents would disrupt the preferred reading put on offer by these critics. The term "Western," then, was used as a way of simultaneously naming and dismissing what seems to have troubled many critics—the film's more or less open class conflict.

MAN AGAINST NATURE?

Instead, as Kauffman's comments indicate, the dominant interpretive orientation that characterized the film's initial reception was formulated in terms of a confrontation between Humanity/Civilization and Nature/Savagery (which, ironically, is also characteristic of the Western—a connection similarly unremarked upon in the film's reception). This opposition constituted the central issue for critics who arrived at otherwise completely divergent understandings of the film. For example, Jay Cocks argued in *Time* that "in *Deliverance*, man must become one with nature in order to survive," which "for Boorman and Dickey…apparently means becoming bestial." Richard Schickel, however, contended that the film presents the argument that "perhaps we are now far enough from the savage state so that we can resist it without loss of self-esteem," and therefore that there is "no social or psychological deliverance to be found in the currently fashionable belief in the retreat to primitivism." Even reviews of the film that focused on the film's treatment of masculinity were guided by this opposition between civilized humanity and savage nature. Penelope Gilliatt, who described the film's narrative as "a ragbag of all the myths about maleness that an analyst's couch ever put up with," archly observed, in an orientalizing gesture, "I doubt if it would go with a bang in, say, India, but in overcivilized, overanalyzed countries it works like a very smooth and exciting piece of toy machinery for men at Christmas."[22]

There are several reasons why this opposition served as the lens through which *Deliverance* was interpreted by its initial audience, not the least of which is Dickey's original novel, and his *oeuvre* in general, with its explicit concern with the self's relationship to "natural" experience. In addition, the film was released on the heels of Sam Peckinpah's *Straw Dogs* (1971), and the similarities between the two films—both narrative (in each film, a middle-class man is pushed to engage in violent behavior of which he would otherwise not think himself capable) and stylistic (the films' willingness to depict extreme and disturbing acts of violence)—led many commentators to explicate *Deliverance* via the two films' presumed shared conflict between the civilized and the savage.[23] And it must be noted that many of the film's own textual elements put this interpretive paradigm on offer. The first line spoken in the film, after all, is "You want to talk about the vanishing wilderness?"—which foregrounds the dam's effect on nature, rather than the valley's residents. In addition, Lewis's survivalist monologues and his pseudomystical aphorisms, such as "You don't beat this river," make available a kind of back-to-nature perspective through which the film's action can be understood—although more perceptive critics, noting Lewis's debilitating injury and near-disappearance from the last third of the film, did suggest that the film was more interested in critiquing this viewpoint than championing it. Finally, Vilmos Zsigmond's highly praised location photography—which, in Moira Walsh's words, makes the "wild natural setting…serv[e] as an additional performer"—also presses the importance of the film's wilderness milieu, thus emphasizing the contrast between the suburban canoers and the environment in which they find themselves.[24]

My point in outlining this reading of the film, and the textual and intertextual justifications for it, is to acknowledge the ways in which *Deliverance*, as a heterogeneous text, with many cinematic and literary intertexts, offers possibilities for multiple readings. However, my question is why *this* reading was produced for the film by its initial reviewers (and therefore suggested as an interpretive lens for the potential audience of the film), as opposed to one that would focus upon the social conflict between the film's opposed class groupings. One answer might be found in the way this understanding of the film recasts the terms of this conflict. Many critics aligned the hill people with nature, as suggested by Cocks's comment that the locals "watch the city men like weasels guarding a burrow." Thus, the violence visited upon the middle-class vacationers by the mountain men is described as an expression of nature—an alignment Cocks himself makes explicit in his claim that "it is nature in all its untamable force that finally rapes man" in *Deliverance*. Even those reviews that did not directly identify the mountaineers with nature often discussed them under the sign of "primitive man" and found the canoers' struggle against nature to be homologous with their battle against the hill people, as in Walsh's summary of the film's many "theses": "man against the elements, technology vs. nature, primitive vs. civilized man." The effect of this recoding of the film's economic conflict, of course, is to render it naturalized and ahistorical—to assert, with Kauffman, that the antagonism between the middle-class men and the hill people would have happened if bulldozers had never been invented. In place of a story about a historically contingent and economically determined battle over resources and sovereignty, the critical reception of *Deliverance* produced a tale in which an innocent group of PMC men meet with a set of natural and quasi-natural enemies whose threat is deemed to be as old as the hills themselves.[25]

A TALE OF TWO SOUTHS

Yet this apparently ahistorical battle of civilized men against both their primitive counterparts and savage nature must, as Fredric Jameson points out, "realize itself in a social world through actions and choices invested with social and historical values."[26] In fact, Jameson's 1972 essay on Dickey's novel offers a useful starting point for rehistoricizing our understanding of the film and the cultural work it does. Jameson notes that when the novel's hill people are contrasted with the protagonists, "those standardized plastic men of our own business society," the hill people produce "a curious feeling of aesthetic anachronism": "these ghosts from an older past, from the Dust Bowl and Tobacco Road, faces that stare at us out of the old Evans and Agee album, that listened to Roosevelt over the old radio speakers and rode the Model-T Ford and voted for Huey Long." Jameson identifies these anachronistic figures with "the Thirties…the great radical tradition of the American past" and suggests that they serve as "a disguise and a displacement" for the then current "threat to the middle-class way of life" posed by third-world anti-imperialist movements, African American freedom struggles, and "the intransigent and disaffected young." In this understanding, the attack and rape of the canoers makes a kind of allegorical sense, "for the propertied classes have always understood the revolutionary process as a lawless outbreak of mob violence, wanton looting, vendettas motivated by ignorance, senseless hatred and *ressentiment*, terms which are here translated into degeneracy and general disrespect for life." The novel, for Jameson, "is a fantasy about class struggle" in which the hill people's anachronistic status enables the PMC's victory over its opponents to be "draped in the mantle of historical necessity."[27]

This conclusion conforms to the narrative of PMC rejuvenation—one in which the class enemy is depicted as an atavistic social force—that I traced in the previous chapter. In fact, although Jameson himself does not mention it, the revalorization and relegitimation of PMC cultural capital that I described as the other key component of this cultural narrative can also be found in Dickey's novel. James J. Griffin notes that "as an advertising executive, Ed works in the manipulation and realization of images," and as such he uses these skills in order to kill the second mountain man: "[Ed] does not descend to instinct and become a primitive hunter; rather, he imaginatively projects himself as a primitive hunter—as if he were playing the role of a stalker in an ad he was designing." After this successful deployment of his professional skills, Griffith argues, Ed returns to his suburban life, but he "takes the river with him…and everything about his work and his personal life is revitalized." Indeed, the ennui and alienation Ed felt toward his advertising job in the beginning of the novel is gone, as he describes how "the river underlies, in one way or another, everything I do. It is always finding a way to serve me, from my archery to some of my recent ads." Therefore, Beaton argues, even with all its "deadly ironies," the novel's conclusion suggests that "the journey down the Cahulawassee River was a providential experience, bringing [Ed] back to life" both psychologically and socially. Thus, the PMC defeat of its class enemies Jameson reads in the novel finds a counterpart in Ed's renewal in his faith in his professional abilities.[28]

Yet despite the fact that Dickey's screenplay further emphasizes this renewal—Suarez notes that one of its final scenes features Ed at his office, where his "creative energies are reignited, for now he works 'busily...seems vigorous and very much in place'"—the film does not offer a rejuvenated protagonist. Indeed, not only does the film refuse to suggest that Ed bests the mountaineers through his professional abilities—here, Ed's killing of the hillbilly is accomplished largely through luck rather than skill—but it also ends on a far from reassuring note. Why, then, does a film that goes to significant lengths to foreground the class conflict Jameson finds in the novel not complement this class narrative by offering its PMC protagonist a sense of vindication from his completed trials? Why, in short, does *Deliverance* not valorize Ed's cultural capital in his confrontation with his class other?[29]

To answer these questions, we must investigate further how the film alters the relationship depicted in the novel between the canoers and the hill people. For if the articulation of PMC identity in *Joe* and *Five Easy Pieces* depended on an imaginative identification with working-class experience, much of *Deliverance*'s negotiations of these issues involves the refusal of such an imaginative identification. This, again, is in sharp contrast with the novel. As Griffith's commentary points out, when the novel's Ed deploys his professional skills, it is in order to "imaginatively project himself" into the mindset of the "primitive hunter" whom he is stalking. The novel is quite explicit on this question: "I had thought so long and hard about him [the second mountain man] that to this day I still believe I felt, in the moonlight, our minds fuse."[30]

Yet the film offers no such attempt at psychic fusion. Instead, as many critics observed, it emphasizes the psychic and cultural distances separating the middle-class men and the hill people.[31] One could read in the sharp disjunction between the hill people and the canoers a faithful echo of the novel's depiction of the Cahulawassee river valley as a kind of anachronistic space. Yet when Ed looks back anxiously at the Griner brothers, the men hired to drive their cars down to Aintry, and the camera zooms in on the rifle in the gun rack of the Griners' truck, the historical signifiers alluded to seem more akin to those of *Easy Rider* than Jameson's radical thirties. Indeed, Jameson himself notes that "since the beginning of the civil rights movement, the redneck as a political symbol has changed his meaning, and tends rather to set in motion associations of knownothingism and reaction, than of the agrarian populism of an older era." Jameson asks us to see these associations as "useful camouflage" for the novel's real political narrative.[32] Yet I would argue that these associations of southern white resistance to and violence against the black freedom movements are very much on the film's mind. For what are the film's insistent implications of degenerate inbreeding but a figuration of a pathological form of whiteness, a Faulknerian

reductio ad absurdum of a racial strategy based on the exclusion of other-
ness? Consider, too, the historical resonance—after the jury nullifications
practiced by all-white southern juries in cases associated with civil rights
workers—of Lewis's argument that they could not turn themselves in after
they had killed Bobby's rapist because they would never get a fair trial from
a local jury. So while I agree with Margie Burns, who complains, in an essay
comparing *Easy Rider* and *Deliverance*, that the attacks by southerners on
outsiders in both films are a "trivializing echo" of the violence visited upon
civil rights activists, we nevertheless must acknowledge that this echo finds
its originating sound in that then still-fresh historical moment.[33]

In this way, *Deliverance*'s depiction of its hill people casts the space of
the Cahulawassee river valley as that of the South's recent, violent past. The
temporal disparity between it and the apparently "modern" (yet unseen)
location from which the middle-class men travel—Atlanta, a key Sunbelt
city—signals the implied historical distance between an Old South and a
New South. In other words, the film's encounter and conflict between the
hill people and the canoers can be read as the cinematic transcoding of the
historical juncture between the civil rights era South and the Sunbelt that
came to take the former's place in the national imaginary.

Indeed, this new vision of the South as an attractive, renewed space for
industrial and demographic growth had to overcome the region's strife-torn
previous two decades. As James C. Cobb and others have shown, one of
the most pressing concerns for southern political and business leaders in
those decades was to promote "a peaceful transition to token desegregation"
in order to ensure the region's economic growth.[34] During the controversies following the *Brown v. Board of Education* decision, Florida governor
Leroy Collins noted that "nothing will turn investors away quicker than the
prospect of finding communities...seething under the tension and turmoil
of race hatred,"[35] while, speaking more frankly, another southern developer
remarked, "One lynching and we've wasted two hundred thousand dollars
in magazine advertising."[36] Southern "moderates," in order to encourage the
region's economic growth, worked to avert the more violent confrontations
arising from court-ordered desegregation and thus to recast the image of
their cities and states as "too busy to hate" (in Atlanta mayor William B.
Hartsfield's oft-quoted phrase).[37]

This moderate strategy, as outlined by writers such as William H. Nicholls,
Leonard Reissman, and Samuel Lubell, was to be led by a "new urban
middle class." The development of this class, according to this "emerging
orthodoxy," would enable the South to break free from the tradition-bound,
agrarian-oriented values of its past and spur "an even more rapid rate of
regional-industrial development" that would inevitably, it would seem, both
modernize the southern economy and reform its racial hierarchies.[38] Of

course, this strategy did little to forestall the continued paroxysms of protest and reaction that marked the civil rights movement's hard-won abolition of Jim Crow social and political structures. Furthermore, it was this black-led (and largely working-class) social movement that secured these sweeping changes, rather than an (implicitly white) urban professional class. Yet when several white southern gubernatorial candidates who had run campaigns more or less friendly to the civil rights movement were elected at the turn of the 1970s—elections that were seen as ratifying the movement's successes—*Time* asserted the importance of "a new managerial class and the formation of strong business leadership" to the "emerging moderation" that made these victories possible. In the case of Georgia governor Jimmy Carter in particular, the magazine argued, in language that seems directly borrowed from the southern moderate theorists of the previous decade, that "the landed gentry from the antebellum mansions who had so long manipulated the state's agrarian economy have yielded to commercial captains from suburban split-levels."[39]

As the coverage of the South's growing economic power proliferated during the 1970s, the oft-commented-upon ascendance of an urban, growth-oriented professional-managerial class came to be linked to, and often made identical with, the overcoming of the South's racist and backward past. Note, for example, the imbrication of these two events in *Ebony* editor Lerone Bennett's sardonic survey of white journalistic depictions of the New South:

> Wherever one turned, in *Harper's*, in the *New York Times*, in the *Atlantic Monthly*, there were rhapsodic litanies on the New South—a South that had turned its back on the horrors of the past; a South that was too busy to hate, a South that was hard at work out-doing the Yankees, a South of hustle and bustle, of new buildings, new roads, and new factories.[40]

In a like manner, *Time*'s 1976 special issue on "The South Today" proclaimed that "the ugly confrontations of the '50s and '60s, the bombings and Klan revivals, the school riots and the statehouse harangues seem as remote as the Dred Scott decision"—and then quickly noted the increasing migration of "white-collar workers, middle management and an intellectual elite from the North."[41] Marshall Frady, in a 1975 *Newsweek* column bemoaning the South's loss of its cultural distinctiveness, also articulated this loss as one signified by the new, PMC-centric image of the South. Where the South had once been "something like America's Ireland, or rather America's Corsica—an insular sun-glowered latitude of swooning sentiment and sudden guttural violences," the region was now swept up in "an almost touching lust for new chemical plants, glassy-mazed office parks and instant subdivisions." Its "chigger-bitten tabernacle evangelists who presided over the South's muggy religious dramaturgies" had been replaced by "manicured young bank accountants in horn-rim glasses," who instead preached "Dale Carnegie devotionals," while "that long pageant of splendidly gargoylish, musky old demagogues [from] the South's age of tribal politics" had been halted by southern moderate figures like Jimmy Carter and Arkansas's Dale Bumpers, both of whom Frady described as "circumspect stockbrokers." As a result, Frady argued, this new class's "barbecue patios and automatic lawn sprinklers are pushing out the possums and moonshine shanties in a combustion of suburbs indistinguishable from those of Pasadena or Minneapolis."[42]

This last image—of the PMC's obliteration of atavistic backwoods spaces—vividly echoes those of *Deliverance*, which may now be fully unpacked as an allegory of this upheaval. The social narrative that I have traced here, and that undergirds the individual events of the film, is one that posits the construction of the Sunbelt cities through the displacement and erasure of an earlier, rural, violent South. In the "sudden guttural violences" of the film's mountain men, one finds the condensed historical residue of not only the actual, contemporaneous battles over land development but also the vivid images of regressive white brutality against the forces of social modernity. In the PMC canoers from the "glassy-mazed office parks and instant subdivisions" of the Atlanta suburbs, the film presents us with the exemplars of the region's new order, graced with the same social amnesia that made their emergence as the saviors of the New South possible in the first place. The material condition that generates the narrative, and sets these two groups into conflict—the damming of the Cahulawassee—is not only the engine of the Sunbelt's power but also the means by which that region's past will be submerged. Just as the corpses produced by the film's violent confrontations—the two mountaineers, but also Drew—are to be covered over by the "big dead lake" made by the dam, so are historical traumas of the South's (unfinished) battles for social justice drowned underneath the boosterish baptism of the region as, in the words of the *Saturday Review*, "the New America."[43]

This last journalistic sobriquet also suggests what is at stake in the period's larger cultural rearticulation of the South, of which *Deliverance* is a key part: that is, the frequently declared integration (as it were) of the region into the nation. Of course, the notion of a "vanishing South" is an old one, and what is of interest here is more the terms under which this integration is said to occur; as I have already suggested, the key terms at play in this particular moment were those of class. What *Deliverance* offers—in addition to its allegory of how the South was won—is a crucial instance of how, under the sign of PMC identity, the distinctions of region are effaced. The film's trailer is especially germane here. Trailers, of course, not only imply a particular audience but also propose a way of reading the film. *Deliverance*'s accomplishes the former by introducing the four canoers as "suburban guys, like you or your neighbor." The latter task, meanwhile, is suggested in its intercutting of brief, elliptical clips from the film's more tense and dramatic moments with a deadpan voice-over that delineates each of the protagonists' PMC occupations—a strategy that underlines the degree to which the events depicted in the film diverge from the familiar, middle-class life that the main characters share with the implied viewers. This invitation to identify the canoers as middle class, rather than as southerners, seems to have worked. Despite the numerous textual elements that signify the protagonists' regional identity—their southern accents, their vaguely good-ole-boy camaraderie, Drew's campfire performance of traditional folk standards, and their relatively frontier-ish interest in bowhunting—the film's reviewers universally described them almost exclusively in terms of their class status and urban origin. One cannot help but see this as a figure for the "vanishing" of the South into the Sunbelt—the latter of which is, in turn, represented as the PMC's new frontier. As former *Atlanta Constitution* editor Reg Murphy put it, "The old pluralism that made a Southerner entirely different from his Northern or Western counterpart has disappeared in a blend of leisure suits,…corporate transfers, and predatory acquisitions."[44] In short, the South's reentry into the union is signified by its status as a region made safe for the dominance of the professional-managerial class.

"ARE YOU SURE THAT'S HIM?"

When I initially conceived of this chapter, I expected my discussion of *Deliverance* to characterize the film as the depiction of the PMC's remasculinization, wherein the confrontation forced upon a group of soft middle-class men by a violent proletarian other produces a kind of regeneration through violence, in which the PMC men recover their "primitive" masculinity in order to reassert and legitimize their class dominance. As I've already noted, I was in agreement with Jameson that Dickey's novel offers us precisely this, and I planned to suggest that the film's adaptation underlined the "historical necessity" of the PMC's recasting of the South as the Sunbelt—especially in the infamous rape sequence, whose visual rendering caused *Deliverance*'s narrative to resonate in popular memory in a manner that the novel did not. Yet many elements of the film, upon closer inspection, turn out to refuse any triumphalist reading of its PMC heroes. These elements, largely unremarked upon in the film's original reception, suggest the powerful historical work that *Deliverance* can still do in unraveling the social history of the Sunbelt.

Think, first of all, of the film's deeply unsettling final images. Ed attempts to return to sleep after being awakened by a nightmare, in which he has seen a blood-drained hand emerge from the dammed-up Cahulawassee. The film's last shot, at the end of the closing credits, returns to this view of the river—a river one now imagines to be harboring a restless corpse—and the ominous tones of the soundtrack underline the film's uneasy absence of closure. Furthermore, Ed's clumsy dispatching of the second mountain man—in a suggestive and somewhat confusing detail, he manages to penetrate himself with his second arrow as he shoots the first—present us with a PMC hero who has neither recovered his masculine prowess nor emerged regenerated from his battle with his class antagonist. If we are to understand *Deliverance* in light of the larger narrative of the Sunbelt as a PMC-centric South, what are we to make of these elements?

To begin, we might note that one of the features of this social narrative is the PMC's identification with socially progressive reform, whereas the working classes come to signify the violent resistances to this reform—a feature that *Deliverance's* narrative encodes in the seemingly unmotivated violence of its hill people. Yet as historians have amply demonstrated, the massive resistance to the civil rights movement found partisans in every social class and, in the white Citizens' Councils established throughout the South during the 1950s, many leaders from the southern middle class. No less than J. Edgar Hoover celebrated the professional membership of these Councils, citing the "bankers, lawyers, doctors, state legislators and industrialists" that made up many of the groups' leadership. And while these groups officially rejected violence in order to pose as the "responsible" segregationist's antidote to the Klan, a few Councils eventually split over this question, and the memberships of the two organizations were not entirely distinct.[45] Furthermore, even those business and political leaders who did not actively support these groups were often in agreement with their principles: a 1963 survey of eighty business leaders in five southern cities found almost universal support for continued segregation.[46] Therefore, the narrative of the Sunbelt that plots a middle-class reformation of an agrarian landscape of redneck violence surely misrepresents the working class's exclusive culpability for the region's reactionary defense against social change.

It is precisely this element of the Sunbelt narrative that many of *Deliverance's* textual elements work to disrupt. In particular, the sequences involving Drew's drowning, and Ed's hunting down and killing of the second hill person, muddy the film's ethical waters. As in the novel, it is left entirely ambiguous as to whether Drew falls out of his canoe because (as Lewis claims) he was shot by the mountain man or because he threw himself in (presumably out of despair over their cover-up of the first murder). This ambiguity persists in Ed's murder of the suspected hill person. Inspecting the freshly killed corpse, Ed gasps "No!" in horror when he sees that the corpse has a full set of teeth—in contrast to the toothless man who had tormented him during Bobby's rape. Even upon discovering that the man is wearing a set of false teeth, Ed is still uncertain as to his identity—as is the viewer; responses to the film have sharply disagreed over both the cause of Drew's death and the identity of the man Ed kills.[47]

Again, this is all more or less faithful to the novel, and Dickey's hero managed to find a sense of renewal (admittedly, a darkly ironic one) from these morally ambiguous events. But the film does more than merely render these events ambiguous: *Deliverance* insists that the viewer, in a gesture that breaks with the film's otherwise meticulous efforts to maintain its cinematic realism, confront the unanswerability of these questions. After lowering the body down the cliff to where Bobby is waiting, Ed says that he "think[s]" it is the right man. When Bobby presses him: "It wasn't some guy just up there...up there hunting or something, was it?" Ed angrily responds, "You tell me!" and turns the corpse's face toward Bobby (and away from the viewer). But as Ed does this, he looks directly into the camera, and his eye contact with the viewer is held just long enough for us to register this startling, unexpected address, this sudden recognition of our position as viewers—a position that is otherwise unaddressed in the film (see figure 2.2). Ed's look, returning ours, marks a crack in the film's realist surface and opens the question of who is guilty and who is innocent onto the viewer ("You tell me!"). And where the camera had before guaranteed the truth of the film's events, by testing and evaluating the claims of its individual characters against this visually authorized Real, the camera here refuses to sanction one interpretation over another. As a result, the viewer is made an unwitting collaborator in the film's inability to adjudicate moral responsibility. This corrosive sense of indeterminacy works to frustrate any possibility of closure.[48]

Figure 2.2. From *Deliverance*. "Are you sure that's him?" *Deliverance* interrogates the viewer.

This indeterminacy, I would argue, rebounds back onto the Sunbelt narrative that subtends the film. In clouding the issue of the second mountain man's guilt—and, perhaps more damningly, suggesting that the hill person killed by Ed is an innocent scapegoat for Drew's death—the film unsettles the allegorical equation of its working-class figures with the violent past of the South. Furthermore, in finding itself unable to justify the violence of the canoers under the guise of necessary self-defense, *Deliverance* encourages us to read the actions of its middle-class protagonists through the lens of class self-interest—an interpretive strategy that subverts their privileged moral position in the larger cultural narrative of the Sunbelt. At the same time, by turning these epistemological uncertainties on the viewer, the film forces the audience to confront the unsatisfactory nature of the canoers' attempt to resolve the film's narrative—and, perhaps, the unsatisfactory nature of the social narrative that undergirds it. In this way, *Deliverance* constitutes at once an allegory of the Sunbelt and, in its narrative swerves and filmic apertures, its critique. As the hand emerges at the film's end from the big dead lake created by the Sunbelt economy, the film asks its audience to consider what has been violently repressed and effaced to secure the PMC's sovereignty over this transformed landscape. *Deliverance*, in short, causes us to look again to where the bodies are buried and to recognize the social antagonisms that produced them.

3

KEEP ON TRUCKIN'

The Southern Cycle and the Invention of the Good Ole Boy

Deliverance's Ned Beatty soon appeared on screen in a canoe once more. During the opening credits of 1973's *White Lightning*, in what would seem to be a deliberate allusion to Boorman's 1972 film, we see Beatty paddling with a partner in a canoe down a still, tree-lined river while another canoe follows closely behind. When the name "Burt Reynolds" appears in the credits, one could be forgiven for thinking that what was unfolding on screen was a sequel to *Deliverance*. Upon closer inspection, though, the second canoe is revealed to be tied to the first, its two young, long-haired male passengers bound and gagged. Beatty, it turns out, is no middle-class vacationer but instead a vicious southern sheriff, who, at the close of the opening sequence, shoots a hole in the young men's canoe, causing them to sink and drown. Reynolds's character is also not a member of the Sunbelt's rising PMC; instead, he plays an easygoing, fun-loving moonshine runner, who nonetheless seeks revenge against Beatty's sheriff for killing his brother. In short, despite the film's almost uncanny resemblance to *Deliverance* in its opening moments, *White Lightning*'s central conflict is not between a southern past, figured as a regressive working class, and the Sunbelt present, embodied by the PMC. Instead, the film, like the great bulk of films in the Southern cycle, turns on a battle between two representatives of southern white working-class masculinity: the redneck and the good ole boy.

Richard Thompson argues that what separates the Southerns of the 1970s from earlier films set in the South is the Southern cycle's impulse "to humanize the redneck figure and prepare him for action as a hero"— that is, to turn him into a good ole boy. Thompson illustrates this point by comparing 1955's *Phenix City Story* to 1973's *Walking Tall* (both directed by Phil Karlson):

In *Phenix City*, the implication is that the rednecks are the source of villainy and so the solution is to Northernize the town in order to save it...In *Walking Tall*, the hero is a redneck—the best of the rednecks—and the implication is that the corruption of the town has to do with cities insinuating their practices into the clear values of the country South.[1]

Thompson's model indicates that *Deliverance* functions as a liminal or transitional text, one that adopts the Western-like generic features of the Southern yet still uses its sole representatives of the southern white working class as its "source of villainy." However, Thompson somewhat overstates his case here in characterizing the humanized rednecks of the Southern. These films are still well stocked with figures of redneck menace, as exemplified by Beatty's sheriff in *White Lightning*. What the Southern offers, then, is not a simple transvaluation of southern white working-class masculinity; instead, the films of the cycle are characterized by a *splitting* of this identity into two, well-nigh Manichean opposites. The negative qualities associated with southern white working-class masculinity, so vivid in popular memory after the civil rights movement, are identified emphatically with the film's villain (often a police officer), while another, sunnier kind of southern white working-class masculinity is offered by the film's protagonist. Through these opposing characterizations the Southern film acknowledges the historical baggage that this classed masculinity had to overcome, and then presents a reconstructed version of this identity.

In this way, we can see the Southern cycle as performing a function similar to that of the nearly contemporaneous blaxploitation cycle: both groups of films attempted to construct a post–civil rights identity, especially as it pertained to masculinity. Just as the blaxploitation cycle has been described as a quasi-nationalist rejoinder to the largely desexualized incarnations of black masculinity associated with such civil rights-era figures as Sidney Poitier,[2] so did the Southern cycle confront the previous decade's mass-mediated imagery of hostile, racist southern white working-class men. Indeed, *Walking Tall* evokes this analogy explicitly by pairing its good ole boy hero, Buford T. Pusser (Joe Don Baker), with a Black Power-aligned deputy, Obra (Felton Perry), whose confrontation with drunken rednecks in an otherwise all-black bar seems to come straight out of a blaxploitation film. That Buford more than once reminds Obra of his "proper" role as a deputy, even as he accepts Obra's black nationalist leanings, also suggests the implicit competition between the Southern cycle's good ole boys and blaxploitation's protagonists as they both sought to establish an authentic masculinity.

Jon Kraszewski has recently argued that blaxploitation's racialized politics of masculinity cannot be understood in isolation from the class dynamics of the period, in which some blacks ascended into the middle class (due to the expanded opportunities of the post–civil rights era) while others found their working-class positions threatened by deindustrialization. While the blaxploitation cycle is usually associated with working-class audiences, since they focus on heroes from working-class or poor backgrounds and their modest production values and sensationalist aesthetics situated them on the lower end of the cultural capital spectrum, these films' marketing strategies were often designed to appeal to middle-class viewers as well. Given these mixed class codes, Kraszewski suggests that the blaxploitation cycle should be seen as negotiating the fault lines between the black nationalist movement's vocabulary of resurgent, proletarian black manhood and the more moderate, "black capitalism"-oriented discourses of class mobility.[3]

The Southern cycle's reconstruction of white working-class masculinity operates along somewhat similar lines. Despite their working-class protagonists and milieus, the Southern films were often marketed to middle-class audiences (especially after they had proven track records with southern and rural audiences). Yet their low budgets and exploitation-oriented visual and narrative modalities located them on a different cultural register than that of their upper-middlebrow precursor, *Deliverance*, which meant that these audiences were encouraged to have a different spectatorial relation to them. This spectatorial relation—one significantly shaped by the films' marketing strategies and critical reception—offered a complicated mix of identification and distanciation for middle-class viewers. In addition, the new kind of southern white working-class masculinity put on offer by these films also articulated the new class identities that were being made possible by the Sunbelt's emergence. In other words, what the Southern cycle's good ole boy introduced to the U.S. cultural landscape was not just a new form of white southern manhood but also a class modality that would come to reorganize the country's electoral politics.

EXPLOITATION FILMS AND THE SOUTHERN STRATEGY

It is no coincidence that Thompson uses *Walking Tall* to outline the Southern's revaluation of the redneck, for the film was central in making the Southern's rise visible to national film critics. An initial failure at most theatres, especially those in urban areas, *Walking Tall* found a second life in smaller, more rural outlets, and it eventually became so successful in these areas that it scored among the year's top twenty rentals. In fact, *Variety* observed that the film's appeal in the South was such that it outgrossed *The Godfather* in many locations. *Newsweek* declared that the film's nontraditional route to box-office success "only underscores a radical change in the film business over the past few years: the rise of the special audience." Many Southerns followed precisely this route in their marketing and distribution. Rather than opening the films in first-run theaters in major urban areas, Southerns were usually first released throughout the South—and in more rural areas of nonsouthern regions—where they often made the bulk of their money, before appearing (if ever) in largely northern urban centers.[4]

I will return to *Walking Tall*'s landmark marketing strategy—as well as the film's provocative content—a bit later. But first, we should note how the Southerns' "special audience," as *Newsweek* described it, and the inventive distribution methods utilized to reach this audience, situate the cycle within the logic of the "exploitation" film. Thomas Doherty explains that exploitation films are usually associated with "controversial content, bottom-line bookkeeping, and demographic targeting," qualities exemplified by the Southern's often violent and sexually suggestive textual elements, its low-budget production and canny marketing, and its southern- and rural-directed release schedule. In addition, the exploitation film's emphasis on cinematic formula, largely of low-budget necessity, means that what is perhaps most telling about such films is the qualities they share, rather than their individual points of divergence. Therefore, in contrast to the previous chapter, which engaged in an extended close reading of a single film and its reception, I will examine here a number of films in order to delineate their mutual reliance on a set of shared ideological principles and tropes. Such a treatment also conforms to the films' contemporary critical reception, which usually discussed each individual film largely through reference to the cycle as a whole. In order to understand the cultural work that this cycle performed, we need to grasp the cumulative effect of the entire body of films rather than the textual features and reception of each individual film.[5]

There is another reason why it is useful to read the Southern cycle through the lens of the exploitation film. Doherty notes that the term was initially used, as a 1946 *Variety* article explained, to designate "films with some timely or currently controversial subject which can be exploited, capitalized on"—a meaning that still obtains for many exploitation films. Indeed, in a 1977 article on the current "descendants of the low-budget movies" of the 1930s and 1940s, *Newsweek* reported that "a shrewd eye for fads and lurid newspaper stories is the key ingredient of success" for these new exploitation films. With this in mind, let us turn to the social and political events that formed the source material for a kind of cycle within a cycle—that is, the cluster of trucker- and CB-related films that constituted one of the main exponents of the Southern cycle during the latter half of the 1970s.[6]

THE "LAST AMERICAN COWBOY"

This minicycle of films is important not only because they are a central component of the Southern cycle—as *White Line Fever*'s (1975) director Jonathan Kaplan joked, "Every picture I'm offered is boy meets truck, boy gets truck, boy loses truck"[7]—but also because the trucker often functioned as the characteristic occupation of the good ole boy. In keeping with the Sunbelt's imagination of the South-as-New-Frontier, the trucker was frequently dubbed "the last American cowboy," as in the title of Jane Stern's 1975 book-length photo essay on trucking life.[8] This association was consolidated and reinforced by Southern films, with their characteristic adaptation of Western generic elements. For example, Vincent Canby noted that *Convoy* (1978) "asks us to admire the free spirit of the truckers who own their own rigs, who love their trucks as cowboys used to love their horses."[9] That cinema's preeminent good ole boy, Burt Reynolds, experienced his greatest success as one half of a fast-driving trucker pair in 1977's *Smokey and the Bandit* tells us that, to understand the filmic construction of this key representative of the Sunbelt, we need to pay special attention to this occupation's role in this construction.

In addition, the trucker films remind us that the working-class figures imagined by 1970s film were not created in a vacuum. Instead, these figures served to "manage," in the many senses of that term, the collective working-class actions of the time. In this instance, the trucker minicycle can be understood as a cinematic negotiation of the dramatic series of nationwide trucker shutdowns that marked late 1973 and early 1974. In response to a number of issues, especially the skyrocketing price of diesel fuel and the newly instituted lower speed limits, groups of truck drivers, communicating through Citizens' Band radios, began blocking interstates in Ohio and Pennsylvania with their rigs on the evening of December 3, 1973—a practice that quickly spread to a number of different states. After the success this largely spontaneous demonstration had in promoting the truckers' concerns, another forty-eight-hour shutdown was called for the following week. When that failed to produce significant government action, a further work stoppage began at the end of January 1974. This last shutdown, which lasted over a week and a half, proved to be the most crippling. *Time* described "dangerously disrupted road transport, closed factories and mines...100,000 people out of work, and...scarcities of food, gasoline, and other critical supplies throughout the East and Midwest." It was the most violent shutdown as well: there were dozens of incidents involving shots fired and bricks thrown through the windows of trucks operating in defiance of the shutdown, as well as numerous tire slashings, and the dynamiting of at least one highway bridge.

Before it ended, eight states had called out the National Guard to attempt to ensure safe passage for nonstriking drivers.[10] Federal negotiators reportedly threatened to utilize the army to deliver freight if the strikers did not accept the government's final proposal. As mediator Pennsylvania governor Milton Shapp put it, "We barely averted martial law in this nation."[11]

This was not the first time that there had been violent protests associated with the trucking industry. In 1967 and 1970, the Teamsters had staged trucking strikes during contract negotiations that were similarly marked by attacks against nonstriking drivers and threatened shortages of food and other supplies. Yet it appears that it was the later series of shutdowns that constituted the relevant background for the minicycle of trucker films. For example, *White Line Fever*, in true exploitation film style, opens with a faux television news report in which the announcer discusses the "recent" shutdown and interviews a trucker, who explains the economic difficulties of owning and operating a truck—material which is presented as the timely context of the story that follows. Similarly, *Convoy*, based upon the C. W. McCall novelty hit that narrates a trucker protest against the fifty-five-mile-an-hour speed limit, depicts a government official threatening to call out the National Guard against the film's trucker-protesters. Even *Smokey and the Bandit*, despite its insistently light tone and rather attenuated relationship to conflicts in the trucking industry, prominently displays the banners of *Overdrive* magazine—whose publisher and editor was credited as one of the chief architects of the 1974 shutdown—in the film's opening sequences at a truck "Roadeo."

But perhaps what most clearly affiliates the films of this minicycle with the 1973 and 1974 shutdowns is the fact that, without exception, the truck driver-protagonists are all independent "owner-operators"—that is, drivers who own their own trucks and contract out their services, and who are largely nonunionized (as opposed to the almost universally Teamster-affiliated "company" drivers, who operate trucks owned by their employers). The 1973 and 1974 shutdowns had been instigated and carried out by owner-operators, not unionized drivers. In fact, it was this nonunionized status that prompted many commentators' surprise at the militancy of the shutdowns. *Time* magazine asked, "What could cause the truckers, normally strong law-and-order men, to become a bunch of traffic-blocking guerrillas?"[12] As this quote suggests, the paradox presented by the collective, solidaristic actions of men (and it was mostly men) whose reputation was one of fierce independence[13] destabilized the dominant understanding of the working class as reactionary hard hats. As such, the 1973 and 1974 shutdowns can be described, in Stuart Hall's well-known formulation, as the sort of "new, problematic or troubling events" that "breach our expectancies and run counter to our 'common-sense constructs,' to our 'taken-for-granted' knowledge of social structures," and which must therefore "be assigned to their discursive domains before they can be said to 'make sense.'"[14] The importation of the trucker-protagonist into the narrative and visual codes of the Southern suggests just this sort of management of troubling social events by locating them in an already-known discursive domain. Tellingly, the trucker films are all set in the South and Southwest (that is, the Sunbelt), despite the fact that most of the shutdowns' disruptions occurred on highways in the Northeast and Midwest, as the Southern transported this newly relevant social figure to the cycle's generically determined environs.

As I have already noted, the adoption of the trucker as Southern protagonist made a certain kind of generic sense, given his cowboy-like identity—an identity underlined by his owner-operator status.[15] And, in fact, the films' emphatic identification of their protagonists as independent owner-operators—usually remarked upon in the opening ten minutes, with occasional disparaging references to unions throughout—could be read as a kind of ideological management. Consider, for example, the following, oft-quoted exchange from *Convoy* between Rubber Duck, the trucker-protagonist, and Dirty Lyle, a corrupt cop:

> Rubber Duck: Hey Lyle, gonna be one of us pretty soon, you know?
> Dirty Lyle: How's that?
> RD: Ain't ya heard? The Teamsters are gonna be organizing the cops.
> DL: Not this one. I don't want no part of your damn union.
> RD: It ain't my damn union, Lyle. I'm independent, remember?
> DL: At least we got one thing in common.
> RD: Two. There ain't many of us left.

The multiple allusions to Western traditions here—the assertion of adamant individualism, the begrudging respect between hero (Rubber Duck) and villain (Dirty Lyle), the intimation of a passing form of life—should not blind us to the other functions of such an exchange. By either downplaying or explicitly negating any connection between independent owner-operators and larger traditions of organized working-class collective action, the trucker films address the political anxiety provoked by the 1973 and 1974 shutdowns—that is, the threat of labor militancy in the face of the energy crisis and concomitant recession. For example, despite the fact that the Teamsters had largely not participated in the shutdowns (in fact, they had officially denounced them), the union used the protests as an opportunity to demand that their wage contracts be reopened before the next round of contract negotiation. The *New York Times* Sunday Business section warned that this move "may be only the beginning of an explosion of labor unrest." In an article that also worried over the possibility that other unions might follow the Teamster's example, *Business Week* described the truckers' protests as proof that "there is more militancy in organized labor now than there has been in years"—even though, of course, the protests were not organized by any union. The threat posed by the shutdowns seems to have caused the *New York Times* editorial page to blur independent owner-operators and unionized company drivers into one unified menace to national stability: "If the truck union—through highway blockades by owner-drivers or strike threats by over-the-road haulers—can force indemnity for its members, it will have matched on the domestic scene the economic coercion used by the Arab oil-producing states to bludgeon the West." Seen in this light, the trucker films' insistence on distinguishing its heroes from organized labor begins to make more than just generic sense.[16]

Yet it was the collective militancy of such nonunionized truckers that the trucker films needed to address in their negotiation of these destabilizing social events. And, despite their resolutely individualistic protagonists and explicit derogation of unionism, these films still turn on crucial actions of working-class solidarity. *White Line Fever*'s protagonist, for example, gathers a following among his fellow nonunionized truckers, who then act together to resist a crime syndicate's control over the trucking industry. *Breaker! Breaker!*'s (1977) hero is saved by a hastily assembled (via CB radio) posse of truckers who descend upon the corrupt town in which he is unjustly imprisoned, leveling the various offending institutions (the court house, jail, etc.) with their trucks. Even the comedic *Smokey and the Bandit* features a climax in which the protagonist is able to complete his run only by enlisting various supporters (again, via CB) in an effort to delay and block the pursuing police. In these examples and others, largely spontaneous, CB-facilitated displays of multiracial working-class solidarity—displays that often carry echoes of the shutdowns—are pitted against either (or both) the police and/or organized crime, which can be read as displaced, degraded figures for the state and monopoly capital, respectively. In these moments, the trucker films incarnate and give form to the disruptive class antagonisms that serve as the social ground of their narratives.

But something curious happened to this social ground when these films were reviewed in dominant journalistic outlets: it was explained away. The elements of the films that refer most directly to social life were consistently downplayed, and questions of genre came to the fore. The reviews of *White Line Fever* provide the most vivid examples of this phenomenon, especially since, one could argue, it is the most explicitly political film of the cycle. In his *Newsweek* review, Charles Michener derided how the film's opening sequence explicitly connected the events of the film to the 1973 and 1974 shutdowns: he claimed that "if the viewer keeps his mind on the formula—and ignores the social trappings—he might just have a feverish good time."

Stanley Kauffman praised director Kaplan's "use of tradition" and suggested that the "veristic details" allow the viewer to "salve his conscience. He knows that the filmmakers really know the life they are dealing with…and he knows that they are 'only' making a movie." Of mainstream critics, only Richard Eder emphasized the ways in which the film "is about poor people who have to work brutally hard for a living" and argued that the "widely unfavorable reviews" that deplored the film's violence refused to recognize that it is "the violence of social protest." With this exception proving the rule, it seems that the interpretive lens offered for PMC viewers was one that, perhaps anxiously, directed their gaze away from the cinematic traces of class conflict and toward the generic formulas that framed these socially signifying elements. Indeed, Vincent Canby went so far as to assert that "today's country movies depict a land quite as far removed from reality as the universe of Bugs Bunny." Such critical declarations mark an interpretive strategy that is in direct opposition to the one suggested by critics for *Deliverance*. There, the Western influences that might imply the material antagonisms between the PMC canoers and the hill people were routinely denigrated as below "the obvious ambitions" (as *Variety* described them) and painstaking realism of the film. Here, the trucker films' presumed lack of ambition gives PMC critics license to insist that the generic form—not the social content—is all that is worth noting.[17]

THIRTEEN WAYS OF LOOKING AT *WALKING TALL*

There were some Southerns, however, whose content occasioned a great deal of analysis by PMC critics. This was particularly the case with the watershed Southern *Walking Tall*—a based-on-a-true-story depiction of a former wrestler who becomes sheriff of his hometown in order to rid it of organized crime and corruption—which was read by many reviewers as yet another sign of working-class conservatism. Yet this interpretive work turns out to be just as revealing of PMC class anxiety as the response to the trucker minicycle.

Walking Tall was originally advertised as a violence-filled action picture (which it is). Under this marketing campaign, though, the film failed in both major urban areas as well as most southern and rural theaters. Yet Cinerama, the company that released the film, noted that it was doing well in a few small areas—areas, they later discovered, in which the theaters had advertised the film by comparing it to 1971's *Billy Jack*.[18] The company then incorporated this comparison in a revised advertising campaign (figure 3.1), which asked, "When was the last time you stood up and applauded a movie?" The text of the ad, which ran alongside a still

Don't walk away from
"WALKING TALL"

".Might just turn out to be this years sleeper and emulate the runaway success of 'BILLY JACK'."
— *Kevin Thomas L.A. Times*

MIAMI	OGDEN, UTAH	MEMPHIS
MULTIPLE	CINEDOME THEATRE	PARK THEATRE
FIRST 3 WEEKS	FIRST 4 WEEKS	FIRST 4 WEEKS
AND CONTINUING	AND CONTINUING	AND CONTINUING
$203,316	$33,724	$97,483

(All-time record surpassing THE GODFATHER)

THIS NEW CAMPAIGN IS DOING IT!

When was the last time you stood up and applauded a movie?

When was the last time you were so impressed and involved that you spontaneously cheered?

At previews everywhere across the country, audiences have responded with a thunderous reaction to "Walking Tall."

It is the deeply moving, contemporary story of a young man who wouldn't surrender to the System . . . and the girl who always stood beside him.

"Walking Tall" is based on the truth and it isn't "just a movie."

"Might just turn out to be this year's sleeper and emulate the runaway success of 'BILLY JACK'."
—*Kevin Thomas, L.A. Times*

CINERAMA RELEASING presents

WALKING TALL

Starring
JOE DON BAKER   ELIZABETH HARTMAN
ROSEMARY MURPHY Written by MORT BRISKIN
Music by WALTER SCHARF Executive Producer CHARLES A. PRATT
Produced by MORT BRISKIN Directed by PHIL KARLSON
A BCP Production
In Color

 FROM CINERAMA RELEASING

R RESTRICTED

NOW "WALKING TALL" IS COMING BACK!
FIRST RETURN ENGAGEMENT · PRESTON II THEATRE, DALLAS, MAY 16th
AND THEN ACROSS THE COUNTRY!

Figure 3.1. Cinerama ad for *Walking Tall* in *Variety* (May 9, 1973, p. 16). This ad promoted the marketing campaign that turned *Walking Tall* into a sleeper hit in southern and rural areas.

from the film that showed Buford and his wife solemnly embracing each other, described *Walking Tall* as "the deeply moving, contemporary story of a young man who wouldn't surrender to the System...and the girl who always stood beside him." Only after this new marketing strategy was employed did the film enjoy its breakthrough success.[19]

This success puzzled Twentieth Century Fox president Gordon Stulberg, who declared, "I just don't understand why a violent film that advertises itself as a violent film suddenly starts doing business when it starts advertising itself as a love story."[20] But while it is true that the revised ad campaign emphasized the relationship between Buford and his wife, these ads also foregrounded *Walking Tall*'s populist politics.[21] By aligning the film with the counterculture-affiliated *Billy Jack* and stressing Buford's struggle against "the System," the new ads prompted potential viewers to anticipate and pay closer attention to elements of the film that Peter Biskind has described as "liberal, even radical."[22] Biskind argues that for significant stretches of its running time, *Walking Tall* "envisions an interracial movement of the poor, albeit Hollywood style, against vested interests." In its representation of the friendship and political alliance between Buford and Obra, *Walking Tall* makes "an explicit appeal to racial brotherhood."[23] Moreover, in its refusal "to vindicate the system by demonstrating that honesty prevails at higher levels"—the "red-neck vice lords" who run Buford's town are revealed to be "appendages of the Big Boss in Nashville, [whose] power reaches on up to the capitol"—the film emphatically insists that genuine reform can only come "from the bottom up."[24] The revised ad campaign encouraged viewers to see these elements as central to the film. When we consider how this marketing campaign reorients *Walking Tall*'s violence by situating it in the context of a grassroots resistance to a corrupt elite, the change in the film's popularity begins to seem less confusing.

However, virtually every PMC commentator on the film, Biskind included, concluded that the film is ultimately a protofascist celebration of unrestrained masculine power and vigilante lawlessness; tellingly, they presumed that this reactionary content accounted for its popularity among southern working-class viewers. Describing *Walking Tall* as "so durned Amurrican [*sic*] that only a quote from Nixon seems lacking from its publicity," Judith Crist accounted for its popularity in the "non-urban country" by asserting that "it's not just a case of different strokes for us different folks: it's an entirely different set of values." Similarly, Jay Cocks sneered in *Time* that "anyone looking to set up a neighborhood vigilante group can get a good jolt of moral inspiration from this extravagantly violent saga." Pauline Kael characterized the film as having "fundamentalist politics" and noted with some horror that "in parts of the South it is a ritual that at the end audiences stand in homage and cheer." Of course, I am not arguing that such rightist meanings are not present in—and, indeed, made eminently available by—the film. What I am arguing is that, as Biskind's analysis and our understanding of the film's marketing history suggest, there are other meanings to which the audience could be drawn as well. Yet these meanings seem to have been illegible to the vast majority of PMC critics at the time.[25]

CLASS ANXIETY AND THE OTHER SPECTATOR

These meanings remained illegible because of the sort of anxiety the films seem to have produced in PMC critics, who, as the responses quoted above suggest, spent as much time looking nervously over their shoulder at an imagined southern working-class viewer as at the films themselves. Indeed, Southerns were almost always discussed with reference to their implied audience—an audience that was assumed to be working-class as well as southern. The *National Observer*, for instance, argued that the Southern films that are released in the North "clean up in Dee-troit and Akron, Ohio, playing to disenfranchised Southerners who work the line and dream of the grean [*sic*], green grass of home." Similarly, Vincent Canby described *Smokey and the Bandit* as "not the sort of movie that's talked about at cocktail parties," but he argued that it and other "country" movies like it

> tell us about the state of the mind of a large part of our union. They are
> the movies supported by people who live in the rural South, Southwest and
> Middle West, people who see most of their movies in drive-ins and respond, I
> suspect, to the non-stop action (which is often just movement), to the colorful,
> heightened vulgarity of the language and who feel most at home in the country
> movie's principle setting: the automobile.

The condescension of these accounts—the redneck minstrelsy of the *Observer*'s "Dee-troit," Canby's droll aside that what non-cocktail-party-going viewers enjoy as action, he discerns to be "just movement"—highlights the critics' notion that this other spectator is a considerably less sophisticated one, and one less capable (as Canby implies) of achieving the proper critical distance from the material on the screen.[26]

Yet this alleged lack of distance (by film and viewer alike) is often an occasion for anxiety as well as classist put-downs. For, in commenting on the Southerns, PMC critics frequently expressed a fear over the effect that the films might have on this supposedly undiscerning audience. Furthermore, their revulsion at the films' ostensibly conservative values often served as a cover for the discomfort they felt over the Southerns' more populist elements. Consider, for example, Kael's account of her unease during a viewing of *Walking Tall*:

> The blood-pounding excitement that most of the street Westerns aim for is simply box-office excitement, but in *Walking Tall* it is integral to the fundamentalist politics that probably all of us carry inside us at some primitive level—even those of us who watch this picture appalled. Buford has a galvanic effect on the audience because he incarnates the blood rage that can so easily be worked up in frustrated people. The visceral impact of this shrewd, humble film makes one know how crowds must feel when they are being swayed by demagogues.

There is a fascinating slippage between "us" and "the audience" in this passage, as the referents to these (usually synonymous) terms seem to shift under Kael's feet—a slippage we will return to in a moment. For now, though, note Kael's apprehension over the "ease" with which the "blood rage" of "frustrated people" can be "worked up," as if "swayed by demagogues." The deliberately vague terminology here reveals as much as it conceals: this is a textbook case of class anxiety, the fear of the anger of the oppressed and disempowered. The above passage, in fact, ends a paragraph that begins by describing the film's conclusion, in which the townspeople dismantle and set fire to the headquarters of the town's organized crime syndicate. Of similar interest is Kael's description of the physique of Joe Don Baker:

> he seems Southern redneck—a common man who works outdoors in the sun—to the soul. He has that heavy flaccid look that Southern white men often get early in life; it goes with a physical relaxation that can fool Northerners like me, who don't always recognize the power hidden in the flab.

The attempt to destigmatize the term "redneck" by qualifying it as a simple term of class identification only underlines the specificity of Kael's anxiety: the fear that "Northern" (read urban; read, especially, PMC) observers may miss the "hidden" threat posed by the working-class bodies of the film. Kael's avowed distaste for the "fundamentalist politics" of *Walking Tall*, which people in the South apparently cheer, might therefore be better understood as a broader, unacknowledged abhorrence of the spectacle of working-class anger, resentment, and defiance—and the apparent approval such a spectacle draws from the working-class viewer.[27]

That this abhorrence is articulated through metaphors of the body—the menace implicit in redneck flab,[28] the "visceral impact" of *Walking Tall*'s "blood-pounding excitement"—is similarly revealing. The familiar implication of this rhetoric—that, by working directly on the body, the Southern film bypasses the critical faculties of the mind—is also one that is persistently reproduced in reviews of other Southern films, including those of the trucker minicycle. Lawrence Van Gelder, for example, surmised that *Smokey and the Bandit* is

> for moviegoers likely to use one hand to pound arm rests with sheer zest
> of a race against time involving 400 cases of Coors beer and the other
> hand to smite thighs with glee at what happens when a couple of good
> old boys and a passel of pursuing redneck sheriffs and state troopers match
> alleged wits.[29]

As in Kael's passage, the imagined working-class viewer is conceived here as a body unable to control itself, one who is resistant to any claims of the intellect (the apparently mindless pleasure in the "alleged wits" of the characters). Of course, this opposition between mind and body, so omnipresent in Western thought, has taken on a particular class valence under the development of advanced capitalism. For the rise of the professional-managerial class was of a piece with the division of labor into "mental" and "manual" categories, as one of the PMC's central roles in the relations of production is precisely to deploy its mental labor to direct, supervise, and discipline the manual labor of working-class bodies.[30] This classed understanding of the distinction between mind and body relates to the PMC class anxiety I have explored above. For, as the PMC viewer's gaze is directed away from the cinematic traces of class antagonism, the class anxieties prompted by the Southern emerge once again, in a kind of return of the repressed, as this gaze turns instead to the imagined viewing experience of the other, working-class spectator—who is figured as a body that refuses to be directed by a mind. The Southern film, by addressing the body, not the mind, of its audience, thus threatens to evade the PMC's critical efforts at class management. As a result, the Southern film's spectacles of working-class bodies operating in excess of the law engender a fear of the working-class viewers in the audience—and their potential unmanageability.

WORKING CLASS LIKE ME

But the Southern's appeal to bodily pleasures did not produce only anxiety in their PMC reviewers. In fact, many accounts of these films praised their facility in providing certain lowbrow pleasures, especially those derived from the action sequences. Of course, such compliments were often back-handed ones, as in Richard Schickel's description of *Smokey and the Bandit* as "fairly tacky" but also "jaunty fun"; he added that even though the "primary market for pictures like this is the rural drive-ins … city slickers should also enjoy *Smokey's* transitory pleasures." These "transitory pleasures" are often bodily ones. Schickel, again, on the southern-prison-football-game film *The Longest Yard* (another Burt Reynolds Southern [1974]):

> [Director Robert Aldrich] fills the sound track with the crunch of every bone, the sight track with every splay of blood he can manage—terrible stuff, but viscerally stimulating. In a simple-minded way, it is also very effective, literally capable of making an audience stand up and cheer just as if they were in the stands at a real game.[31]

Once again, the appeal of the film is bodily ("viscerally stimulating"), rather than intellectual ("simple-minded")—and it seems to produce a well-nigh involuntary physical response. It is an experience, then, that seems to parallel the one Kael describes in the first passage from her I quoted above. For the body she is describing in that passage, during those uneasy oscillations between "us" and "the audience," is often that of the *middle-class* viewer, who seems to be moved against her better judgment. Even those "appalled" by Southerns, she argues, respond to them "at some primitive level," feel them in the "blood," even. In moments like this, the middle-class "us" is joined, through the experience of the film, with the implicitly working-class "audience" that had made the "us" uneasy just a moment earlier. The experience of the Southern—which comes to middle-class viewers (thanks to the work of PMC critics) with associations of its redneck fans—affords them something like a momentary affective communion with an imagined working class. In other words, watching a Southern—many of which, as I have noted, were eventually released in theaters outside of their original target market, frequently with considerable success—offers the PMC viewer an opportunity to inhabit, through the body, the experience (and related pleasures) of working-class spectatorship.[32]

In this way, Southern films can be seen as the cinematic counterpart to the CB craze. After the 1973–1974 shutdowns, during which truckers demonstrated for television cameras how they had used CBs to organize the protests, this form of communication that had hitherto been used only by truckers was increasingly adopted by middle-class drivers, as applications for CB licenses exploded from less than 15,000 per month before the shutdowns to 200,000 a month by 1975.[33] *Newsweek* offered the following testimonial of a steel salesman to explain this middle-class interest in CB use: "I try to talk like a trucker and pride myself on being able to help them."[34] As commentators on the craze noted, all CB users, no matter what their class or regional background, adopted a working-class, middle-South accent in their transmissions. This impersonation was accompanied, of course, by the use of the "demotic jargon" (as *Time* described it) of CB slang. And much of the appeal of CB use was the opportunity to invent a persona through the anonymity of the communication form (an appeal dramatized in the 1976 Southern film *Citizen's Band/ Handle With Care*).[35] Thus, just as viewing a Southern offered a way to share in the visceral pleasures of working-class cinemagoing, so did the adoption of a redneck accent and vocabulary enable middle-class CB users another form of bodily identification with an imagined working-class other.

Much of this cross-class identificatory desire, of course, was that of middle-class men, who seemed motivated by the familiar, homosocial impulse to remasculinize themselves through an affective connection with laboring bodies—a desire exemplified in Harry Crews's explanation in an *Esquire* article of how "truckers are different from you and me":

> Sure, he may have a wife and children and a mortgage somewhere, complete with all the domestic trivia that every real man is supposed to carry on his back with such humiliating eagerness, but by God, when he fires up that diesel he becomes a sudden and beautiful *wheel*, rolling beyond the reach of bill collectors, and even beyond the sweet, necessary love of a good woman.

Such a passage resonates uncannily with *Time*'s description of the good ole boy:

> The core of the good ole boy's world is with his buddies, the comfortable, hyperhearty, all-male camaraderie, joshing and drinking and regaling one another with tales of assorted, exaggerated prowess. Women are outsiders...
>
> What he really loves is his automobile. He overlooks his wife with her hair up in pink rollers, sagging into an upside-down question mark in her tight slacks. But he lavishes attention on his Mercury mistress, Easy Rider shocks, oversize slickers, dual exhaust. He exults in tinkering with that beautiful engine, lying cool beneath the open hood, ready to respond, quick and fiery to his touch.

Crews's awed account of how the trucker becomes one with his machinery ("he becomes a sudden and beautiful *wheel*")—escaping the apparently castrating influences of economic necessity, the domestic sphere, and women in general—is matched by *Time*'s more snide (but equally misogynistic) articulation of the good ole boy's male-only world of car worship. Both, however, testify to the homosocial energies that combine with a fantasy of unalienated labor in the eroticization of working-class masculinity. Such gynophobic energies are equally on display in Southern films. In *Smokey and the Bandit*'s opening moments, we are introduced to Bandit's (Burt Reynolds) buddy-sidekick Cledus (Jerry Reed) as Bandit breaks into his bedroom (against Cledus's wife's protestation that "you can't have him!"). Bandit then straddles Cledus on the bed, and helps groom and dress him. This homosocial connection, reinforced through their shared machinery (they make the Coors run in order to earn enough money to buy a new truck), is interrupted only once, when Bandit leaves his car to make love with Carrie (Sally Field). During this interlude, Cledus is thrashed in a barroom brawl, demonstrating the dangers of superseding the primacy of the male-male bond.[36]

Crews's desire for cross-class identification is clearly motivated by a longing to enter this homosocial circle (since, apparently, his profession does not allow him to escape the "humiliations" of the domestic sphere). But there is another reason for this particular kind of identificatory impulse, one that causes Crews, a freelance journalist and author, to claim that *my own life has caused me to have an almost blood-kin feeling for the trucker. Or at least a certain kind of trucker: the independent, over-the-road owner/operator.*"[37] As many commentators on trucking life have noted, owner-operators are in "limbo between labor and management."[38] Although their ownership of the means of production would seem to place them in the latter category, the fact that they must contract out their services to a trucking company means that they often had little control over many aspects of their working conditions—a situation characteristic of labor. In traditional Marxian class taxonomies, they would be described as petty bourgeois—i.e., self-employed small businesspersons. But journalistic accounts of trucking life continually returned to the contradictory character of their work experience—the mix, as *Newsweek* put it, of "cowboy-like freedom to move along when he wants" and the legal and economic pressures of the "tedious, wearying job" that make it "hardly so independent."[39] This contradictory experience found articulation in the cinematic form of the Southern: the open-road autonomy is rendered in the fast-driving action sequences, while the constraints on this autonomy are figured in the depictions of mobbed-up trucking companies and corrupt, vengeful police. Such contradictions also realized themselves on the level of narrative modality. Southern films often oscillated between action and comedy on the one hand (modes indicative of freedom) and heavy-handed melodrama on the other (a form concerned with the ineluctable limits of social life)—a divided film form that responds to the trucker's seemingly contradictory location in class relations.[40]

The student of Marxist sociology will recognize the phrase "contradictory location in class relations" as the one that Erik Olin Wright uses to characterize not independent owner-operators, but the PMC.[41] The PMC's role in capitalism, after all, is at once exploiter, in their organizational role as agents who discipline and control labor, and exploited, in that the surplus value they generate is expropriated by capital. Furthermore, as Johanna Brenner and others have emphasized, this contradictory class location has a profound experiential dimension, since PMC labor is characterized by a series of paradoxical imperatives: for example, PMC workers are often granted wide occupational autonomy, yet they have little or no control over the conditions under which this autonomy is granted.[42] In this way, the fascination middle-class observers had with the antitheses of trucking life—the mix of cowboy-like freedom and proletarian powerlessness—can be grasped as a misrecognition of the contradictions of their own laboring position. The bodily abandon offered by the trucker film's pleasures can be seen to offer the PMC viewer a way to live out these antinomies of autonomy and servitude, of individualism and solidarity, in blue-collar clothes and southern accents. This would certainly explain why *Variety*'s A. D. Murphy described the emphatically working-class protagonist of *White Line Fever* as "a middle-class, average-guy protagonist" whose plight "is timely in an era when individuals seem helpless against organized everything."[43] It therefore makes sense that the trucker films came to form the heart of the Southern cycle's appeal to and success with nonsouthern, and non-working-class, audiences—and also became so central to the invention of that cultural icon, the good ole boy.

CLASS ON LOCATION

The invention of the good ole boy, though, had roots in more than just the inherent fascination of the trucker shutdowns of 1973 and 1974. This regeneration and revaluation of southern white working-class masculinity was also shaped by developments within the political economy of 1970s American filmmaking. For the rise of the Southern cycle was enabled through Hollywood's increased reliance on location shooting—a shift that also changed the way the South was represented on screen. Southern location shooting—which meant shooting in "right-to-work" states that were hostile to unions in ways both official and unofficial—offered the possibility of cheaper, nonunionized work forces, which, in turn, weakened the power of the Hollywood-based film unions. This development not only affected the balance of class power in the film industry but also helped influence the way that the southern working class came to be represented by this industry. Furthermore, southern location shooting, as a strategy of labor relations, was characteristic of the Sunbelt, in that this momentous shift in economic and political power was accomplished through a kind of internal deindustrialization, a movement away from the highly concentrated, unionized sectors of the United States toward the dispersed, fragmented, and largely nonunionized workforces of the U.S. South and West. In this way, Hollywood

filmmaking practices can be viewed as homologous with the larger transformations of U.S. political economy that provided the ground for the New
Right's rearticulation of class identity.

Technological developments in cinematography and sound recording
during the 1960s and 1970s enabled the increased use of location shooting. As David Cook puts it, these developments made "filmmaking lighter,
more flexible, and therefore more responsive to the wide variety of location
contexts in which production now took place." But, as Cook points out, if
these technical advances made more kinds of location shooting possible,
the "primary force" behind their increased utilization was an interest in cutting down on "soaring studio overhead."[44] Yet many filmmakers in the 1960s
hesitated to shoot their films on location in the South, even when the script
called for a southern setting. Often, this hesitation was based on the difficulties that such productions encountered from local authorities and residents,
who took issue with the negative portrayals of the South offered in the films.
Roger Corman, for example, described how he had been "run out of a town
in southern Missouri by the police on one-hour's notice" while making *The
Intruder* (1961), a film about a southern racist demagogue. Producer-director
James Goldstone related how he had been warned, while filming the anti-
pollution television film *A Clear and Present Danger* (1970) in Birmingham,
Alabama, that "the mayor is an honorable man, and he will not withdraw
his permission for you to shoot in this city, but he cannot be responsible for
your well being." As a result of such threats and harassment, many filmmakers shot their films about southern race relations in nonsouthern locations,
such as Illinois (*In the Heat of the Night* [1967]) and Northern California
(*...tick...tick...tick* [1970], *Brother John* [1971]). As Goldstone noted, "You
can work [in Northern California] and not have that feeling of intimidation and constantly looking over your shoulder that you do in the South."
However, as *Variety* noted in an article on the phenomenon, "non-contem-
porary, non-disputatious dramas" found that "the ole (*sic*) southern hos-
pitality [wa]s still in effect." Corman himself acknowledged that he "could
not have received more cooperation" while filming *Bloody Mama* (1970), a
nonracially themed period piece about Ma Barker and her family.[45]

The making of *Deliverance* proved to be no exception to this rule. From
the beginning of its filming on the Chattooga River in northern Georgia,
many locals protested both the film's representation of backwoods residents
and its depiction of homosexual rape.[46] Christopher Dickey, James's son, who
worked as an extra and stand-in on the film, recounted in his memoir that
as the production went on, "we started to hear from our trailer-park friends
that there were a lot of people in these mountains who didn't like this film we
were making." A few days later, cast and crew "arrived on the set to word that
someone had been shooting at the trucks the night before...add[ing] to the

sense that the whole production was racing against time."[47] The resentment of the locals did not abate after the shooting had concluded. *Deliverance*'s popularity spurred a flood of novice canoers to the Chattooga, who then overtaxed the local sanitation and rescue facilities; despite the efforts of the latter, seven people died on the white-water rapids of the Chattooga in the first year after *Deliverance*'s release.[48]

Despite these many difficulties, though, *Deliverance* helped inaugurate a filming boom in Georgia—which was in turn part of the newly expanding use of location shooting in the Sunbelt. The central reason for this boom was the potential economic benefits of location shoots, which came to outweigh the public relations concerns of many Sunbelt leaders. *Atlanta Constitution* editor Reg Murphy admitted that *Deliverance* "won't do much to enhance the reputation of Appalachia. It will confirm the prejudices of some outsiders." But he contended that the film's release, and especially its premiere in Atlanta (as opposed to the normal premiere sites of New York and Los Angeles), would be "an epochal event" for a city "on the very edge of becoming a movie city."[49] Noting the amount of money that *Deliverance*'s production had pumped into the local economy (roughly half of the film's $2 million production budget), Gov. Jimmy Carter and the Georgia legislature established a Motion Picture and Television Advisory Committee in order to spur further film and television production in the state. In doing so, they joined what the *New York Times* referred to, in 1974, as the "ever-spreading though undeclared war for location shooting." As the *Times* reported, state film commissions, eager to stimulate their local economies by attracting Hollywood dollars, offered "all sorts of special services and cooperation." These included various tax breaks and exemptions, state-supported transportation for location scouting, and other kinds of enticements, such as the Arizona film commission's arrangement to haul a five-ton generator, as well as photographic and electrical equipment, over unpaved terrain to aid a film production's shoot in an uninhabited section of the Superstition Mountains. Such enthusiastic cooperation prompted the Entertainment Industry Committee of Hollywood's Chamber of Commerce to worry that California was being "robbed of an estimated $400 million in 'runaway' production."[50]

Yet the greatest attraction southern location shooting offered was the availability of nonunion labor. While states from every part of the country created (or expanded already existing) film commissions in the 1960s and 1970s, it was the "right-to-work" Sunbelt that exerted the strongest attraction to the film industry. Aida Hozic explains that the increasing power of "merchants" (such as financiers and agents) over studios and producers during this period "turned 'below-the-line' costs into the only variable costs which studios and producers could manipulate," thus forcing "producers to take production to the southern 'right-to-work' states" as well as to certain foreign locations.[51] Indeed, Charlotte-based independent filmmaker Bob McClure bragged about not only his ability to use nonunion labor in North Carolina but also the ways in which the right-to-work environment enabled him to avoid paying union rates to guild members: "when we ran into an actor who belonged to the Screen [Actors] Guild, we just changed his name."[52] In fact, the benefits of the South's nonunion workforce were so thoroughly expected that producer Ed Pressman actually complained in the *New York Times* when the Texas Film Commission failed to locate an old theater that would allow him to avoid paying extras and stagehands at union rates.[53]

The Hollywood unions fought these kinds of labor practices vigorously. In 1974, Ben Loveless, secretary-treasurer of Teamsters Local 399 and co-chairman of the National Conference of Motion Picture and Television Unions, attacked the film commissions of Texas, New Mexico, and Colorado for encouraging film productions to "ignore certain parts of [union] contract[s] while in those states."[54] Similarly, representatives from SAG and the American Federation of Television and Radio Actors (AFTRA) complained that, in Texas, "there are a lot of actors, non-members, who do a lot of work and won't join the union, using the right-to-work law as an excuse."[55] That same year, IATSE sued AMPTP, Columbia, MGM, Warner Brothers, AIP, and Twentieth Century Fox over their practice of acquiring for distribution films already made by independent, nonunion producers— a violation of the union's 1973 contract. Many of these films were made in the Sunbelt, including *Abby/Possess My Soul* (1974, made in Kentucky), *Buster and Billie* (1974, Georgia) and the Burt Reynolds Southern *W. W. and the Dixie Dancekings* (1975, Tennessee).[56]

Despite these efforts by the film unions, nonunionized domestic filming proliferated. *Variety* estimated that, in 1975, about one hundred films were made in the United States with nonunion labor, roughly equal to the number of films produced under the standard union agreements. Furthermore, the threat of moving film productions away from the unionized environs of Hollywood to the right-to-work South (and to foreign countries) was often used to discipline the Hollywood unions.[57] Addressing the 1974 IATSE convention, AMPTP executive vice president Billy Hunt warned that "labor problems will do more to discourage or eliminate local and domestic film production and film exhibition than any other single factor other than diminished box office receipts."[58] When IATSE supported an AFL-CIO-endorsed bill in the California legislature that would limit the ability of employers to force "mandatory overtime" on their employees, the AMPTP lobbied against the bill, maintaining that it would spur runaway production in states with fewer labor regulations—an argument that helped to kill the bill in committee.[59] Meanwhile, southern state governments worked to limit the reach of unions in their jurisdictions. When SAG tried to stop its members from working for North Carolina-based independent producer Earl Owensby, whose productions utilized nonunion labor, the state's attorney general ruled that North Carolina's right-to-work law forbade the refusal of employment to nonunionized workers, and he suggested that union members who were being fined for working on nonunion productions "retain private counsel for [their] defense." Owensby, emboldened by the state's defense of his labor practices, ordered his attorneys to bring suit against SAG if they put him on their list of "unfair" employers.[60] In short, southern location shooting not only enabled cheaper film productions through the use of nonunion labor but also restricted the ability of the film unions to defend and advocate for the interests of its members both in and out of Hollywood.

In addition to shifting the balance of class power away from organized labor in the film industry, these developments also influenced the way that the southern working class came to be figured in the films of the Southern cycle. In the first place, since many filmmakers were eager to cash in on the lower costs of location shooting, but knew that films which had depicted the South negatively had faced hostility from local residents, it made economic sense to pursue film projects that would have an easier time being made in these southern locations. Furthermore, much was made of the pliancy of nonunionized southern film crews in comparison to those of the Hollywood unions. Owensby himself published an article in *Variety* describing how "labor problems encountered by producers in Hollywood are minimized" on his productions largely due to the flexibility of the crews (and, of course, the lower labor costs). In contrast to the rigidly demarcated work rules of unionized sets, where each task may be performed only by the craft worker assigned to that task (i.e., only camera operators may operate the camera), "when someone is on the payroll at E. O. Studios," Owensby wrote, "he works. If there is no need for his services immediately on a film, he will be utilized by one of the other companies associated with the studios....So a grip today could be tomorrow's assistant director."[61] With a work force that was both cheaper and more compliant than that found in Hollywood, it is not surprising that the representations of the southern working class found in the Southern cycle increasingly took on the sunny characteristics of the good ole boy. If the obstinate and hostile "rust-belt" workers of *Joe* are to be understood as the product, in part, of the New Hollywood's confrontations with the aging, exclusionist film unions, then we can take the affable, easy-going blue-collar men of the Southern cycle to be partially generated by the right-to-work, employer-friendly labor context of Sunbelt location shooting. (Here, too, we might find another determinant for the good ole boy's consistently anti-union identity in the Southern cycle.) Add to these conditions of production the fact that most of these films considered southern audiences to be their initial (and sometimes only) target market, as well as the fact that many filmmakers negotiated film content with local residents (as was the case with *Walking Tall* and *Buster and Billie*, among others),[62] and the reasons behind the Southern cycle's shift from the murderous, degenerate rednecks of *Deliverance* to the playful, fast-driving good ole boys of *Smokey and the Bandit* come into sharper relief.

THE SUNBELT, CLASS, AND THE RISE OF THE NEW RIGHT

Hollywood's practice of relocating production away from demographically concentrated and largely unionized sectors toward dispersed sites in the right-to-work South and West was a development that characterized the new political economy of the Sunbelt as a whole. As Kim Moody explains, after the "decade of class confrontation that climaxed in the 1946 strike wave"— which occurred for the most part in the densely populated industrial centers of the Northeast and Midwest—corporations sought either to move their operations entirely to the anti-union South or at least to concentrate new investment in the region. The strategy was not only to move production away from unionized areas to settings with legal and cultural barriers to labor organizing but also to scatter these new sites of production so that "the solidarity engendered by the earlier massive concentrations of workers and their families" could be kept to a minimum. Such a dispersal of production sites also presented the unions with "increased problems of communication, information gathering, and...the weakening of pattern bargaining"; this last, Moody explains, meant that various plants in any given industry were able to pay "a variety of wages and benefits [that] could only increase the competitive pressure on union wage and benefit rates" in a way that they could not have in the earlier, more centralized regimes of Fordist production.[63]

Thus, by moving production to areas that were both geographically scattered and removed from the histories of trade unionist struggle that produced the film unions in the first place, the studios, like other U.S. corporations, limited the ability of Sunbelt workers to build solidarity with each other and connect with the larger traditions of the film unions. Decentralized production also made it more difficult for the film unions to monitor and enforce union pay scales and work rules. Location shooting's erosion of the latter, according to Michael Storper and Susan Christopherson, was particularly damaging since "work rules were arguably more important than wage rates in the unionization struggles of the 1930s, and the employers' attempt to weaken them represents an attack on one of the major sources of union legitimacy and inter-craft solidarity."[64]

These kinds of industrial strategies did more, though, than just contribute to the sharp decline of union density in the postwar United States.[65] They also changed the political economic landscape in such a way as to destabilize old class identities and create the possibilities for new affiliations. Such possibilities were then harvested by the New Right. Mike Davis argues that the New Right was able to mount its takeover of the Republican Party and, with Reagan's presidential victory in 1980, eventually the nation, through an alliance of "the entrepreneurs and suburban elites of the emergent 'Sunbelt.'" This alliance fueled a political movement within the Republican Party that worked to attract elements of the Democratic coalition through a focus on "bipartisan single-issue campaigns with a rightist dynamic, rather than on frontal ideological clashes."[66] As Davis's Gramscian rhetoric suggests, this realignment tended to occur through cultural struggles over so-called "social issues"—school busing, abortion, welfare, gay rights, and so on—which, as many critics have pointed out, relied on the coded vocabularies of racialized and gendered backlash for their political effectivity. But, Davis argues, without an *economic* rhetoric that would be "acceptable to Western entrepreneurs and Eastern skilled workers and professionals," the New Right would have "remained primarily a sectional phenomenon." This economic discourse was soon furnished by the antitax movement catalyzed by California's Proposition 13 movement. Rather than directly attacking government spending on various New Deal programs—which had been the traditional (and electorally unpopular) strategy of economic conservatives—the New Right, following the Proposition 13 movement, instead focused its rhetoric on cutting taxes, interpellating its targeted audiences as "taxpayers," rather than, say, workers who are beneficiaries of state investment.[67]

Again, it is impossible to understand the success of this strategy without noting the ways in which race and gender discourses were utilized in such campaigns—in, for example, *National Review* publisher William Rusher's opposition between "producers" (implicitly white men) and "non-producers" (implicitly poor blacks and welfare mothers).[68] But the Proposition 13 movement also took advantage of the way that the "stagflation" (economic recession accompanied by inflation) of the 1970s created divisions *within* the working class. In contrast to the tendency of economic depressions "to achieve a leveling effect in the composition of the working class," Davis explains, stagflation "deepen[ed] and exaggerat[ed] intra-class differentiation," creating "opposing camps of inflationary 'haves' and 'have-nots.'" For example, working-class homeowners found themselves both benefiting (in inflated property values) and suffering (from higher property taxes) from the effects of stagflation in ways that differed from nonpropertied workers and the poor. As a result, public spending and taxes increasingly became a terrain of division between suburbanized workers and middle strata on the one hand, and inner-city workers and non-waged poor on the other...tempting the stronger or more advantaged sections of the working class to abandon traditional solidaristic political alliances to join new inter-class "have" blocs arrayed against the collective "have-nots."

Davis concludes that such a development demonstrates how, as the working class became increasingly disorganized through the Sunbelt's massive relocation and overhaul of U.S. worksites, "secondary distributional struggles thus acquired, at times, a greater political salience than 'old' class-defined alignments."[69]

Davis's account of the shifts in political economy that undergirded the New Right's discursive and electoral strategies is persuasive, but it is important to see these "secondary distributional struggles" as *class* struggles. As J. K. Gibson-Graham, Stephen Resnick, and Richard Wolff have argued, traditional Marxist theory has focused on the way class positions are generated within the relations of production, where surplus value is appropriated from labor by capital. Yet the authors remind us that Marx was equally interested in the class processes that involve the *distribution* of surplus value (which is addressed in volumes 2 and 3 of *Capital*). Thus, we need to recognize the ways in which "distributive flows can be seen as constituting a range of distributive class positions." Doing so allows us to attend to the ways that these different moments of class experience inform each other.[70] And, as Adam Przeworski reminds us, class struggles are always "struggles *about* class formation as well as struggles *among* organized class forces."[71] Therefore, the New Right's rise needs to be understood as a moment in which distributional class struggles came to reshape and rearticulate class identities in order to forge new class formations.

By recognizing the class nature of these struggles, we can begin to grasp the specifically class-based cultural work done by the Southern cycle—especially the trucker films, which visualized these class realignments by occasioning a kind of affective communion around a shared structure of class feeling. This hybridized class identity was put on offer by the films through their good ole boy characters who incarnated blue-collar bravado and petty-bourgeois self-sufficiency in tales that combined solidaristic action and individualistic ownership; as the films oscillated between the anarchic freedom of action-based comedy and the tragic limits of melodrama, they gave filmic form to the tensions between self-directed labor and economically determined constraint that could speak to the contradictions of the PMC's position as well as to working-class experience. When these representations found audiences among both working-class and PMC constituencies—and when the latter imagined a connection with the former by inhabiting their presumed spectatorial location—they incarnated a potentially mutual class habitus that could enable subsequent political interpellation.

Indeed, the cultural precipitate of these representations—the numerous accounts of the good ole boy celebrated in the journalistic encomia to the Sunbelt—also manifested a recombinant class identity that partook of working-class earthiness and middle-class amenability. *Time* insisted that "being a good ole boy" was "not a consequence of birth or breeding; it cuts across economic and social lines; it is a frame of mind that life is nothing to get serious about." Yet the magazine's subsequent descriptions of the figure were laden with class-specific signifiers. On the one hand, *Time* described the leisure pursuits of the good ole boy as those of *Deliverance*'s middle-class vacationers: "Between good ole boys on a fishing, hunting, canoeing or camping weekend, distinctions of class or income are secondary to expertise or camaraderie." On the other hand, its ensuing description of the good ole boy's sartorial habits suggests a specifically blue-collar resistance to bourgeois taste that characterizes the films of the Southern cycle: "He disdains neckties as a form of snobbery; when he dresses up, it is to wear a decorated T-shirt with newish jeans or, for state occasions, a leisure suit with a colored shirt."[72] Of course, such claims to classlessness in the midst of accounts of class-specific phenomena are common to U.S. ideology; what is striking here is the palpable mix of class affects that are used to characterize this figure. The good ole boy, as a kind of bourgeoisified redneck, marks a location from which a new class modality could be experienced—one made possible by the economic and political terrain of the newly PMC-controlled Sunbelt.

It is from this class modality, it seems, that Bill Fries, an Omaha adman, sought to rename himself C. W. McCall and record "Convoy," the smash hit country song about a trucker rebellion on which Sam Peckinpah's movie was based. Noting the song's success, Fries/McCall told *Newsweek* of his plans to use his new-found fame to "make a few statements—about how regulated our lives have become and how many of our freedoms we have lost."[73] Just as Fries/McCall sought to deploy the character of the trucker to articulate his PMC-influenced antiregulatory interests as blue-collar resistance, so too did the New Right capitalize on the cross-class affiliation made visible by the good ole boy. After all, Rusher's opposition between "producers" and "non-producers" that I noted above described the former as made up of "businessmen, manufacturers, hard hats, blue-collar workers and farmers" while the latter featured "a semi-permanent welfare constituency." Similarly, Paul Weyrich, the direct-mail mastermind behind many New Right campaigns, referred to the "blue-collar, middle class origins of the New Right." Even allowing for the notoriously confused U.S. rhetoric concerning class identity, these descriptions of a common class interest between the working class and "businessmen [and] manufacturers" are striking.[74]

That this conservative movement's ascendance proved disastrous, politically and economically, for the working class subjects in whose name it often spoke is one of the crueler ironies of recent U.S. history. But while it is frequently bemoaned by liberal and leftist commentators that the New Right was able to achieve power through a focus on "cultural issues" that succeeded in distracting public discourse away from questions of economic and class interests,[75] my analysis of the class-oriented cultural work that the Southern cycle accomplished tells a different story. For rather than evading class, the New Right took advantage of a new vocabulary of class that was being generated by the cultural and political economy of the Sunbelt and made dramatically visible by the films of the Southern cycle. In doing so, they seemed to have acknowledged the multiple moments of class identity and the various processes of class formation—especially their articulation in the cultural realm—far more effectively than left movements had.

Yet this rightist articulation of the class vocabulary evinced in the Southern cycle was not a necessary or foregone conclusion. As I have also demonstrated, the films of this cycle, for all of their conservative elements, were often powered by the radical energies of working-class militancy and solidaristic action as well. Even the apolitical Burt Reynolds defined the typical hero of his films as "a good ole boy who fights the system with dignity and, above all, a sense of humor." It is worth recalling, after all, that many of the period's film critics saw Easy Rider as the first Southern. Yet the class anxiety that many PMC critics felt toward Southern films suggests that they often identified more with the "system" being assailed in these films than with their good ole boy protagonists. Such an identification points toward the importance of leftist cultural analysis that engages with, rather than ignores, class conflict and antagonism. What we find in the Southern cycle, finally, is not an inevitable rightward turn but a new set of class identities that could have traveled down any number of roads.

PART III

MACHO MEN AND THE NEW NIGHTLIFE FILM

In part II, we saw how the deconstruction and eventual disappearance of the Western was accompanied by the rise of a cycle of films that adapted the genre's themes and concerns to a changing political and economic landscape. This part begins with another genre's decline during the 1970s—that of romantic comedy. In a 1978 *Film Quarterly* essay on the genre, Brian Henderson treated Michael Ritchie's film from the previous year, *Semi-Tough*, as a symptom of what he declared to be "the death of romantic comedy." This was a familiar concern during the decade. Molly Haskell observed, in her landmark 1974 book *From Reverence to Rape*, that "from the evidence on the screen, most people have given up trying to make movies about love"—suggesting that it was not just romantic comedy but romance itself that was disappearing from U.S. film screens. This concern was shared by David Denby, who lamented that "most of the big hits as well as the movies that have earned critical raves and awards in recent years have done without romance, and an amazing number have dispensed with women." Henderson, Haskell, and Denby all complained, to different degrees, that contemporary films offered fewer and more one-dimensional roles for women. But Denby feared that such developments portended not only an absence of compelling heroines and the end of romantic comedy as a genre but also "the decline of heterosexuality" itself in U.S. cinema.[1]

These dire predictions seem to have been spurred in part by the immensity of the social changes that, these critics claimed, were responsible for such cinematic developments. Denby, for example, laid the blame for this alleged decline of heterosexuality squarely on the shoulders of the women's movement. He asserted that

women's liberation has paralyzed the movie companies. In New York and
Los Angeles, where movie projects are hatched, relations between the sexes
are a battleground on which all previous rules of warfare have been thrown
out. What's happening between men and women is now so charged-up,
improvisatory and bewildering that the movie companies are afraid to touch it.[2]

Henderson and Haskell also argued that feminism had challenged traditional representations of heterosexual interaction. But for Haskell, it was
not paralysis but fear and hostility that generated the consequent absence of
heterosexual romance:

> The growing strength and demands of women in real life, spearheaded by
> women's liberation, obviously provoked a backlash in commercial film: a
> redoubling of Godfather-like machismo to beef up man's eroding virility or,
> alternately, an escape into the all-male world of the buddy films from *Easy
> Rider* to *Scarecrow*. With the substitution of violence and sexuality (a poor
> second) for romance, there was less need for exciting and interesting women.[3]

Both Denby and Haskell also expressed great anxiety over the emergence
of a new model for cinematic relationships: homosexual romance.[4] Denby
angrily denounced the critical practice of detecting, in the virtually all-male
"buddy" films, a "subtext of *repressed* homosexuality," which he declared to
be "a nasty, invidious game." (In support of this claim, he offered, of all
things, *Midnight Cowboy* (1969) as an example of a movie that disproves
such speculations.[5]) Haskell did admit that these cinematic male-male
relationships were about love (among other things), but she also described
such relationships as "a delusion…the easiest of loves: a love that is adolescent, presexual, tacit, the love of one's *semblable*, one's mirror reflection."
This "homophile impulse," she continued, "like most decadent tropisms,
like incest, is, or can be, a surrender, a sinking back into one's own nature."[6]
It's hard to decide which is uglier—Denby's panicked refusal to see same-
sex love when it is right there in front of his eyes or Haskell's equation of
homosexuality with incest. My point simply is that these accounts illustrate
how dramatically the twin movements of women's and gay liberation disrupted the cinematic codes of gender and sexuality during the 1970s. The
romance plots on which onscreen relationships between men and women
had been based for decades had come under thorough critique by feminism, while the new visibility of post-Stonewall gay communities revealed
the (almost exclusively male) homosocial energies that had shaped and
continued to shape many Hollywood films. As a result, American cinema
no longer knew how to represent heterosexuality in the wake of feminism
and gay liberation.

The group of films that this next section examines can be seen as attempts to address and navigate this new social and cinematic context. *Saturday Night Fever* (1977), *Looking For Mr. Goodbar* (1977), and *Cruising* (1980) can all be understood as responses (albeit strikingly different ones) to these dilemmas of gender and sexual representation, as they each struggle to offer an image of contemporary heterosexual romance—and/or its impossibility. *Fever* tries to revive the traditional romance not only by adopting and updating the genre of the musical but also by setting its film in a working-class enclave of Brooklyn, "a world," as the *Village Voice*'s Frank Rose put it, "where it's like the 60s never happened."[7] *Goodbar*, however, *is* set in a world where the 1960s happened—its protagonist, Theresa Dunn (Diane Keaton), readily partakes of the new-found freedoms of casual sex and recreational drug use—and portrays Theresa's difficulties in trying to negotiate heterosexual relationships while also maintaining her protofeminist independence. *Cruising*, in contrast, represents the withering away of heterosexuality that Denby feared by literalizing the homoerotic motifs of so many buddy movies. The film depicts the police force and the gay male sadomasochist community as mirror images of each other, sites in which intramale relationships are enacted over scripted rituals of power and submission. Accordingly, the relationship between the film's undercover cop protagonist Steve Burns (Al Pacino) and his girlfriend (Karen Allen) becomes eclipsed as Steve finds himself seduced by the homosocial context of the station house and the homosexual scene of the leather bar.

Despite their different approaches to the possibility of heterosexual romance, all of these films utilized the space of the bar or nightclub to explore the period's dislocations of gender and sexual identity. In this way, they can be considered what I am calling "new nightlife films," because they all demonstrate how the new nightlife of the 1970s offered spaces for identity transformation, locations where one could inhabit a persona or mode of existence at odds with one's "daytime" self. In *Fever*, Tony Manero (John Travolta) attempts to transcend his dead-end life working in a Brooklyn paint store through his masterful command of the dance floor at the local disco. *Goodbar* goes to significant lengths to contrast Theresa's responsibility and dedication as a teacher of deaf children with her apparently risky and self-destructive behavior in singles bars. The leather bars of *Cruising* not only become sites of sexual disorientation for Steve but also serve as places of parodic identity play, as in the "Precinct Night" sequence, in which a leather bar's denizens dress as police officers. In short, these films locate their action in settings where new gender or sexual identities can be tried on, where signifier and signified can become detached from each other, as the possibilities opened up by women's and gay liberation are investigated by characters and filmgoers alike.

What is striking about this identity play, though, is that all three films make conspicuous use of the same figure—the white, working-class male—in order to represent and respond to these gender and sexual shifts. *Fever*, set entirely within a white ethnic milieu, devotes considerable energy to eroticizing white working-class masculinity—an approach that complicates its avowedly heterosexual plot. *Goodbar*'s Theresa spends much of the film oscillating between the affections of a wild, unpredictable working-class lover, Tony (Richard Gere), and a more staid (but equally volatile) professional boyfriend, James (William Atherton)—only to be killed by a self-loathing gay man, Gary (Tom Berenger), who is Gere's blue-collar double. *Cruising*'s world is one inundated with the signifiers of working-class delinquency (especially that of motorcycle gangs) that were adopted by gay male sadomasochistic culture to articulate a more masculine brand of homosexuality. In each of these films, the white working-class male body serves as a kind of switchpoint in the new networks of gender and sexual identity.

Part III explores why this particular body was so crucial to the period's renegotiations of gender and sexuality. I take as my starting point Peter Biskind and Barbara Ehrenreich's persuasive account of working-class masculinity in late 1970s American cinema, "Machismo and Hollywood's Working Class." They characterize the films that focused on working-class characters during this period (including *Saturday Night Fever*, as well as *Bloodbrothers* [1978] and the first two *Rocky* films [1976, 1979], among others) as "middle-class male anxiety dreams in which class is no more than a metaphor for conflicting masculine possibilities."[8] They argue that in these films the "working class becomes a screen on which to project 'old-fashioned' male virtues that are no longer socially acceptable or professionally useful within the middle class—physical courage and endurance, stubborn determination, deep loyalty among men."[9] Yet these virtues are still "secretly admired" by the movies as a "powerful cultural image of [masculine] defiance."[10] Ultimately, though, these films treat this brand of masculinity as outdated, frozen in a previous era of gender, sexual, and economic relations, and the films' narratives work to supplant this form of male identity with a more modern, reconstructed, and implicitly middle-class version. Therefore, these films deploy the white working-class male body so that they may nostalgically embrace a certain kind of masculinity while also making its disappearance seem both necessary and salutary.

There is much that is persuasive in this account—indeed, it informs my earlier discussions of the anachronistic character of the working class in the decade's cinema. However, Biskind and Ehrenreich tend to treat these representations of working-class masculinity as static portrayals, fixed symbols of a stable gender and sexual identity. In the new nightlife films, though, the problem seems to be that the signifiers of white working-class masculinity are not nearly static or fixed enough. For the embrace of the "clone" look by gay men, who adopted working-class clothing and affect in order to rearticulate gay male identity, threatened to disrupt any untroubled association between these signifiers and traditional, heterosexual masculinity. Rather than guarantee this masculinity, the white working-class male body (and its simulations) served in these films as an index of the period's dis- and reorganizations of gender and sexual identity, as this body signified multiple, occasionally contradictory forms of male identity in the same film— sometimes in the same scene, or even the same shot.

My inquiry into the reformulations of masculinity in these films will frequently engage with the argument, promulgated most famously by Judith Butler, that the "queer" performance of seemingly heteronormative identities enables a subversion of the "natural" status of these identities—an issue foregrounded by the identity play made possible by the films' nightclub settings. But I also will relate this critical conversation about the performance of gender to the crises in class representation I have discussed in earlier chapters. For the decline of the manufacturing base and concomitant dismantling of the Fordist regime left significant traces on the period's cinematic representations of class and gender identity. The shift from industrial to service production in U.S. political economy, partial and uneven as it was in this period, meant that the working class was coming to be distinguished from the PMC not by virtue of the divide between manual and mental labor but rather by the divisions between different forms of what Michael Hardt and Antonio Negri describe as *"immaterial labor*—that is, labor that produces an immaterial good, such as a service, a cultural product, knowledge, or communication."[11] In other words, the U.S. working class was beginning to look less like the hard hats of *Joe* or *Five Easy Pieces* and more like the low-skill service workers of *Saturday Night Fever*; which is to say, they were starting, in some ways, to be less easily distinguished from the high-skill, high-value service workers of the PMC. The investment of both straight and gay communities in the iconography of the industrial-laboring male body, then, speaks not only to crises over masculinity but also to those concerning class identity. After all, gender and sexuality were not the only social categories being recast during the 1970s.

If the new nightlife films endeavored to depict the decade's brave new worlds of gender and sexual dynamics, their focus on white working-class male characters meant that they brushed up against dilemmas about class identity as well. In doing so, these films prompt us to ask: once the material relations that helped engender a certain brand of masculinity no longer obtain—or, more precisely, move from dominant to residual status in the national political economy—what happens to the signifiers that once broadcast this kind of gender identity? Are they necessarily consigned to the dustbin of history, as figures for an outdated form of existence, or can they take on a new life, with a different set of associations? If the latter is the case, what are the political consequences of such a rearticulation of class and gender identities? To answer these questions, we must explore the central role played by the cinematic vocabulary of class in the period's imagination of new masculinities.

4

SATURDAY NIGHT FEVER AND THE QUEERING OF THE WHITE, WORKING-CLASS MALE BODY

Saturday Night Fever now seems so representative of its cultural moment —an entire late 1970s structure of feeling is evoked by the iconic, oft-parodied image of John Travolta in that white suit—that it is worth remembering that the film was initially viewed as something of a throwback. Director John Badham explicitly cited Busby Berkeley musicals and *West Side Story* (1961) as influences on the film, and many critics echoed Richard Corliss's observation that its love story corresponds faithfully to "the tradition of the Fred Astaire-Ginger Rogers musicals of the thirties."[1] Furthermore, the film's social world of outer-borough white ethnics was often taken to represent a bygone era, a milieu rooted more in the 1950s than the 1970s. Yet *Fever* also positioned itself as a film very much about the contemporary world of disco nightlife, and in some ways about the future as well—the nightclub, after all, is called 2001 Odyssey. We can see the film's restless traversal of signifiers of the past, present, and future as a symptom of the difficulty it faces in attempting to offer a viable, contemporary heterosexual romance. By situating its traditional love story in the apparently anachronistic space of the Brooklyn neighborhood of Bay Ridge, and by utilizing the older generic structure of the musical, *Fever* clearly hopes to avoid the difficulty of depicting contemporary gender relations even as it broadcasts its up-to-dateness by focusing on disco music and nightclubs. Yet the film's deployment of various class and sexual identities to signify this conflicted temporality, as we will see, often threatens to work against its avowedly heterosexual orientation.

Indeed, the preeminent problem facing *Fever* is that disco music and nightclubs were strongly identified with gay men in the mid-1970s. If Bay Ridge is understood by the film as a neighborhood where the values of the 1950s are still dominant, the dance floor of 2001 is nevertheless a space that could connote more contemporary, and less heterocentric, gender and sexual norms. This dilemma for *Fever*'s heterosexual romance is compounded by the fact that much of the film's visual pleasure is derived from its strategy of making a male body (John Travolta's) an object of the camera's gaze—a strategy that, as a good deal of feminist film theory suggests, threatens the heterosexual stability of the implicitly male spectator. Therefore, I take *Fever*'s central representational problem to be its attempt to craft a heterosexual narrative out of cultural resources and filmic practices that would seem better suited to gay male themes. The hurdles that the film must clear, and the tactics it must use, in order to do so end up telling us a great deal about the surprising centrality of class to the articulation of gender and sexual identity in this period.

GAY MEN AND DISCO

The importance of disco to gay male self-understanding in the 1970s is well established. Walter Hughes argues that the experience of disco played a vital role in what he describes as the "post-Stonewall project of reconstituting those persons medically designated 'homosexuals' as members of a 'gay' minority group, and of rendering them visible, individually and collectively."[2] Hughes traces the origins of disco—not only as a style of music and dancing but also as a site-specific experience of dancing to DJ-created music in nightclubs—to predominantly black gay clubs of the late 1960s, where songs were spliced together to provide "a predictable, unbroken rhythm conducive to long spates of dancing."[3] As the phenomenon spread to nightclubs throughout the gay communities of U.S. urban centers, discos began, in Dennis Altman's words, to "represent for many gay men an important way of expressing both a sense of solidarity and a celebration of their sexuality; at their best, discos generate[d] a communal eroticism that [wa]s very powerful."[4]

What is perhaps less well known now is the degree to which these origins and associations were recognized in dominant journalistic accounts of disco, as the movement transformed from an underground institution of urban gay communities to the multibillion-dollar industry it became at its peak in the late 1970s (not coincidentally, after the runaway success of *Fever*).[5] A year before *Fever*'s release, *Newsweek* claimed that "the group most responsible for keeping discos alive was the homosexual community. Gays wanted places where they could lose themselves dancing—and at the same time make the scene."[6] The practice of straight voyeurism at gay discos formed the topic of an impressionistic piece by Sally Helgesen in a 1977 *Harper's* essay (the topic was also briefly remarked upon in a 1976 *Forbes* article about the burgeoning disco industry).[7] These acknowledgments of disco's gay genealogy did not abate after the release of the film. In 1979, *Newsweek* noted that, pre-*Fever*, disco was primarily the provenance of "small urban groups of blacks and Hispanics, homosexuals and Beautiful Insomniacs," and that the industry continued to rely on gay tastemakers: "These trend-setting discos are usually owned and operated by homosexuals and most of the deejays, as well as the lighting crews, are also gay." The magazine even noted the liberationist roots of the music, quoting Fantasy Records executive Nat Freedland's declaration that disco "is a symbolic call for gays to come out of the closet and dance with each other."[8]

Interestingly, there was a persistent fascination in these and other journalistic accounts with how the experience of disco clubs tended to destabilize the sexuality of clubgoers. *Newsweek*'s Maureen Orth remarked that these clubs were "environment[s] where technology throws a cloak of non-threatening anonymity over insecurities and hangups."[9] Similarly, Helgesen described how the straight patrons at gay discos often seemed to move beyond mere voyeurism: "their presence had about it an ambiguity of purpose, for while they might say that they were there only as watchers, only as voyeurs, they were also becoming participants." Helgesen went on to suggest that such boundary crossings are provoked by the ambience and music of the clubs themselves:

> After you've been in a disco for a while, after your senses have been operated upon by those *bodies*, those Objects from which Hobbes deduces all our fancies arise, you may begin to feel a disorientation of fancy within yourself, and you may attune yourself to the repetitive shifts of this electronic music of the spheres and fall into a kind of disco trance in which your brain turns off and you give yourself up to the sensations which envelop you. And suddenly whoever you thought you were when you walked in the door may no longer seem very important.[10]

Hughes makes a similar point, arguing that the physical sensation of disco's bass line—which is felt in the body, as a result of the nightclub's powerful sound-systems—penetrates and controls dancers to such an extent that "the beat" destabilizes dominant identity positions and opens up the space for sexual dissidence: "When we allow the beat to become part of us we disturb the very foundations of conventional constructions of masculine selfhood."[11] Such an experience seems to explain Albert Goldman's vituperative attack on disco in a 1978 issue of *Esquire*, in which he disdains its "overt tendency to spill over into orgy, as it has done already in the gay world." Declaring that disco music "is meant to be experienced subliminally, not so much in the mind as in the body," Goldman complained of its "phallically probing bass line," which contributes to the "final rape of the human sensorium" that (he claimed) occurs in a disco club—suggesting precisely the sort of threatened masculine selfhood Hughes describes.[12]

THE OPPOSED TEMPORALITIES OF GAY MEN AND THE WORKING CLASS

Given this context, how was it that the makers of *Saturday Night Fever* thought that they could set their updated musical—and accompanying heterosexual love story—in a site so heavily associated with non-heteronormative practices and identities? To begin to answer this question, we must turn to Nik Cohn's 1976 *New York* article, "Tribal Rites of the New Saturday Night," on which *Fever* was based. As the article's title implies, Cohn approached his subject matter as if he were traveling to an exotic culture, perhaps made even more mysterious by its close proximity to the "civilized" world of Manhattan: "Moving from neighborhood to neighborhood, from disco to disco, an explorer out of my depths, I have tried to learn the patterns, the old/new tribal rites." In keeping with this ethnographic tone, Cohn described the Bay Ridge disco culture as a world of (somewhat) noble savages who have yet to be ruined by the excesses of the counterculture:

> While Manhattan remains firmly rooted in the sixties, still caught up in faction and fad and the dreary games of decadence, a whole new generation has been growing up around it, virtually unrecognized. Kids of sixteen to twenty, full of energy, urgency, hunger. All the things, in fact, that the Manhattan circuit, in its smugness, has lost.
>
> They know nothing of flower power or meditation, pansexuality, or mind expansion.…In many cases, they genuinely can't remember who Bob Dylan was, let alone Ken Kesey or Timothy Leary. Haight-Ashbury, Woodstock, Altamont—all of them draw a blank. Instead, this generation's real roots lie further back, in the fifties, the golden age of Saturday nights.

Untouched by recent social history, and unaware of the "pansexual" possibilities produced by this history, these white working-class ethnics presented Cohn—and the makers of *Fever*—with suitably traditional, heterosexual subjects. Yet it should be noted that, rather than admire the freshness or authenticity of this exotic, unspoiled culture from an earlier time (the fifties), Cohn seemed fascinated by the mass-produced, prepackaged tackiness of their leisure pursuits: the overwhelming cologne, the "automaton chugging, interchangeable" disco songs, and the brightly colored, often clashing clothes ("His shirt was pink and scarlet and yellow; her dress was pastel green. His boots were purple, and so were her painted lips."). In contrast to this apparent garishness, Cohn maintains his distinction by continually referring to himself, New Journalism-style, as "the man in the tweed suit"—a signification of class difference that neatly encapsulates the article's constant oscillation between prurient fascination with and smug condescension toward its subjects' working-class hedonism. While Cohn seemed to value the anachronistic 1950s traditionalism of Bay Ridge disco culture, it was also a world that he held at a sardonic distance—a narrational stance, we shall see, that *Fever* also maintained.[13]

There is one other important fact about Cohn's article that should be noted here: he made the whole thing up. In a 1997 *New York* essay commemorating the twentieth anniversary of *Fever*'s premiere, Cohn confessed that, despite the fact that his original article carried a prologue which pledged that "everything described in this article is factual and was either witnessed by me or told to me directly by the people involved,"[14] much of it was in fact fabricated. Cohn, who had moved from England to New York just a few months before visiting the 2001 Odyssey disco, explained that he had had such difficulty interviewing its denizens—"Quite literally, I didn't speak the language"— that he "faked it." He recounted how he seized upon a fleeting image, "a figure in flared crimson pants and a black body shirt, standing in the club doorway" who had "a certain style about him—an inner force, a hunger, and a sense of his own specialness," and based the fabricated article around him. Informing the ensuing portrait, Cohn explained, was his belief that

I knew that look well. I'd seen one version as a child, in my hometown of Derry, when I came across a teen gang outside a coffee bar and watched one of them, their leader, do tricks with a rubber snake. And again, in London, around 1965, when I turned up one night to see the Who and met a Mod named Chris, just turned 17, who claimed to buy three new suits a week and change his shirt five times a day.

Therefore, even though he "knew nothing about this world," he took these British figures (whom he also met only briefly) and "translated them as best as I could to Brooklyn....I imagined about how it would feel to burn up, all caged energies, with no outlet but the dance floor and the rituals of Saturday night." In short, the source material for *Fever* was almost solely the product of middle-class, male homosocial fantasy about working-class desire, rebellion, and hedonism—imported from Britain, no less.[15]

There are powerful reasons, though, why this particular fantasy found an eager audience in the United States. As I have demonstrated in previous chapters, there was a persistent investment in the idea of the white working class as a backward, provincial social group unable or unwilling to adapt to rapidly changing modern life. The contemporary sociological and journalistic discourses about "white ethnics" also offered a quasi-racialized understanding of the working class to explain this "fact": the failure of working-class whites to assimilate into middle class institutions and norms was characterized as a feature of their ethnic ties to Old World traditions rather than a product of class stratification. Furthermore, as Barbara Ehrenreich has argued, this white ethnic identity took on two distinct but reinforcing forms: the liberal version, which saw the group (especially the men that almost always stood for the entire group) as "a psychic dumping ground for such unstylish sentiments as racism, male chauvinism, and crude materialism," and a more conservative view, which held the group to represent "the 'traditional values' which the middle class saw slipping from its grasp" thanks to its immersion in the permissive, cosmopolitan world of consumerism.[16] While the former conception imagined the white ethnic working class as a sort of national id, and the latter saw it as a collective superego, both perspectives characterized the class as stranded in an essentially archaic way of life, a group whose members might display, at different moments, vicious bigotry, charming tackiness, and old-fashioned loyalty. In other words, this was a group very much like the one that populated Nik Cohn's invented Bay Ridge—and therefore *Saturday Night Fever*.

In fact, screenwriter Norman Wexler (who also penned *Joe*) added a scene not found in Cohn's *New York* piece that neatly epitomizes this understanding of an out-of-date working class. We first meet Tony Manero's family—his abusive, unemployed construction-worker father, his devoutly Catholic mother, and his grandmother, shrouded in black, who keeps shouting "Basta!" and "Mangia!"—as they gather for a Friday night dinner. During this meal, the film drives home the family's outmoded, traditionalist ways, which are rooted not simply in their ethnic habits but also their precarious economic location. In between slapping various family members, Tony's father attacks his wife for daring to question him—and for suggesting that she get a job herself. Much like the nightlife Cohn described as having its roots "in the fifties," the father's slightly pathetic desperation to cling to his role as breadwinner—and thus his claim to patriarchal authority—seems rooted in a previous era's view of work, family, and gender. *Fever's* emphasis on the family's, and particularly the father's, brutally dysfunctional refusal to grasp the increasing untenability of this worldview seems to be the film's way of demonstrating the inability of such working-class families, and especially working-class men, to adapt to the modern, postindustrial world.

Contrast this to contemporaneous understandings of homosexuals. Susan Sontag, in her "Notes on Camp," proclaimed that "Jews and homosexuals are the outstanding creative minorities in contemporary urban culture."

Similarly, George Steiner argued that "Judaism and homosexuality...can be seen to have been the two main generators of the entire fabric and savor of urban modernity in the West."[17] This implication of a cultural vanguardism on the part of homosexuals (usually gay men) was also one that certain gay male writers embraced. Edmund White bragged that "New York gays are justifiably proud of their status as tastemakers for the rest of the country, at least the young and up-to-date segment of the population," while Jeremy Seabrook went one step further to claim that "the homosexual has become a kind of pathfinder; a pioneer of the new kind of human being that has come into existence under the protective shelter of plenty."[18] This narrative of gay male cultural vanguardism is one that also informed dominant understandings of disco, as suggested by *Newsweek*'s discussion of disco's gay trendsetters, and made even more explicit in Helgesen's brief history of the disco club Infinity:

> Infinity drew a gay crowd when it opened, but as so often happens at discos in New York, the party crowd followed them there, the straight society people. After the place had been written up, and everybody knew it was chic, what is known on the scene as 'the scurve' arrived, singles who live with their roommates on the Upper East Side or in the middle-class neighborhoods of New Jersey and Long Island.... Now middle-class men cruise the banquettes each weekend.[19]

The hierarchy of hipness recounted here implies a hierarchy of class position as well: whatever the "real" class identity of Infinity's gay crowd, their wealth of cultural capital seems to give them a de facto upper-class status. In contrast, the working-class residents of the New York's outer boroughs do not even register in this hierarchy, so degraded is their cultural position. These accounts of disco and its surrounding culture treated gay men as members of the social and sexual cutting edge, forging new identities and cultural forms, not just adapting to the future but also actively shaping it. In other words, they are located on the opposite end of the cultural and temporal spectrum from the blue-collar ethnics that populate *Saturday Night Fever*.

QUEERING THE WHITE, WORKING-CLASS MALE BODY

Fever played upon this association of the working class with parochial, outdated gender and sexual practices, then, as it used the working-class bodies and settings of Cohn's Bay Ridge to elude disco's associations with homosexuality. (For added insurance, the film includes a scene entirely extraneous to the narrative in which Tony and his friends threaten to bash a stereotypically effeminate gay male couple.) However, developments within gay male culture during the period made this strategy more problematic than it might first appear. As I have already mentioned, post-Stonewall gay male culture increasingly came to signify its identity through the use of working-class clothes and affect. As a result, the signifiers of working-class masculinity no longer automatically denoted heterosexuality. Furthermore, the kind of working-class masculinity portrayed in the film was understood to deviate from "proper" (that is, middle-class) modes of development in ways that offered curious parallels with homosexuality's supposed divergence from paths to mature heterosexuality. What this meant was that *Fever*, for all of its overt efforts to project a neoconservative world from "the golden age of Saturday nights," was a film besieged on all sides by signifiers of nonnormative gender and sexual identity. The ideological consequences of these queer and/or nonnormative associations come into sharpest relief around those scenes in which Tony quite literally makes a spectacle of himself. These moments, in which *Fever* positions and films Tony's body as an eroticized object of its desiring gaze, demonstrate not only the difficulty of representing a heterosexualized masculinity at this moment but also the important class desires that inform these understandings of gender and sexual identity.

The unexpected overlap between working-class and queer masculinities first becomes visible early in the film. Tony asks his boss at the paint store for an advance on his wages, complaining that his payday should be Friday or Saturday, like everyone else's. His boss replies:

"And they're broke on Monday—boozing, whoring, pissing away their money all weekend. This way you're paid on a Monday, you got money all week. You can save a little, build a future."

"Oh, fuck the future!"

"No, Tony, you *can't* fuck the future. The future fucks you. It catches up with you and it fucks you if you ain't planned for it."

The class narrative that undergirds this exchange concerns a key marker of class difference: the capacity for "deferred gratification." Starting with what Ehrenreich has called the "discovery" of the poor in the late 1950s, sociologists and journalists continually asserted that what distinguished the professional-managerial class from the lower orders was not, say, access to higher education, family business contacts, and similar class-based advantages but instead an ability to exercise self-discipline, save money, and plan for the future. Those beneath them on the socioeconomic ladder, it was claimed, suffered from a "'present-time orientation' and an insufficiently developed 'deferred gratification pattern'"—conditions that rendered them incapable of transcending their inherited class position. If the working-class was trapped in the past, it would seem, part of the reason was that they were unable to imagine a future. And, as Ehrenreich points out, "a person who lives entirely in the present, unable to wait for the next anticipated pleasure, is, of course, a child."[20] In this sense, the working classes and poor not only embodied historically outdated worldviews but also suffered from arrested development, unable to "grow up" into a world of middle-class maturity. This same class narrative informs the entirety of *Fever*'s storyline, which equates Tony's coming of age with his rejection of his "present-time oriented" friends and their working-class childishness for the kind of class mobility embodied by Stephanie (Karen Lynn Gorney), his middle-class-aspirant dancing partner and love interest. Unsurprisingly, this logic was favorably commented upon by PMC reviewers: *Newsweek*'s David Ansen praised Tony's realization "that there is more to life than gang bangs, gang wars, and dance contests," while Pauline Kael approvingly noted that the film was "a celebration of individual climbing, as a way out of futureless squalor."[21]

Of course, there was another narrative about male "immaturity"—one advanced by psychiatrists, rather than sociologists, which located the failure to embrace "responsibility" in one's sexual orientation rather than one's class position. In *The Hearts of Men*, Ehrenreich's genealogy of what she terms the "male revolt" against the breadwinner role, she discusses what was, until at least the early to mid-1960s, the ultimate sanction against male "irresponsibility": an association with, or quite often an outright diagnosis of, homosexuality. "In psychiatric theory and in popular culture," she explains, "the image of the irresponsible male blurred into the shadowy figure of the homosexual. Men who failed as breadwinners and husbands were 'immature,' while homosexuals were, in psychiatric judgment, 'aspirants to perpetual adolescence.'"[22] Tony, in fact, spends a great deal of the film trying to avoid being forced into taking on the role of breadwinner. For example, he rejects Annette's (Donna Pescow) advances because, he tells her, all she ever talked about were her "married sisters," and that he "got the idea that all you were interested in was being a married sister yourself."

However, it should be noted that the gay liberation movement's project of depathologizing homosexuality—such as its successful campaign to persuade the American Psychiatric Association to remove homosexuality from its list of diseases—had caused this cultural narrative to lose a considerable amount of its currency by the time of *Fever*'s release. In fact, Ehrenreich argues that gay liberation's (and feminism's) successes ironically enabled straight men to refuse the breadwinner role, as Tony does. As many gay activists came to identify lesbians and gay men as a distinct minority population, Ehrenreich suggests, "homosexuality began to recede as a possibility inherent in most men and congeal[ed] into a condition specific to some." Thus, "the social deviant—who departs from standards of masculine maturity—was no longer an automatic suspect for sexual deviance."[23] The immaturity demonstrated by Tony's refusal to practice deferred gratification or embrace the breadwinner role therefore tended to read primarily as a class dysfunction, especially given the film's other class-based discourses. But the association of homosexuality still hovers faintly, ghost-like, in the background throughout the film. Consider the scene in which Tony struts around his room, wearing only black bikini briefs, chanting "Al Pacino! Al Pacino!" and then "Attica! Attica!" Pauline Kael characterized this scene, and not incorrectly, as a moment of Italian-American and working-class identification—she describes Pacino as "their saint...the boy like them who became somebody without denying who he was."[24] But the Pacino character (from *Dog Day Afternoon* [1976]) whom Tony is imitating is a bisexual man who tries to rob a bank in order to pay for his male lover's sex change—which gives the scene a secondary, albeit less visible association with queer identity. In short, it seems that whenever the film attempts to secure Tony's traditional sexuality through a performance of his working-class identity, the specter of homosexuality returns with an almost uncanny regularity.

In fact, the biggest threat to Tony's presumed heterosexuality may be those very signifiers of working-class masculinity. For the period of *Fever*'s release also witnessed what Martin Levine calls "the birth of the gay clone."[25] This identity was so named for its uniformity of dress and appearance, almost all of which was borrowed from traditionally working-class accoutrements: short hair, thick mustache or closely-trimmed beard, muscle T-shirts, tight Levi jeans, flannel shirts, denim or leather jackets, leather or work boots, and an incipient body-building ethic. Levine suggests that this adoption of working-class style was motivated by the association of "traditional closeted homosexual culture" with "the affect and pretensions of an aristocratic upper class," which was often understood to be "feminized and effeminate." Therefore, Levine reasons, post-Stonewall gay men, in a desire to "prove [their] masculinity...embrace[d] the rougher, coarser masculinity of the common laborer."[26]

The development of clone culture, furthermore, was produced by not only the imperative to counter the image of gay men as effeminate but also the desire to celebrate the erotics of masculine beauty—a strategy that Richard Dyer claims has subversive effects on straight masculinity: "By taking the signs of masculinity and eroticizing them in a blatantly homosexual context, much mischief is done to the security with which 'men' are defined in society, and by which their power is secured."[27] Many commentators have emphasized the ironic valence of this new gay masculinity, what Levine calls the "doubleness of clone style—its self-conscious, almost parodying references to stereotypically traditional masculinity, and its self-conscious embracing of that very stereotype at the same time. Clone style was both parody and emulation."[28] Dennis Altman claimed that the clone look's insistence that "to be gay is not, as is often thought, to be a man who would be a woman," constituted "a new form of drag, a parody of the social expectations of homosexuals."[29] This "new form of drag" reached its apotheosis with the Village People (another important artifact of disco culture), who, in hit songs like "Macho Man," performed various types of working-class masculinity (construction worker, biker, sailor, soldier, policeman) with a campy abandon that seemed to parody both these masculinities and gay male culture's adoption of them.[30]

Such developments might lead one to posit, following Judith Butler, that the clone look's parodic performance of working-class masculinity in contexts of gay male desire and practice served as a potential disruption of the "heterosexual matrix": the "grid of cultural intelligibility through which bodies, genders and desires are naturalized."[31] Butler argues that when sexual desire for men, which is supposed to inhere in female bodies, is found instead attached to male bodies—bodies, moreover, which exhibit masculine appearance and behavior—these signifiers of maleness and masculinity are revealed to be what they are: social constructs, rather than a "natural" set of traits. Therefore, if the conservative iconography of the hard hat (discussed in chapter 1) signified a seemingly "natural" masculinity that contrasted with the "unnatural" androgyny of the counterculture, then the Village People's "queering" of this figure (in the form of its flamboyant construction worker, David Hodo) suggested that this supposedly natural form of masculinity was also a mere performance, one that bore no automatic affiliation with heterosexuality.

But what kind of impact did clone culture's queering of working-class masculinity have on the reception of *Saturday Night Fever*? Surprisingly, despite the fact that no reviewer commented on disco's association with gay culture, more than one noted *Fever*'s affinity with the homoeroticism of a well-known avant-garde film. Pauline Kael described *Fever* as possessing "a feeling for the sexiness of young boys who are bursting their britches with energy and desire…which recalls Kenneth Anger's short film *Scorpio Rising* (1963)."[32] This comparison is especially suggestive, since *Scorpio*'s queer eroticization of biker culture is characterized by Juan Suárez as foreshadowing "the leather, metal studs, butch posing, and other outer signs of radical gay difference deployed by 1970s clones."[33] *Scorpio*, Suárez notes, also features a "homoerotic circuit of looks," with its male characters "constructing their appearance in front of the camera, turning themselves into spectacles that tend to freeze the narrative flow."[34] This aspect of Anger's film seems to have prompted Al Auster and Leonard Quart to claim that *Fever* alludes directly to *Scorpio* in a sequence in which Tony prepares in front of his mirror before an evening of dancing.[35] Yet Kael still insists that *Fever* is "a straight heterosexual film"—a conclusion agreed upon, implicitly or explicitly, by every other reviewer. This reception seems to undercut the subversive power Butler would grant the parodic performances of clone culture, despite the multiple traces of this culture—some of which are openly acknowledged by its reviewers—that are scattered throughout the film.[36]

MASCULINITY, NARCISSISM, SELF-CONSCIOUSNESS, AND CLASS

In order to better understand *Fever*'s heterosexual orientation, as it were, we need to look more closely at the predisco preparation scene cited by Auster and Quart. For this scene is not only one of the film's most famous—Susan Bordo declares that "never before *Saturday Night Fever* had a heterosexual male movie hero spent so much time on his toilette"[37]—but it is also exemplary of the film's larger strategy of treating Tony as an object of the camera's gaze while also signifying his heterosexuality. Granted, this last claim may seem puzzling, since this scene in particular would appear to illustrate D. A. Miller's distinction between the "macho straight male body and the so-called gym-body of gay male culture":

> The first displays its heft as a *tool*…as both an armored body and a body wholly given over to utility, it is ultimately aligned with the unseen body of the bossman, the dick in boxer shorts and business suit; whereas the second displays its muscle primarily in terms of an *image* openly appealing to, and deliberately courting the possibility of being shivered by, someone else's desire.[38]

According to this distinction, it would be impossible *not* to read Tony's body, in this scene and others, as aligned with gay male culture. Both Tony's prenightclub primping and the camera's relationship to these activities are motivated by a desire to treat his body as an alluring image. Indeed, the very fact that Tony spends the entire scene in front of a mirror, taking evident pleasure in and admiring his reflection, underlines this focus on image (figure 4.1). Even when Tony flexes his muscles and strikes a martial arts pose, the film's cut to a shot of his Bruce Lee poster makes clear that this pose is an imitation of an image he hopes to replicate—that these muscles are meant for display, not use.

Furthermore, during this sequence, the camera often shoots Tony's body from below, as if lying prostrate at Tony's feet in a sort of mock supplication. This perspective emphasizes his black bikini briefs, which hang a bit below his hips. As Jeff Yanc notes, "the spatial perspective of the shot

Figure 4.1. From *Saturday Night Fever*. Tony Manero (John Travolta) contemplates his image.

makes the crotch appear larger and more prominent than any other part of [his] body"—which leads Yanc to claim that the shot "appears to have been included in the sequence solely to fetishize the male 'package.'"[39] In this way, the scene recalls Miller's argument that "the entitled man, or boy aspirant to entitlement, is less inclined to contour his genitals in briefs than to make them invisible in boxer shorts"—a practice Miller criticizes as part of a middle-class resistance to male embodiment that seeks to hide "the penis, which disappears into a cool rectangularity that (already anticipating the *suit* that is such underwear's 'logical' and ethical extension) only apotheosizes it as the phallus."[40] Tony, it is safe to say, is never intent on hiding his penis. A scene from the following morning emphasizes his insistent embodiment: Tony awakens, again wearing only his black briefs, sits up, moves the sheets out of the way, and reaches into his underwear to scratch himself. Tony's "crude" handling of his body refuses any middle-class inclination toward disembodiment and, if Miller is right, could signal an alignment with the gay male "refusal...*to closet our bodies*."[41]

Of course, Miller appears to equate working-class and queer embodiment in this argument, which itself is symptomatic of the confusing overlap of signs that I am trying to disentangle here. So what was the distinction between straight and gay significations of working-class masculinity that enabled the reviewers of *Fever* to conclude that the film is a "straight heterosexual" one?[42] Yanc argues that Tony's straight masculinity is secured during the bedroom grooming sequence because "he is fully aware of his own image." Therefore, Tony's body is not feminized, as much feminist film theory would predict, since the viewer is denied true voyeuristic pleasure in subjecting him to an objectifying gaze, and his overtly displayed narcissism is positioned for the viewer as a display of macho self-appreciation, which the viewer recognizes as stereotypically masculine, despite the image of his near naked body.[43]

Yanc sees this strategy as of a piece with the film's efforts to suppress disco's "homosexual origins" via its "constructions of hypermasculinity."[44] But there is something strange about these claims. In the first place, clone culture was nothing if not a "hypermasculine" affair, in which the signs of masculinity are stylized and exaggerated for both erotic and parodic purposes. Similarly, the "narcissism" Yanc notes in Tony's performances had, since Freud, been described as a homosexual quality, both for its denotation of an arrested sexual development and its connotations of a queeny obsession with appearance and style.[45] As Susan Bordo argues, "the man who cares about his looks the way a woman does ... is unmanly, sexually suspect."[46]

   In fact, while Yanc is correct to note that Tony is "fully aware of his own image," the narcissism of this sequence was frequently interpreted as an illustration of Tony's inability to achieve any form of critical self-awareness. David Ansen singled out the "grim and hilarious vanity of Tony's preparations at the mirror" as one of the film's most enjoyable moments, while Frank Rich described Tony as "ignorant of the world, narcissistic and, except on the dance floor, aimless."[47] As these comments suggest, what is striking about Tony's narcissism is not its macho-ness, nor any association with nonnormative gender or sexual practices; rather, it is Tony's complete unself-consciousness. But if Tony seems to lack any critical awareness of his concern for his appearance, the film is at pains to establish *its* critical distance. As Jenny Taylor and David Laing argue, during Tony's predisco preparations "the camera's gaze is ironic, tongue in cheek, self-referring, and the audience both participates in the process of narcissism and at the same time sees it as a *display* of narcissism."[48] This spectatorial distance is reinforced during the dinner sequence, when Tony arrives swathed in a sheet to prevent any stains on his clothes, and he yells at his father not to muss his hair—a sequence that, as Andrew Sarris put it, "turns Tony once more into a low ethnic clown."[49] In other words, *Fever* characterizes Tony's narcissism not as the dandyish affectation of a man who cares about his looks but as a sign of the character's deeply limited, almost solipsistic worldview—a worldview that we, by virtue of our privileged, knowing spectatorial position, are able to transcend.

   This distinction is consonant with Levine's suggestion that one way clones signified a subtle difference from the working-class masculinities they were imitating was by "stylizing these looks" in a manner that differed from their "less self-conscious" straight iterations.[50] And who better to represent the "less self-conscious" straights than the working class? Kael, in fact, asserts that Travolta's appeal in *Fever* comes from "a thick, raw sensuality" that "seems almost *preconscious*," which gives him the appearance of "an Expressionist painter's view of a young prole."[51] Richard Corliss is less demure in this appraisal of Tony's working-class cognitive resources: "Before prehistoric man could talk, he communicated by dance; then by grunts; then, failing all else, fists. And these are pretty much the modes of expression favored by Tony Manero," whom he calls a "proletarian stud."[52] Thus, it was not just the working class's association with outdated sexual and gender identities that informed *Fever*'s use of blue-collar characters and settings but also a perceived disparity in critical self-consciousness, which enabled a form of narcissism for its protagonist that would not be confused with the knowing self-fashioning of gay male culture. The homoerotic implications of *Fever*'s visual strategies, therefore, are circumvented by the narrative's class condescension, which treats Tony as too mired in his backward-looking, parochial worldview to play his masculinity as anything but straight.

Yet *Fever*'s positioning of class capabilities also produced in its PMC reviewers an intense, even avid visual pleasure in Travolta's performance of Tony. For this pleasure was generated by the spectacle of not merely an attractive male body, but an attractive *working-class* male body. Kael's fondness for Travolta's "almost preconscious…thick, raw sensuality" was merely the most transparent (or honest) expression of this class-based pleasure. Molly Haskell lovingly described the way Travolta's "ethnic face—pale, porcine, sensual—concentrates" during the dance sequences, while Corliss admitted to enjoying the "raw, belligerent, Neanderthal energy and grace" that Tony's proletarian stud brought to the movie.[53] Corliss goes on to say that "Travolta is, perhaps, an Astaire of the hustle, substituting his own carnal magnetism for Astaire's precision and artistry."[54] One cannot deny the evident pleasure behind these comments, their delight in the spectacle of working-class embodiment that the film offers. Yet their vaguely backhanded nature—representing Tony's charms as animalistic, or at least characteristic of an earlier stage of human evolution, but above all as reflective of bodily "magnetism" rather than intellectual "artistry"—testify to the spectatorial position of class superiority offered by the film. Indeed, Haskell, in commenting on the Cohn piece that inspired *Fever*, describes the Bay Ridge men as "steeped in an ignorance so profound that they could not imagine themselves as possessing possibilities, or a visa of potential, that would carry them over the Brooklyn Bridge and into the future"—giving us a movie with "a sad, funny story of bigotry and bravado."[55] The reception of *Fever* is thus marked by both attraction and condescension to Tony's working-class masculinity—or, to put it more precisely, attraction that is to some degree generated by condescension. Tony's solipsistic narcissism, and the larger cultural backwardness of his working-class milieu, are not only signifiers of ineluctable heterosexuality; they also invite a gaze that takes pleasure both in the inarticulate, visceral physicality of working-class male bodies and a spectatorial experience of cultural and intellectual superiority to them.

If Tony's exhibitionism avoids the suggestion of homoeroticism that Laura Mulvey's "Visual Pleasure and Narrative Cinema" predicted, it is because it performs at the service of a particular kind of class pleasure. In fact, the invitation both to see and to control—to take pleasure both in looking and in dominating—offered to the implied middle-class spectator of *Fever* suggests an interesting parallel to Mulvey's distinction between "woman as image" and "man as bearer of the look" in dominant cinema.[56] I have argued elsewhere that films often imply a middle-class spectatorial position by granting the viewer a sense of epistemological superiority over their working-class characters, thus replicating the knowledge relations of the capitalist workplace (where manager functions as brain, while worker functions as hand).[57] We can see that *Fever*'s reception indeed testifies to the enjoyment produced by the idea of the working class as a backwater of outdated social forms and limited cognitive abilities—a setting that sometimes invites envious nostalgia but more often smug superiority. In this way, *Fever* and its reception indicates that the spectacularization of the male body— which would only accelerate in popular culture in the decades following the film—was more than just a mainstreaming of homoerotic forms from an emergent gay male culture, although it very much was this as well. It was also a symptom of middle-class desire for working-class embodiment, which takes an unusual degree of visual pleasure in the allegedly unself-conscious physicality of these bodies. These intertwined pleasures, both epistemic and erotic, of *Saturday Night Fever* would have been unthinkable without the discourses of class that underpin its narrative and visual strategies.

5

Extra Masculinity

Looking for Mr. Goodbar *and* Cruising

Saturday Night Fever may have largely eluded the gender and sexual disorder of the 1970s, but it did so only by depicting its working-class characters as mired in a pre-1960s worldview. (Such strategic nostalgia was aided, no doubt, by the film's adoption of many musical generic conventions.) But not every new nightlife film chose to avoid the 1960s. Richard Brooks's *Looking for Mr. Goodbar* (1977) and William Friedkin's *Cruising* (1980) both confronted contemporary gender and sexual relations more directly. In doing so, they seemed to indicate that this new social terrain could not be mapped using the old cinematic tools, whether those of the musical or romantic comedy—in large part because the terrain itself was so bewildering. Molly Haskell argued that the achievement of *Goodbar* came from its recognition of the "social nightmare" of heterosexual dating in the late 1970s, a world "in which there are no mutually understood signals, no rituals, no codes for deciphering the intentions of another individual."[1] *Cruising*, in turn, made visible another set of mixed social codes: the film's persistent comparisons of gay S/M practices to law enforcement procedures (and vice versa) caused the *New Yorker*'s Roger Angell to be so unsure of the line dividing them that he wondered, "Are all cops, or most cops, gay?"[2] Gender and sexual identity was being revised so quickly and so utterly in the late 1970s, it seems, that one needed a scorecard to keep all the players straight (as it were).

Of particular interest is the way both of these films depict—and worry over—the new possibilities of working-class masculinity in this transformed social setting. Like *Fever*, *Goodbar* and *Cruising* share an intense voyeuristic interest in this kind of masculinity, an interest that often drives their visual strategies even as it troubles their narrative coherence. In fact, Robin Wood has argued that both *Goodbar* and *Cruising* can be considered "incoherent texts," in that they "do not know what they want to say."[3]

I will contend that this incoherence is often produced by the confusing unreadability of the blue-collar-attired men that inhabit these films. Do these men signify the traditional, if outdated, masculinity of *Fever*'s "golden age of Saturday nights," or do they indicate a new (and, for these films, troubling) world of queer sexuality? In pondering this dilemma of gender and sexual interpretation, both films end up generating, in different ways, what I am calling an "extra masculinity": a new kind of working-class male body that exceeds the traditional meanings of this body, and not just in the manner posited by post-Stonewall gay male culture. The reception of this extra masculinity reveals some of the roots of middle-class fascination with working-class masculinity during this period—a fascination informed by the idea that this body was disappearing from the economic scene. My closing discussion of the controversial production history of *Cruising*, and its effects on the resulting cinematic text, will therefore focus on the following question: to what political uses might the white, working-class male body be put—both onscreen and off—in this emerging post-Fordist moment? Before grasping the new and potentially liberatory possibilities of this body, though, we must first understand the semiotic disorder it engendered in *Looking for Mr. Goodbar*.

LOOKING FOR MR. GOODBAR'S STRATEGIC INCOHERENCE

Just as *Fever* was frequently taken to be "an authentic statement…about America's newest crop of alienated youth," with the "fresh bead" it drew "on the rituals of the disco life," so was *Looking for Mr. Goodbar* often hailed as an accurate portrayal of the experiences—and dangers—of the contemporary singles bar.[4] In fact, Haskell suggested that the movie "may even be an important film" for its apparently realistic rejoinder to those "who propound the glories of swinging singlehood and sex-on-demand without ever setting foot in the bars, and who remain comfortably immune from the demons that the rhetoric of liberation has unleashed."[5] Similarly, just as *Fever*'s quasi-documentary status was established by the supposedly ethnographic article that inspired the film, so too was *Goodbar* authenticated by the fact that it was based on a true story—that of Roseann Quinn, a twenty-eight-year-old schoolteacher who was killed by a man she had taken home from a singles bar. Yet just as *Fever*'s founding story turned out to be more fantasy and speculation than journalistic investigation, the *New Times* article by Lacey Fosburgh, "Finding Mr. Goodbar," that inspired Judith Rossner's best-selling novel *Looking for Mr. Goodbar*—which, in turn, was the basis of screenwriter and director Richard Brooks's film—was revealed to be a journalistic reconstruction that had little actual fact to go on.[6] Clearly, Quinn's murder provided a particularly inviting screen for various ideological projections regarding the new gender and sexual possibilities enabled by the space of the singles bar—a fact testified to by the multiple iterations (Fosburgh's article, later expanded into a book; Rossner's novel; Brooks's film) of the story.

What seems to have spurred these repeated articulations of Quinn's murder was the uncertainty of gender relations that the singles bar embodied, particularly the absence of "mutually understood signals...rituals...[and] codes" that Haskell described.[7] The film's reception also suggests the absence of a master code for understanding and interpreting the new sexual mores. While many critics, both academic and popular, described *Goodbar* as a patently antifeminist film, a reactionary morality tale in which a sexually liberated and financially independent woman is punished (via murder) for her transgressions against patriarchal authority,[8] at least two (notably male) writers described the film as antimale, with one going so far as to claim that *Goodbar* "really goes beyond the most highly politicized feminism, beyond even radical lesbianism, in its advocacy of female independence."[9] Such a drastic divergence of opinion on the film's political valence points to an equally dramatic cleavage in understandings of contemporary gender politics.

One might argue, following Wood, that *Goodbar*, as an incoherent text, invites such divergent readings. Rather than treat the film as presenting a univocal ideological viewpoint, then, we should explore the contradictory energies that drive the film and examine how these conflicting impulses are treated by the film's reception. This seems especially necessary since *Goodbar* is deeply divided in its attitude toward its protagonist, Theresa (Diane Keaton), who is based on Roseann Quinn. Does the film's contrast between her caring, dedicated teaching of deaf children during the day and her promiscuous, drug-taking hedonism at night imply a value judgment, with the former (appropriately feminine) role acting as a moral rejoinder to the latter, liberationist practices? Or, as the film (especially Keaton's performance) often suggests, are her nighttime activities substantially pleasurable and even fulfilling in their own right? Does her eventual murder amount to the film's condemnation of her double life? Or does it instead suggest a more subtle indictment of male violence and domination? These questions, in turn, pose the central conundrum of the film: which is the "real" Theresa?[10] Is the schoolteacher her "true" self and the singles bar persona a masquerade born out of desperation, or is this latter, more consciously devised personality actually a better representation of her chosen life? That the film offers evidence to support each of these opposed options indicates not only the contradictory nature of the film but also, I suggest, the unreadability of the social landscape it is trying to represent.

GOODBAR'S MEN

If the film can't decide what to think of Theresa, it is remarkably consistent on its male characters, who all engage in forms of patriarchal domination and violence, regardless of their class position. The film sets out the class oppositions of the men in Theresa's life early on. Her father is a working-class white ethnic patriarch—he lectures Theresa about how, as a poor Irish child, he worked in a coal yard—while the man with whom she has her first sexual relationship is a college professor. However, neither the father, who is domineering and emotionally abusive toward Theresa, nor the professor, who tells her at one point, "I just can't stand a woman's company right after I've fucked her," is represented as an adequate figure of male authority. As the narrative progresses, and Theresa leaves both her father's house and the professor, she takes up with two similarly class-divergent men: Tony (Richard Gere), whose (possibly illegal) occupation is left unclear, but whose self-presentation is that of a slick working-class delinquent, and James (William Atherton), a welfare agency social worker. Except for the fact that James is a lawyer in Rossner's novel, these sets of oppositions are all more or less faithful to the book, including Theresa's passionate sexual attraction to Tony, and her lack of it for James.

Something happens, though, to James's character in the move from page to screen. Where, in Rossner's novel, James was an understanding and emotionally supportive suitor who was contrasted with the sexually compelling but misogynistic and violent Tony, the film's James is more or less as pathological as Tony (as well as all of the other men in the film). At one point, James tells Theresa that, as a child, he saw his father brutally beat his mother after she had taunted him for his impotence; after a failed attempt at lovemaking with Theresa, James tells her that he made the story up—implying suppressed violent impulses associated with his sexual anxieties. These suggestions are confirmed later in the film, as James begins stalking Theresa—particularly when she goes out with other men—and he eventually tears apart her bedroom after she refuses to be in a monogamous relationship with him. That James's violent outburst is visually rhymed, in the next shot, with a similar fit of anger from her father—he throws her Christmas present back in her face for not marrying James—only confirms that James, for all his talk of being a "liberal" who wants "to save the world," offers just another version of male domination and control.

Goodbar also draws a connection between James's desire for control over Theresa and his PMC occupation. When we first meet James, he is telling Mrs. Jackson, the mother of one of Theresa's students, that if her lover (to whom she is not married) continues to live with her, he will file a report that will cause her to lose her welfare benefits. Mrs. Jackson angrily responds that, given the hardships of being a poor single mother, she has a right to the pleasure her lover gives her. As such, the sequence quite explicitly articulates the feminist critique of the welfare state's role in policing the sexuality of poor women.[11] James's avowed intentions to help and support women are therefore shown to be related to a desire to discipline their sexuality, which is in turn linked to his professional-managerial class identity. While James's attempts to control Theresa are, for the most part, less violent than those of Tony (who physically beats her after catching her with another man), *Goodbar* makes clear that the actions of both men—one working class, one professional—are similarly motivated by a will toward male domination.

However, many reviewers of the film refused to acknowledge James's pathological impulses. Vincent Canby called James "a good young Catholic man Theresa should love," while Betsy Erkkila argued that it is the "genuine love and respect of [Theresa's] social worker boyfriend that turns Terry off; his desire to marry her rather than to make her leaves them both dry and limp."[12] Academic critics of the film have often concurred with this understanding of James: E. Ann Kaplan described James as the "nice, stable, protective man," whom Theresa rejects "just *because* he wants monogamy, just *because* he wants to 'protect' her."[13] Indeed, Joan Mellen claimed that, rather than critique the desire for male control that drives James's character in the film, *Goodbar*'s "Victorian" sensibility asserts that "domestic protection, of the kind that would be provided by Theresa's pallid social worker admirer, is necessary for a woman's well-being."[14] Unable or unwilling to see James as just as threatening to Theresa as Tony, these critics seemed to rely on his professional occupation (and accompanying manners) to guarantee his status as the "proper" object choice.

Granted, this misreading of the film was probably encouraged by the intertext of Rossner's novel, in which James is indeed a middle-class, sensitive (if sexually dull), and eminently marriageable man who acts as a foil to Tony's volatile blue-collar bad boy. Yet those reviewers who did note this recasting of James's role in the film saw this not as part of a larger critique of male domination but instead as a sign of the film's muddled or ill-tempered motives. Calling the film "a general diatribe against alleged American decadence" that "lashe[s] out against the young," Frank Rich complained that "Theresa's one appealing suitor...whose sweetness should leaven the story, becomes as cruel as the rest."[15] John Simon argued that Brooks's apparent desire to turn the novel's psychological study into a sensationalistic thriller makes "even a perfectly nice lawyer" turn "into a voyeuristic, presumably impotent, social worker."[16] Richard Corliss bemoaned the fact that, since "every man Theresa meets is a schmuck or a prick," Brooks offers the viewer no "opposing moral force," no representative of the "sensible, joyful middle ground" that the film "utterly exclude[s]." In fact, Corliss imagines that the only way the film's lack of balance could be righted would be by the inclusion of a character very much like the reviewer himself:

> Diane Keaton is just too lovely, fresh, huggable to be taken advantage of by such creeps. A girl who looked as good as she does would be taken advantage of by much more high-class creeps; she might even be taken to heart by someone as fascinating as Woody Allen—or you, or me. If *Goodbar* is a hit, it will be because millions of men respond to the sweet vulnerability and promise of Keaton's Theresa the way they did on hearing of Marilyn Monroe's death: if only she'd met *me*! I'd have understood her, comforted her, taken her to string quartet recitals, and marvelous undiscovered restaurants, been a friend in need, loved her as a person, helped her love herself.[17]

Without a sympathetic male figure with whom to identify, Corliss implies in this self-mocking passage, the only pleasure left for male viewers is to imagine themselves as the proper middle-class, string-quartet-attending suitor for Theresa. Perhaps the absence of a reassuring representative of one's class also explains the unhappy responses of other PMC male critics.

In fact, the film's unsparing view of male domination as a cross-class affair led Wood to suggest that *Goodbar* makes the radical argument that "violence is inherent in sexual relationships under patriarchy." One of the film's key narrative strategies, after all, is to present a number of (ultimately false) moments of foreshadowing in order to give us "the feeling that any of [the men] might go berserk and kill her," as Haskell puts it.[18] James's story about his impotent father beating his mother echoes the scenario of Theresa's eventual murder (which would be known to those who read Rossner's novel), leading us to suspect later, as he silently stalks her, that he might kill her.[19] Tony, for his part, not only beats Theresa, but later, after she refuses to let him back into her apartment, shouts, "You are dead!" Given that we have earlier seen Tony wildly wave a switchblade at Theresa and "jokingly" threaten to stab her, the chance that Tony will turn out to be the killer seems equally likely, if not more so.

It is worth noting that during the scene in which Tony menaces Theresa with a knife—which is the first night that she takes him home—we spend a great deal of time admiring Tony's/Gere's body: he first paces about the apartment wearing only a jock strap and an unbuttoned, tight blue denim shirt, then drops to do push-ups (drawing attention to his bare ass, framed by the straps of his supporter), and finally strips off his shirt to dance around with the knife. The scene bears not a little resemblance to the bedroom grooming sequence in *Saturday Night Fever* in its eroticization of a physically energetic and seemingly unself-conscious white, working-class male body, although here the gaze is "safely" marked as that of a heterosexual woman. As Betsy Erkkila observed, in "scenes such as these, Brooks invites the audience to indulge their voyeuristic fantasies."[20] Pauline Kael agreed, claiming that the film plays on the desire of "moviegoers...to see how other people are making out—in sex, at work, in the city," and that the *Goodbar* narrative was popular because "it's about something that most women have probably done at some time—or, at least, have wanted to do."[21] And, since our perspective is so closely aligned with Theresa's—we even experience her daydreams and fantasies as if they are actually happening, only to be brought back to "reality" by a later, correcting shot—*Goodbar* encourages us to take vicarious pleasure in Theresa's explorations of the possibilities of the new nightlife, which in this scene involves taking home some rough trade, and enjoying a working-class male body that also seems capable of violence—a complicated pleasure we will return to later in this chapter.

SEX, GENDER, AND UNDECIDABILITY

However, the working-class man that ultimately kills Theresa is Gary (Tom Berenger), whom we first see dancing and making out with his male lover in a gay bar. As Kael notes, Gary appears as "a second Richard Gere": "he holds his lips slack and takes more from the young Brando than from De Niro, but it's the same kind of programmed working-class lowlife."[22] Indeed, when Gary enters Theresa's apartment, he swings on a pipe and jokes around in a manner very similar to Tony. Why, then, does *Goodbar* produce a second working-class man to carry out the violence augured by the first (not to mention by Theresa's middle-class admirer)? Furthermore, why is Tony's double gay? In Rossner's novel, Gary was living and sleeping with a gay man, yet he seemed to do so only in exchange for money and housing, and he had a pregnant wife in Florida. In addition, the novel's Gary is able to achieve an erection with Theresa and "successfully" have sex with her, and only kills her after she will not let him stay the night. The film's Gary, in contrast, seems initially quite happy in his relationship with his male lover (they are both smiling as they kiss in the disco), and he cannot get an erection with Theresa—even with the help of amyl nitrate "poppers," long associated with gay male sexuality.[23] It seems crucial to the film that Gary is emphatically gay—and that a gay man be the killer. Yet for a film that elsewhere implies that male violence is widespread in heterosexual relationships (no matter what class position the man occupies), the decision to place the responsibility of Theresa's murder on a nonheterosexual man is a curious one.

E. Ann Kaplan posits that *Goodbar* "locat[es] the rage that leads to murder in a homosexual" in order to allow "the dominant class of men to avoid identification with the final, most brutal act."[24] This seems somewhat persuasive, but if Gary's homosexuality serves as a kind of escape hatch for straight male viewers, why does the film's portrayal of the murder allude to the threats posed by both James (Gary kills Theresa because of his anxiety over his impotence) and Tony (she is stabbed to death with a knife)? Perhaps the answer is related to the fact that, as Kael observed, Theresa "cruises singles bars the way male homosexuals cruise gay bars and S/M hangouts."[25] In fact, Bryan Bruce has argued that

> Theresa's sexuality is consistent with the expression of gay male sexuality which emerged most forcefully around the time of the film's release, and it is no accident that her "cruising" leads her to gay bars.... The emphasis on eroticism in gay culture is, as it is for Theresa Dunne [sic], an expression of defiance, of the overwhelming rejection of the repression and taboo that is directed towards alternative sexual practice.[26]

This connection between Theresa and Gary is also suggested by Wood, who claims that both characters are "victim[s] of a society that assigns people fixed roles, imposing on them notions of what a real man or real woman should be," and that the "catastrophe" of the murder is a sign of the characters' inability to understand "the links between feminism and gay liberation."[27]

Thinking of Theresa and Gary as linked figures—analogues of each others' rebellions against and deviations from normative sex and gender roles—also helps us recognize how Gary functions as a kind of "hysterical" figure, a corollary of the undecidability of Theresa's character. As I have already noted, much was made of the film's emphasis on what Newsweek's Jack Kroll called Theresa's "Dostoevskian double personality."[28] And it is the inability of Tony and James to acknowledge and respect both selves that motivates their anger against Theresa. Tony, furious at Theresa's rejection of him, threatens to expose her nighttime activities to the school administration, in hopes of ending her job; James, in turn, tears down and smashes a glass mobile with sexually explicit line drawings that Theresa had earlier described as representative of the side of herself that he refused to see. In this way, the two characters reflect the film's own confusion as to which of Theresa's selves to valorize—and, in turn, which of Theresa's selves to declare her "true" self. As Goodbar approaches its denouement, and it seems that either man could kill Theresa, it also seems likely that whoever kills her will tell us something about the film's own attitude toward Theresa. If Tony kills her, it will be a sign of the perils of liberated promiscuity; if James commits the murder, it will suggest that the daylight world of middle-class monogamy has its own dangers.

Unable to choose either one of these options—and thus decide upon the "correct" understanding of Theresa's character—*Goodbar* instead produces Gary, who functions as something like a hysterical sign. As Geoffrey Nowell-Smith has argued, hysterical texts are those whose repressed energies, produced by contradictions they cannot resolve, return as textual excesses and incoherencies.[29] In this sense, Gary can be seen as the textual excess generated by the film's failure to resolve its contradictory attitude to Theresa's two selves. Not only is Gary more or less extraneous, unnecessary to the plot (since more than one character has already demonstrated murderous rage toward Theresa), but his body also bears the marks of an undecidable sex/gender identity that is analogous to Theresa's; he appears to replicate Tony's hypermasculine, insatiably heterosexual body, and he seems to *want* to inhabit this body, yet his sexual orientation disrupts these associations, rendering these signifiers unreadable.

It is not a coincidence that this hysterical textual symptom—this sign of the unreadable identities created by new sex and gender mores—is embodied by a blue-collar-looking gay man. Note how, in a film otherwise narrated solely from Theresa's perspective, we are presented with one sequence that occurs outside of her experience: that of Gary's fight with his male lover, which immediately precedes his chance meeting with Theresa.[30] It is as if *Goodbar*—afraid that its audience would be confused by the association of a butch, working-class masculinity, so similar to Tony's, with a panicked homosexuality—breaks with its narrational strategy in order to establish and confirm Gary's sexual orientation.[31] In this scene, we see Gary angrily removing his female drag clothes as he insists upon his masculinity (he yells, "You're the nellie, not me! I'm a pitcher, not a catcher!"). His chosen replacement wear, though—blue denim jacket, jeans, and leather boots—could be read as that of either a straight, working-class man, or a gay male clone. And in the singles bar where he meets Theresa, Gary is actually first approached by another man, who "mistakenly" assumes that Gary is cruising for a male lover. Theresa, though, perhaps recognizing the similarity in appearance to Tony, is also mistaken in reading Gary as straight. In other words, the scene enacts in miniature the social nightmare Haskell described, in which there are no mutually understood signals or codes. Gary's blue-collar, repressed gay man—who signifies both as a butch straight man and a self-affirming gay clone, but in fact is neither—thus serves as the symbol of a new social landscape where signifiers can no longer reliably refer to stable signifieds.

Which is not to say that, in contrast to *Fever*, *Goodbar* works to subvert the "natural" association of working-class masculine signifiers with heteronormativity. Instead, the film underlines the importance of these class signifiers to understandings of sexuality and gender. While James is shown to be an equal partner with Tony in male pathology, it is this latter, working-class character that the camera eroticizes as an exemplar of heterosexual masculinity. Further, when Theresa is first taken to a gay bar by one of her well-dressed, middle-class pick-ups, and she asks him if he is gay, his denial is jovial and unpanicked, and the film seems to treat the question of a middle-class man's sexual orientation as uninteresting. To see a firmly muscled, blue-denim-appareled macho figure as gay, however, is apparently to contemplate the disruption of the gender and sexual symbolic order —a disruption that finds its analogue, one might argue, in the violent and all-but-unwatchable murder of Theresa, which concludes with the gradual disappearance of the cinematic image itself. Gary's sudden and seemingly unmotivated arrival at the end of *Goodbar* signals the film's panic at its own inability to represent the unreadable world suggested by Theresa's new, protofeminist sexuality. That this unreadability finds its expression in an extra working-class male body, whose masculinity is a mystery to himself as well as others, indicates the high cultural stakes attributed to blue-collar iconography for contemporary understandings of sex and gender norms.

CRUISING AND THE SADOMASOCHISM OF CLASS DESIRE

The propensity for violence—and its erotic undercurrent—exhibited by *Goodbar*'s working-class Tony (and his gay doppelganger, Gary) also crops up in Nik Cohn's description of his imaginary Vincent, the model for *Saturday Night Fever*'s Tony. Cohn wrote that "before Saturday night began, to clear his brain of cobwebs and get himself sharp, fired up, [Vincent] liked to think about killing." These thoughts are linked, by Cohn, to the fact that "during the week Vincent sold paint in a housewares store. All day, every day he stood behind a counter and grinned. He climbed up and down ladders, he made the coffee, he obeyed. Then came the weekend and he was cut loose." Cohn goes on to depict Vincent's violent fantasies in detail—imagining them through cinematic models—and notes, at their conclusion, "The week behind the counter has been obliterated. No drudgery existed. He was released. Saturday night has begun."[32]

Fever's Tony, of course, has no such violent fantasies, and in fact he seems less volatile than his working-class friends. Yet his character still seemed to inspire a mix of fear and desire in some PMC critics. Commenting on Travolta's portrayal of Tony, Frank Rich wrote that "at once mean-looking and pretty, he conveys a kind of threatening sexuality that floors an audience." Rich further noted admiringly that when "Tony and his inarticulate chums burn off the tensions of their workaday jobs and Roman Catholic guilts, we see a mindless explosion of pent-up energy that is almost frighteningly hedonistic. The characters become cruel and volatile beneath the strobe lights."[33] Just as Theresa (herself a middle-class observer) takes pleasure in the spectacle of Richard Gere's Tony—who often seemed mindless, frighteningly hedonistic, cruel, and volatile—so too did writers like Cohn and Rich find the apparently implied violence of working-class male bodies to possess an erotically compelling component.

Note, too, that this violence is linked by these writers, either implicitly or explicitly, to class resentment—the invented Vincent's need to be cut loose from his servitude, the "explosion" produced in reaction to the "tension" of "workaday jobs" described by Rich. What motivates this curious spectatorial dynamic, in which PMC observers take pleasure in the spectacle of class-inspired violence (or the possibility thereof) on the part of their class other?[34] The complex—and frequently bewildering—narrative and visual strategies of *Cruising* speak rather vividly to these questions. A film about, among other things, the performance of identity—the plot centers on a policeman, Steve Burns (Al Pacino), posing as a gay S/M aficionado in order to track down a killer—*Cruising* also highlights the class impersonations of gay male S/M culture, thus offering a sort of distorted mirror of this middle-class attraction to working-class masculinity. The often panicked response to the film by (almost all male) critics testifies, in turn, both to their fascination with *Cruising*'s spectacle of unrestrained masculinity as well as the discomfort evoked when this spectacle is located in an explicitly homosexual context. In this way, *Cruising* exposes the homoerotic energies that constitute a crucial element of male PMC investment in working-class masculinity, while also suggesting a new and potentially liberatory articulation of this masculinity.

THE CLASS UNCONSCIOUS OF S/M

About a third of the way into its running time, *Cruising* features a sort of film-within-a-film sequence that, as Simon Watney half-seriously suggested, could be taken as a figure for our own spectatorial experience of the movie—an experience that is furthermore a kind of reductio ad absurdum of the PMC interest in watching violent working-class male bodies that I noted above.[35] This sequence opens, in daylight, with a well-dressed fashion designer closing his uptown store and discussing an upcoming weekend dinner party.[36] The next shot, however, shows him at night, dressed down, and driving to a leather bar. Once there, he slips into a peep show booth, joined by a man dressed as a biker, and they begin watching a pornographic film loop. The film they watch is similar to the one we have been viewing:

both feature captivated, voyeuristic shots of men dressed as working-class delinquents engaged in rough, sexualized displays of domination and submission.[37] The arousing effect of this spectacle of eroticized, proletarian violence on the middle-class viewer is made clear, as he kneels in front of the other man, presumably to perform oral sex. Yet the leather-clad man takes the violence on the screen in front of him one step further and repeatedly stabs the fashion designer in the back, killing him—and thus simulating, Watney implies, the brutal effect *Cruising* has on its spectators, especially its gay viewers.

Watney's argument against *Cruising* is typical of that made by gay (and some straight) critics of the film, especially his claim that "it is precisely the casual, repetitive slippage from 'gay' to 'violence' which is so offensive and dangerous in *Cruising*."[38] And, despite the film's opening disclaimer—that "this film is not intended as an indictment of the homosexual world. It is set in one small segment of that world, which is not meant to be representative of the whole"—*Cruising* often seems to be making precisely this case: that this "segment" *is* representative of the whole (even "respectable," middle-class gay men cruise the downtown leather bars), and that this "world" is inherently violent. Why, then, did screenwriter and director William Friedkin choose gay male S/M culture to act as a synecdoche for gay experience? The 1970 novel by Gerald Walker, on which the film is loosely based, was not set in the S/M scene, yet Friedkin explained in an interview that "I felt that it just wasn't interesting enough to show an ordinary gay bar."[39] Instead, he told Janet Maslin, "I was fascinated by [the S/M bars]...It seemed to me to be very exciting. And unusual. And outside my own experience."[40] What attracted him, he said, was the "macho fantasy" enacted by the clubgoers, since "all the films I've made in one way or another deal with characters who are obsessed, driven, perhaps sexually confused, given over to a macho image, which is generally bluff, and living on the edge of danger."[41] The kind of "macho fantasy" that gay male S/M culture seemed to offer Friedkin thus bears investigating.

As Daniel Harris explains, "the leather community as we know it today originated in the early 1950s, with the rise of the first gay biker clubs," whose members were drawn to the iconography of straight motorcycle gangs, and "who soon began to impersonate them, imitating their snarling, contemptuous masculinity and disdain for middle-class respectability." As with the later development of the clone look (which Harris suggests was inspired by these gay motorcycle clubs), the "implicit purpose of such organizations...was to subvert the prevailing stereotypes of effeminate homosexuals by creating a hypermasculine environment in which members could cultivate the machismo of their heterosexual heroes." Harris claims that "for most of the early participants in the leather phenomenon, rough, unsentimental S/M sex was less a means of erotic fulfillment than a political affectation." Whether or not this (unsourced) assertion is true, what is important to note about S/M's origins in contemporary gay male practice was that it articulated gender and sexual identity through "an elaborate form of transvestism that involved putting on the bogeyman costumes of a new social threat to the bourgeois world" (a social threat cinematically embodied by Marlon Brando in *The Wild One* [1954]).[42]

By the 1970s, S/M culture offered gay men not only a hypermasculine gender and sexual identity but also a set of practices that could parody— and, according to some enthusiasts, exorcise—the unjust power relations of larger society. Answering the charge, made by anti-S/M feminists and others, that S/M scenarios uncritically replicated the most oppressive and exploitative sorts of social relations, S/M defenders argued that these scenarios are undertaken voluntarily, with well-developed etiquettes for signaling consent, and that the positions assumed in these scenarios are reversible. As Pat Califia insisted, in an oft-quoted essay:

> The system is unjust because it assigns privileges based on race, gender, and social class. During an S/M encounter the participants select a particular role because it best expresses their sexual needs…The most significant reward for being a top or a bottom is sexual pleasure. If you don't like being a top or a bottom you switch your keys. Try doing that with your biological sex or your socio-economic status.[43]

Furthermore, Leo Bersani argues, S/M operates as "a kind of X-ray of power's body, a laboratory testing of the erotic potential in the most oppressive social structures."[44] When these social structures are reincarnated in the consensual, equal opportunity zones of S/M practice, Califia suggests, their "uniforms and roles and dialogue become a parody of authority, a challenge to it, a recognition of its secret sexual nature."[45]

It would seem that this last, parodic function is what drew Friedkin, at least in part, to the iconography of S/M. One of the film's earliest scenes features a pair of police officers accosting two male transvestite prostitutes and forcing the sex workers to perform oral sex on them in their squad car. The exterior shot of the patrol car is then blocked by a leather-clad man, whom the camera follows into an S/M bar (we soon discover that he is the killer). As Robin Wood notes, "this introduction concisely states the theme of the interchangeability of the police force and the leather bars."[46] This theme is pursued consistently throughout the film. In one particularly memorable sequence, during a police interrogation of a gay murder suspect, the detectives open a door to reveal a large, heavily muscled black man wearing only a cowboy hat, jock strap, and leather boots, who silently enters the room, slaps

Steve (who is posing as another suspect), and then silently leaves. Neither his presence, nor his attire, is ever explained. This intrusion of S/M iconography into police practice is mirrored in the "Precinct Night" scene, in which gay male S/M aficionados all wear police-styled uniforms (figure 5.1)—a dress policy that ironically prevents Steve from entering the bar, since, although he is a cop, he is dressed as a leatherman. David Savran described this last sequence as one that "flagrantly reveals (long before *Gender Trouble*) not only the necessarily performative nature of identities (sexual, gendered, and otherwise) but also the intense homoeroticism that is sublimated in what passes for normative male homosociality."[47] Friedkin's use of S/M here, therefore, seems to draw upon its implicit political critique, its parodic revelation of the sexualized power relations that structure police (and other disciplinary) practices—a revelation that "says to society: this is the way you really are," in Bersani's phrase.[48]

If S/M operates by theatricalizing oppressive social relations, though, we must recognize that much of its visual effect comes from the spectacle of men coded as working-class subjects—subjects normally forced to submit to various kinds of economic discipline and control—engaged in apparently violent acts of domination. Furthermore, the uniforms utilized, such as various kinds of biker gear, are frequently those of antisocial rebels, working-class male figures that refuse the discipline of the boss and the state. If Friedkin was drawn to S/M because of its "macho fantasy," part of its attraction may have also been its accompanying class fantasy—that of working-class men set loose from their subordinated economic position to pursue a desublimated, sexualized will to power. In other words, the visual imagery offered by S/M practice, which Friedkin deployed to

Figure 5.1. From *Cruising*. "Precinct Night" in *Cruising*.

obsessive effect in *Cruising*, seems to invite, almost hyperbolically, the PMC attraction to the violence of insubordinate working-class male bodies that frequently attended *Saturday Night Fever* and *Looking for Mr. Goodbar*.

THE UNCOMFORTABLE VOYEUR

But where does *Cruising* locate us in this "macho fantasy"? Are we positioned to inhabit vicariously the proletarianized male bodies engaged in this eroticized domination, or are we aligned instead with figures like the ill-fated fashion designer, with his desire to submit to a hypermasculine, working-class man? In other words, does the film ask us to imagine ourselves as perpetrators of working-class-coded aggression or as targets of it? Alternatively, is it the case that, as many gay critics complained, we are meant to recoil in horror from the entire scene, as the spectacle of men loving men is made abject by its association with violence and murder?

Such questions plagued reviewers of *Cruising*, who frequently protested that the film gave little guidance as to how to interpret what was happening on screen. Often, this criticism was voiced as a frustration with Friedkin's refusal to "explain" S/M. As David Ansen complained:

> the ominous bar scenes are butch *grand guignol*, full of sweaty flesh, menacing shadows and barely glimpsed acts of degradation performed by glowering, bearded men in black leather and chains. But who are these people and why are they doing all these kinky things? Friedkin isn't interested in explaining his milieu: he merely offers it up as a superficially shocking tableau for the titillation and horror of his audience.[49]

In a like manner, David Denby asserted that "the movie as a whole seems to have been made by a man who sees everything and comprehends nothing—a voyeur."[50] Yet one might also posit that, rather than spell out *why* people engage in S/M—which would then tell the viewer how one *should* feel about S/M practices, thus keeping the proceedings at a safe distance—*Cruising* instead forces the viewer to confront his or her interest in and/or fear of the S/M scene. This anxious preference for a sociological approach would seem to explain the frequently made observation that, as Vincent Canby put it, the film "describes the s. and m. [*sic*] scene with far more leering detail than most people will find necessary."[51] Thus, when the *Nation*'s Robert Hatch castigated the film because, among other things, "the group scenes contain very little that I could identify as genital contact, however perverse; it looked to me like obscenely infantile messing around," this disapproval could come from the fact that *Cruising*'s blank voyeurism seems to generate a desiring gaze without offering socially sanctioned objects and actions for this gaze. Perhaps most importantly, in refusing to furnish a sociological framework for this gaze, the film also denies the critical distance provided by the knowing, condescending spectatorial position offered in *Saturday Night Fever.*[52]

Denby wondered why Friedkin did not use his protagonist's own ignorance of S/M as an entry point for the bewildered (implicitly straight, non-S/M-practicing) viewer—that as Steve Burns learned about this world, so would we. Instead, Denby lamented, Steve is "a passive observer, distant from us."[53] Indeed, our inability to access, and thus to identify with, Steve's subjectivity was another common criticism of the film. The shift in Steve's character, as he seems to lose interest in his heterosexual relationship and become increasingly drawn to gay men (including his non-S/M-practicing gay neighbor, Ted Bailey), is "left undramatized," Frank Rich remarked, as there are "no scenes that clearly show Burns's descent into a personal hell or his growing sexual ambivalence."[54] Furthermore, the film suggests that Steve himself may have become a killer, when Ted is discovered murdered at the end of the film, after the person who we thought was the killer has been caught. This is consonant with the novel's denouement, but, as Vincent Canby complained, "what happens to the film's cop...is far from clear."[55] As a result, Roger Angell concludes, "Steve Burns is something of an enigma, to himself and to us all."[56]

But perhaps it is precisely this fact—that our unknowing about Steve's inner life may be akin to his own confusion—that explains *Cruising*'s seemingly incoherent narrative and character developments. In fact, the film seems to get more confusing as it progresses, as Steve's motivations become increasingly opaque to both the viewer and himself. He describes this unsettling loss of self, in a deeply shaken whisper, to Captain Edelson: "Things are happening to me, you know? I don't know that I can handle it...It's just, stuff's going down and I don't think I can deal with it."[57] Yet rather than compensate for the increasing incoherence of its protagonist by offering a coherent omniscient narration—or, conversely, by telling the incoherent story through the perspective of its incoherent protagonist—*Cruising*, in a genuinely frustrating gesture, allows its omniscient narration to fracture and fall to pieces as Steve himself does.[58] Since we do not share his perspective, Steve may be too "distant from us," as Denby complained, but our increasing confusion puts us in a situation that is analogous to his.

One is tempted to invoke Jean-Louis Baudry's famous account of the "ideological effects of the cinematographic apparatus" and characterize this difficulty in identifying with a protagonist, and the fracturing of omniscient narration (which would disrupt our alignment, on Baudry's account, with the apparatus itself), as the signs of a breakdown in the position of "transcendental subject" dominant cinema is supposed to offer us.[59] And there is a case to be made that this breakdown could be a symptom of the threat posed by the film's ubiquitous representations of gay male sex, the "seductive and intolerable image of a grown man, legs high in the air, unable to refuse the suicidal ecstasy of being a woman," as Bersani polemically describes it.[60] Following Bersani, one might say that the shattering of straight male self-hood enacted by having one's body penetrated—an act everywhere implied in *Cruising*—generates the apparent fragmentation of the film's protagonist, as well as the film's own inability to make its narrative cohere, thus disallowing the spectator an all-knowing, all-seeing perspective. Such a reading would certainly help explain much of the panicked nature of the film's vituperatively negative reception by straight male critics. And it would also account for the film's frequent equation of gay male sex with death—an association that reaches its nadir with the frames of anal penetration from a pornographic film interpolated into a shot of the fashion designer's stabbing, which visually equates the act of being penetrated with murder.[61]

Despite the persuasiveness of such a reading, the identificatory strategies of *Cruising* seem more complicated than the univocal one (an identification with the apparatus) offered by this account. In fact, *Cruising* asks us to inhabit multiple positions. During one of the first sequences, we find ourselves perched over the shoulder of the killer as he cruises a muscular actor, takes him to a hotel, and has the actor worship him before tying him up and killing him. Later, though, we are located in the position of the victim in the fashion designer sequence I described earlier—a man whose nervous glances at the rough trade sizing him up we share, since we know one of the men checking him out is the killer. Even our identification with Steve, problematic, incomplete, and ultimately frustrated as it is, takes many forms. In one bar sequence, as he is cruised by various men (including one of the cops, now off-duty and dressed in leather, who harassed the transvestite prostitutes), we assume his perspective; the men looking him over peer directly into the camera, their faces taking up almost all of the frame, suggesting their intimate address to both Steve and the viewer. Yet when Steve begins to stalk the actual killer—watching him from outside his apartment window, sitting across from him on a bus, and so on—we are aligned as much with the killer's discomfort under Steve's almost predatory gaze as we are with this gaze itself. Finally, when Steve repairs to a hotel with a suspect, and asks his pick-up to tie him up, we are forced to experience the scene from a distance, as we are located in the police car with the detectives who are listening to Steve's hidden microphone. *Cruising* thus situates us, at various moments, at all points along the S/M circuit—the dominant gazer/cruiser/top/killer, the submissive gazed-upon/cruised/bottom/victim, and the removed voyeur avidly taking in the scene.

CLASS AND THE FANTASY OF MASCULINITY

This fluid, mobile, and even contradictory set of identificatory positions is perhaps yet another sign of the film's much-commented-upon refusal to present the viewer with a stable, coherent perspective from which to understand and evaluate the film's events. But we can also see this network of looks and positions as corresponding to the psychic operations of fantasy outlined by Jean Laplanche and Jean-Bertrand Pontalis and elaborated upon by Elizabeth Cowie.[62] "The fantasy scenario," Cowie argues, "always involves multiple points of entry which are also mutually exclusive positions," and therefore "present[s] a varying of subject positions so that the subject takes up more than one position and thus is not fixed."[63] *Cruising*'s mobile circuit of identification and desire offers just such multiple points of entry into mutually exclusive positions, as we find ourselves, at various points in the film, dominating, dominated, and observers of domination.

But this raises the question: what is the fantasy being worked through here? I take Friedkin at his word and agree that what is being enacted here is indeed a "macho fantasy." The leather bars—like the police station—are all-male settings in *Cruising*. But despite the connections Friedkin wants to draw between the homoeroticism of the two worlds, the station house is associated with repression and hypocrisy, whereas the S/M bars are zones of desublimated activity. There, men can pursue Eros and Thanatos at will, freed, as they are, from both women and the reality principle. The fantasy being figured forth here seems to be one of unrestrained masculinity. It is as if, with relations between heterosexual men and women in such disarray after the seismic shocks of second-wave feminism, the only place that "true" masculinity could fully express itself was in the leather bars of gay male S/M practitioners.

Such a suggestion may seem a bit perverse, but it is one that was asserted by a number of journalists and academics at the end of the 1970s. Donald Symons, in his 1979 book *The Evolution of Human Sexuality*, wrote that the fundamental differences between male and female sexual behavior were illustrated by "the fact that homosexual men behave in many ways like heterosexual men, only more so, and lesbians behave like heterosexual women, only more so." According to Symons, the fact that certain allegedly "male proclivities," such as preference for physical attractiveness, youth, and sexual variety, are "manifested by homosexual men to unprecedented degree" is due to the fact that "their behavior is not constrained by the necessity to compromise with women."[64] Similarly, an alarmist article in *Time* that followed *Cruising*'s release, which asked if "homosexual males consciously seek danger," suggested that they very well might, but largely because they are men: "One explanation is that homosexual male sex is likely to be more aggressive than heterosexual sex simply because two men are involved." The article cites psychologist C. A. Tripp, who claimed that sadomasochism is rare among straights and lesbians but common among gay men because of "the additive effect of two males together." Many straight men may want to engage in S/M, Tripp argued, but they have difficulty finding women who would consent, whereas "in male-male relationships, there is no such shortage of players, and leather bars make them easy to locate."[65]

These arguments dovetail with the contemporaneous critique of S/M made by some feminists, who saw it as the sine qua non of patriarchal domination, and identified gay male culture's efforts to bring "homoerotic sadomasochism out of the closet" as a sign of "the convergence of what was once deemed a 'gay sensibility' with what was once deemed a 'heterosexual sensibility.'" This convergence, they argued, "is conspicuously a male sensibility."[66] All of these discourses, therefore, locate a "truth" of masculinity (particularly of male sexuality) not in the norms of heterosexual male behavior but instead in the theatricalized performances of their excluded other. That post-Stonewall gay male culture's hyperbolic and (at least somewhat) parodic simulations of traditional masculinity came to be associated with what many writers took to be the distilled essence of this masculinity is, of course, not a little ironic.

Cruising's fantasy of masculinity unbound referred not only to these newly minted understandings of gay men (especially gay male S/M) but also to the working-class signifiers in which this fantasy was dressed up. Above and beyond the working-class-coded clothing worn by their denizens, the leather bars in which *Cruising* was filmed—or, in some cases, which were re-created for the film (more on this in a moment)—are all minimally decorated, warehouse/industrial-type settings with names like the Mine Shaft and the Anvil. In other words, they are spaces that mimicked, and eroticized, sites of working-class labor (as many gay male bars did, according to Martin Levine).[67] Yet the dominance and submission of these spaces in *Cruising* is not that of the Taylorized shop floor but instead the sexualized parody of such relationships. In other words, the film simulates a privileged site of traditionally "masculine" labor in order to draw upon its gendered associations, but it then transmutes this space from the realm of economic necessity to that of libidinal freedom—where the apparently quintessentially masculine sex drive may then pursue all of its desires. In the cinematic spaces that *Cruising* creates, the PMC fascination with and attraction to violent (or potentially violent) white working-class male bodies can travel along the circuit of spectatorial alignments that the film makes available, thus allowing the PMC viewer to experience any number of relationships to these bodies: vicarious identification, masochistic submission, and/or scopophilic, voyeuristic appreciation.

Before one celebrates the cornucopia of pleasures that *Cruising* put on offer for the middle-class viewer, it must be acknowledged that these pleasures seem to have been largely rejected, or at least strongly disavowed. The fact that *Cruising* narrativizes these pleasures in a series of murders suggests that the film's investments in working-class male bodies are ones from which it ultimately recoils. And, as I have already argued, the eventual revulsion from the film's orgiastic spectacles of S/M culture registered by both the text and its male critics is surely generated, to a large extent, by the fact that it is *gay* S/M that we are watching. But I would add that some of this aversion may also be produced by class anxiety. David Ansen noted that the film "does succeed in creating a new homosexual stereotype: not the limp-wristed, effeminate pansy of old, but a menacing, macho muscleman who pursues sex with surly ferocity and barely suppressed violence."[68] If the working-class-coded male bodies of the film inspired the sort of desiring gaze that I discussed in relation to *Saturday Night Fever* and *Looking for Mr. Goodbar*, these bodies are also more persistently aggressive, with this aggression directed (*pace Goodbar*) at other men—most often professional men (professors, actors, fashion designers, etc.). Their "surly ferocity and barely suppressed violence," dressed in the signifiers of working-class delinquent rebellion and acting outside any visible disciplinary regime (except for those of their own parodic creation), might have suggested a class-based threat that could have interrupted any unproblematic experience of pleasure.

Still, the accounts that critics gave of *Cruising* suggest that the sorts of desires I have catalogued above were at least alluded to, however obliquely, before they were disavowed. In addition to Ansen's detailed description of the film's "butch *grand guignol*" and Hatch's desperate search for "genital contact," there was Roger Angell's acknowledgment that Friedkin's

> late-at-night glimpses of the gliding, posturing figures along the trashy back streets of the meat rack; his smoky, pounding, earsplitting, overcrowded, sweaty bars, writhing with dancers and sexually clutching male couples, where men loom and hover and stare (glitteringly, through black aviator glasses), like Richard Lindner's monster males…are executed with a power that does away with all our defensively vague prior imaginings and replaces them with a horrendous reality.[69]

Or there is Vincent Canby's observation that

> everywhere the movie goes, it sees nothing but young and not-so-young men who dress as if they were going to a costume ball in a garage for motorcyclists: leather jackets, leather vests, leather jeans, leather boots, leather caps, lots of superfluous chains, everything decorated with the studs that are the sequins to members of the fancy s. and m. crowd.

> When Mr. Friedkin's camera passes through west Greenwich Village on a summer evening, it finds the streets teeming with men, seemingly hundreds of them, all of whom look exactly alike.[70]

These lengthy descriptions of *Cruising*'s fantasy of unrestrained masculinity point to the critics' inability to take their eyes off the screen while this fantasy was being enacted. In fact, the intensity of disdain that the film ultimately provoked from these critics may be a kind of negative sign of the powerful hold this fantasy exerted. That the film also refuses to grant the viewer any sociological framework to explain this fantasy—that "it makes no attempt to comprehend…it just stares," in Canby's words—means that the film also leaves us precious little distance from our reaction to this fantasy. Like the direct address of the leather men as they cruise Steve—which also addresses us, and makes us aware of our own fascinated, desiring, yet uncomfortable gaze—*Cruising* looks the PMC fascination with unrestrained, working-class masculinity straight in the eye, and it leaves us almost no room to look away.

THE WORK OF EXTRA MASCULINITY

Like the Southern films discussed in part II, the new nightlife films I have examined here all utilized location shooting: *Fever* filmed its dance sequences in the actual Bay Ridge 2001 Odyssey disco, *Goodbar* was shot in various Chicago singles bars, and *Cruising* made use of several Greenwich Village street locations and nightclubs.[71] Location shooting, of course, is often deployed in order to bolster a film's authenticity; for example, Travolta described in interviews the significant amount of time he spent getting to know the regulars at the 2001 disco before filming started on *Fever*.[72] However, as Kelly Hankin observes in her discussion of the use of lesbian bars in *The Killing of Sister George* (1968), location shooting can also be used "to know and master" the spaces depicted.[73] And since the new nightlife films are concerned precisely with mapping the bewildering social worlds of these spaces, we must inquire into how the location shoots shaped the films' articulations of new gender and sexual identities. For, if location shooting often results, as Hankin's account demonstrates, in the imposition of a filmmaker's preconceptions on the space depicted, it can nonetheless also enable new possibilities of class struggle over the labor of cultural production, including the production of social identity. By utilizing the spaces and inhabitants of a "real" location instead of those found in the controlled environs of a studio set, filmmakers can unwittingly open the filming process to the meaning-making (and meaning-disrupting) labors of local residents. Even as one of the effects of location shooting is to challenge the ability of film laborers to organize themselves and collectively struggle over the conditions of production, another (largely unintended) effect is to enable other subjects to challenge the filmmakers' control over the shape and meaning of the film production. In the case of *Cruising*, this meant a struggle between the film-makers and gay Village habitués (some of whom acted as extras in the film) over the queer significations of the working-class male body—a struggle that offers a compelling and even politically useful allegory for the larger battles over the articulation of both masculinity and class during the period.

It may seem strange to think of such struggles as *class* struggles. However, Michael Hardt and Antonio Negri's discussions of "affective labor" and its increasingly important role in the "informatization" of late capitalism suggest that the processes of meaning production, and the conflicts that arise over them, can be usefully thought of as class processes.[74] Hardt and Negri argue that contemporary capitalism has been and is being reorganized through the development of information technologies:

> Just as the processes of industrialization transformed agriculture and made it more productive, so too the informational revolution will transform industry by redefining and rejuvenating manufacturing processes....In effect, as industries are transformed, the division between manufacturing and services is becoming blurred. Just as through the process of modernization all production tended to become industrialized, so too through the process of postmodernization all production tends toward the production of services, toward becoming informationalized.[75]

In this new regime of global capitalism, therefore, immaterial labors are "directly productive of capital" and have "become generalized through wide sectors of the economy."[76] Among these immaterial labors is affective labor, which is often typified by health care and "domestic" work, and which Hardt defines as that which produces "communities and collective subjectivities." Hardt identifies the entertainment and culture industries as generators of affective labor, since they are "focused on the creation and manipulation of affects."[77] The communities and collective subjectivities, in other words, that are generated by cultural texts through their address and capture of various audiences can be thought of not just as a stage of consumption (the end point of the productive process) but also as another link in the chain of production (as they also constitute demographics and target markets that can catalyze the reorganization of information-driven industrial production). The struggles between various groups of film workers and audiences over the constitution of collective subjectivities, such as the new gender and sexual communities depicted in the new nightlife films of the 1970s, might therefore be productively explored as class struggles.

Negri and Hardt's account of affective labor provides a suggestive context for Matthew Tinkcom's theorization of the "queer labor" of gay film workers. Arguing against the standard critical understanding of "camp" as a structure of meaning that is generated only through particular *reading* practices, Tinkcom describes camp as a strategy of production as well, one that "provid[es] the opportunity for queers to use their labor to mark the [cultural] product." Tinkcom suggests that camp cultural production can be described, using Hannah Arendt's terms, as work rather than labor—that is, as activity "by which humans create for themselves something recognizably outside themselves by which they know their relation to labor." Textual elements that are identified as opportunities for camp reception—such as the male dancers that appear more like queer fans than heterosexual suitors of Judy Garland during the "Great Lady Has 'an Inteview'" number of *Zeigfield Follies* (1946)—are those in which the queer laborer has established some sort of commentary on both the product of his or her labor (which is almost always heteronormative) and his or her part in that labor. As Tinkcom puts it, "camp stages the moments in which dissident same-sex subjects draw attention to the very labor…required to conceal themselves [and] the labor to produce themselves."[78] Therefore, if, as Eve Kosofsky Sedgwick writes, camp reception is "the moment at which a consumer of culture makes the wild surmise, 'What if whoever made this was queer too?'" then the queer work that invites this response can be best understood as affective labor, in that it establishes a collective (queer) subjectivity through the operations of the text.[79]

Although *Cruising* is not a camp text, something very much like what Tinkcom is describing here occurred in the battles over the film, as various groups of queer subjects, both in and out of the film's production, sought to alter its shape while it was being made in order to shape the communities and collective subjectivities it might generate. In fact, *Cruising* was among the first films to be protested by an organized political group while the film was still in production.[80] After drafts of the screenplay had been leaked to the press and some activists, *Village Voice* columnist Arthur Bell implored his readers "to give Friedkin and his production crew a terrible time if you spot them in your neighborhood."[81] Soon, many gay bars reneged on their agreements with Friedkin, refusing to let the film be shot on their premises, while protests were organized by a coalition of gay and lesbian groups (including the moderate National Gay Task Force and the more radical Gay Activist Alliance); eventually, over 1,000 protestors marched on the film's production sites for several evenings in a row.[82] Furthermore, during filming, activists blew whistles and chanted in order to interrupt sound recording and used mirrors to disrupt the lighting scheme of various outdoor shots.[83] In some cases, they even walked into the middle of scenes and made faces at the camera.[84]

Shots disturbed by mirrored flashes of light, or by intervening bystanders, had to be refilmed on the same location, which had the (intended) effect of raising the cost of making *Cruising*. However, bad sound recordings could be re-recorded, or "looped," in postproduction, and, as Nat Segaloff reported, Friedkin took advantage of this necessity to embellish the aural atmosphere of the film: "Ironically, the disruptive chanting of the demonstrators…forced him to loop dialogue in postproduction, and in enjoying a 'second chance' at making the film he moved farther toward the impressionistic style" he chose for the film. Paul Huntsman, the film's postproduction supervisor, claimed that "there's probably more leather sound [in *Cruising*] than you'll ever hear in a film again." This, along with the foregrounded "sound of clinking chains…and footsteps on streets" in the soundtrack, "forces the viewer/listener into threatening, yet tantalizing, proximity" of the film's events, Segaloff notes. Thus, we hear, with Steve, "the call of writhing leather…seducing" both him and us.[85] In a way, Friedkin's use of sound seemed to symbolize what the mostly gay protestors had feared—that, in place of the voices of the gay community (here represented by their chanting), *Cruising* would offer only a lurid fetishization of their experiences, thus silencing them both figuratively and literally.

As I have already suggested, I take Friedkin's efforts to immerse the viewer in the sensual experiences of S/M to be part of a larger (perhaps unintentional) effect of the film, which is to induce us to confront our own libidinal investments in the scene; therefore, this aural strategy is not necessarily a politically deleterious one. Especially since, in another part of the struggle over the film's community- and collective subjectivity-building labor, many gay men *were* able to shape the representation of gay masculinity in *Cruising*, and in such a way as to suggest a gender and sexual politics that exceeds Friedkin's ambivalent, perhaps even incoherent intentions. These men were the more than 500 extras in the bar sequences—most of whom, by all accounts, were regular attendants at the same leather bars portrayed in the film. Although a handful of extras eventually quit, while a few others stayed on in order to leak information to the protesters, most defended the film and their role in it.[86] Some extras argued, in the February 1980 issue of the gay men's magazine *Mandate*, that their participation in the film would promote a more masculine image of gay men. But, as Alexander Wilson observed, the "most persistent argument made" by the extras was "as much a defense of limitless sexual expression as it [wa]s of the film's attempts to render that expression."[87] In other words, they insisted on a sexual pluralism that many gay activists, concerned with "positive images" of their community, wished to downplay in negotiating popular representations of homosexuality. As if to make good on their promise of making visible sexual diversity, the extras, according to many accounts of the production, turned the filming of the leather bar sequences into all-day parties. For example, Mark Johnson, a production executive on the film, recalled asking one extra how the day of filming had gone, to which the extra replied, "It wasn't bad. I got blown twice."[88] Such playful hedonism clearly translates onto the screen, as a few nonhomophobic commentators on the film have acknowledged. Edward Guthmann described his "startled" response to the bar scenes:

> Instead of menacing images of decadence, the festive, bacchanalian atmosphere in the bars seemed a bright contrast to popular notions that gay life is gloomy and desperate. As one heterosexual woman remarked to me during the film, "It's very alluring." Most of the men are engaged in some kind of activity with one another, be it sex, or dancing, or drinking and laughing. It could even be argued that these scenes are *idealized*.[89]

What the extras seemed to have accomplished was an affiliation of gay male identity with not only traditional signifiers of masculinity but also a polymorphous exploration of bodily pleasure.

In doing so, these men also opened up the possibility that this affiliation could work in both directions, linking this desublimated pursuit of pleasure with the working-class male body. In other words, instead of articulating this body as a figure from a previous era of gender and economic relations, whose charm is tinged with its near-anachronistic status, the extras of *Cruising* suggest a new life for the signifiers of working-class masculinity—an extra masculinity, if you will. Their affective labor works against not only traditional assumptions about masculinity but also those about the possibilities of working class labor, which are too often hemmed in by that labor's gendered clothes. When *Fortune* magazine elegized the "homely, masculine energy" of "Steeltown U.S.A." in its December 1977 issue, for instance, it personified the rapidly deindustrializing region as "the clumsy, plodding prizefighter hero of the movie *Rocky*" only to note that it was "reeling and stumbling—and, quite possibly, dying."[90] Blue-collar masculinity as depicted here no longer has a place in the U.S. political-economic order—its labor has been relocated elsewhere in the globalizing economy. By contrast, the extras of *Cruising* utilize the simulated steel workplace of the Anvil to disassociate blue-collar signifiers from the sadomasochistic logic of capitalist labor relations, and relocate them to contexts of mutually agreed upon erotic play. The queer labor of these bodies (performed, like all working-class labor, under conditions they do not control) becomes newly relevant, directed toward the generation of communities and collective subjectivities that might resist the (re)productivity demanded by heteronormative and capitalist cultures. To borrow a phrase from Bill Nichols's account of Eisenstein's *Strike* (1925), *Cruising*'s extras offer a vision of "workers [who] no longer make commodities for those who steal their labor. They make themselves."[91]

Of course, one could argue that this vision takes part in the class fantasy that Biskind and Ehrenreich identified in many 1970s films about working class men, one that imagines that "the working-class male…possess[es] the autonomy the middle class feels it has lost."[92] What is compelling about the queered working-class masculinity of *Cruising*'s extras, though, is that it reimagines this fantasy of class autonomy without couching it in the image of patriarchy lost. As Leo Bersani reminds us, the "nearly mad identification" with traditional masculinity in post-Stonewall gay male culture is coupled with "*the appeal of its being violated.*"[93] Therefore, the working-class male body of *Cruising* is not that of inviolate male selfhood—Biskind and Ehrenreich's recalcitrant blue-collar ethnic, whose defiant claims to traditional masculine privilege are celebrated even as he is sacrificed to the "progress" of economic development. Instead, the film's scenes of exuberant working-class bodies reenvision the labor that these bodies might do in a post-Fordist, postpatriarchal, and perhaps even postcapitalist future. Rather than mourn the slow disappearance of the traditional white, working-class male, the *Cruising* extras put this body back to work.

It is no coincidence, of course, that working-class masculinity became fetishized during the decline of the U.S. manufacturing base; the post-Stonewall masculinization of gay male identity engaged in just as much of a nostalgic class fantasy about manual labor as the straight commentators who championed the class's allegedly traditional gender and sexual politics did. The queer embrace of the working-class male body, however, literalized the middle-class, often homoerotic investment in this body and its labor. This post-Stonewall project did not so much subvert the naturalness of this masculinity as place alongside it another kind of masculinity, which looked very much like the first—an extra body, so to speak. This new, extra masculinity activated the same circuits of desire that attended the first, only to foreground the erotic nature of this desire. This, I would argue, is why the figures of the clone and the leatherman haunt the films I have analyzed here, and why these films, as well as the reception to them, are marked by panicked responses to their fascination with white, working-class male bodies. *Fever*'s feverish work to downgrade the cultural status of its white ethnics, *Goodbar*'s *homo ex machina* ending, *Cruising*'s murderous disavowals—all of these testify to a libidinal investment in working-class masculinity that dare not speak its name. What post-Stonewall gay male culture's recoding of working-class signifiers demonstrated, therefore, was the degree to which this investment, and its repudiation, are as motivated by structures of class feeling as those of gender and sexuality. In *Cruising*, though, we see not only the fantasies of unrestrained masculinity that inform the PMC fascination with the white, working-class male body but also, in the shots that linger over the extras engaged in an affective labor all their own, a different kind of fantasy—one that refers to this body's past, even as it imagines for it a possible future.

Conclusion

Working-Class Solidarity and Its Others

This book has traced the ways in which American middle-class culture, especially its film culture, was shaped during the 1970s by a fascination with the working class—a fascination that was marked by anxiety, but also desire; repulsion, but also attraction; condescension, but also identification. In the youth-cult cycle, the working class was depicted as the central enemy of the counterculture, but it was also featured as an avenue for middle-class disaffiliation, a site of alleged authenticity that enabled a critique of professional cultural capital. (That this film cycle ultimately recovered such cultural capital under the sign of New Hollywood auteurism is merely a sign of the contradictory energies driving the films' structure of class feeling.) The good ole boy protagonists of the decade's Southerns, meanwhile, were often dismissed and sometimes perceived as threatening by many middle-class critics, yet they offered a spectacle of free-wheeling resistance to the constraints of both working- and middle-class labor to which PMC audiences were repeatedly drawn. These audiences also came face to face with their paradoxical investment in the white, blue-collar male body in the new nightlife films—films which navigated the social terrain that was being transformed by feminism and gay liberation by deploying this body as a figure doomed for the dustbin of history even as its powerful erotic allure suggested the possible futures of sex and gender relations.

As this last group of films vividly illustrates, this PMC identification with working-class figures was energized in no small part by the masculinity (and whiteness) of the body it took as a synecdoche for the working class. Indeed, the white, working-class male characters that populate so many films of the 1970s often serve to mobilize what Sally Robinson aptly describes as an "identity politics of the dominant."[1] Robinson argues that, as the civil rights and women's movements challenged white masculinity's (illusory) position of unmarked universality—revealing it to be a specific, embodied particularity—white men came to characterize their status through the rhetoric of victimization put on offer by the very identity movements that had displaced their hitherto uncontested centrality. In doing so, they attempted to "recenter white masculinity" by drawing on the "symbolic power to be reaped from occupying the social and discursive position of subject-in-crisis."[2]

One of the ways in which white masculinity inhabited and often capitalized on this position of crisis during the 1970s was through its embodiment in working-class figures whose affective appeal often encouraged the kinds of cross-class identification this book has examined. Consider, for example, one of the decade's most popular cinematic depictions of white, working-class masculinity, *Rocky* (1976). The film perfectly illustrates the ways in which white masculinity became "marked" as particular in relation to other emergent identities during the period. Rocky Balboa (Sylvester Stallone) is known as the "Italian Stallion"—underlining his ethnic whiteness as a specific racial identity—and the Muhammad Ali-like heavyweight champion Apollo Creed (Carl Weathers) selects him as an opponent because of his "novelty" as a "snow white underdog." By the time Creed chooses him, Rocky has already lost his boxing gym locker to a rising black contender, and he has unsuccessfully tried to persuade a defiant local teen girl to stop acting like a "whore." In short, he is depicted as a white man whose "normal" race privileges and gender prerogatives have been stripped away. But what truly signifies his underdog status is his class position: his low-rung underground economy job (he acts as an enforcer to a local loan shark) and modest means are relentlessly contrasted to Creed's corporate trappings and dandified elegance.[3] (And, of course, his white ethnic identity has served as a marker of his working-class identity all along.) Thus, Rocky's struggle to prove himself worthy of a title fight—to "go the distance" rather than lose in a knockout—derives much of its energy from the discourse of class uplift that structures the film (a discourse reinforced by Rocky's *Marty*-like romance with the shy Adrian [Talia Shire]). However, the film's concluding boxing match pays out largely in renewed race and gender feeling via the rhetoric of nationalism. At the beginning of the January 1, 1976, fight, Creed enters the ring dressed in cartoonish embodiments of American Bicentennial iconography—first as George Washington, then Uncle Sam—as he taunts the white underdog whom he chose as an opponent necessary for a "good show." Yet the subsequent fight serves as a brutal disciplining of Creed's arrogance, with Rocky wounding the hitherto undefeated champ while also demonstrating his own physical resilience (even as he loses the fight by decision). By the end of both the fight and the film, as Rocky stands with his loyal girl by his side, there is no question which racial and gender identity has reclaimed the position of national representativity.

This logic of white male victimhood can be found in many of the films I have discussed here, from *Walking Tall*'s brutal physical punishment of Buford as he struggles against a pointedly female-led crime syndicate to Tony's frustrated befuddlement at Stephanie's quasi-feminist career ambitions in *Saturday Night Fever*. In these films, class plays a central role in securing this victim status, as the working-class location of the white male protagonists serves as the founding condition of their relative disempowerment. This dynamic suggests some of the politically deleterious implications of the PMC fascination with the working class in this period: namely, that the fascination was, as Peter Biskind and Barbara Ehrenreich argued, primarily with a particular kind of white masculinity, for which class serves as the modifier, not the noun in question.

However, there is much more going on in these cinematic encounters with white, working-class men than the backlash politics identified in these (nonetheless compelling) arguments. To highlight the other forms of political articulation opened up by these encounters, I turn now to a group of films that arrived at the end of the 1970s which imagined working-class life and struggle via largely nonwhite or nonmale protagonists. In *Blue Collar* (1978), *Norma Rae* (1979), and *9 to 5* (1980), the class experiences of its main characters are also imbricated with their race and gender identity, yet here obviously this class location does not operate as a metaphor of the erosion of white masculine authority. Instead, the working-class position of *Blue Collar*'s three central auto workers serves to pose the dilemmas of interracial solidarity, while that of *Norma Rae*'s and *9 to 5*'s female workers provides an opportunity to explore the gendered division of labor (and the labor movement). These three films are also rather apt for this current study, in that they take part in the social and cinematic currents that I have surveyed throughout this book. *Blue Collar* is the first film directed by the young critic-turned-movie-brat Paul Schrader (screenwriter of *Taxi Driver* [1976]) and it had its roots in a tale of generational rebellion similar to that which inspired the youth-cult cycle. *Norma Rae*, for its part, is set in the industrializing Sunbelt that served as the location for the Southern cycle; the relation of the titular protagonist to the good ole boys of those films is indicated by the title of David Denby's review of the film, "Good Ol' Girl Meets David Dubinsky."[4] Finally, while *9 to 5* does not position any of its action in the singles bars or nightclubs found in the new nightlife films, its tale of pink-collar rebellion is absolutely driven by the feminist energies that so bedevilled the films of that cycle. The ways in which the working class is imagined by these films—in particular, in the forms of political and social solidarity that they put on offer—indicate some of the progressive and perhaps even utopian motivations behind the PMC fascination with working-class life during the period. Rather than signifying as a figure for the lost race and gender privilege of white men, working-class experience is articulated in these films as the building block of antiracist and feminist subjectivity. Therefore, while *Blue Collar, Norma Rae*, and *9 to 5* are often faulted by left critics for displacing their class-oriented narratives for more identity politics-oriented concerns, the textual work of these films—and frequently their reception—suggest the mutually constitutive nature of class solidarity and its others. By investigating the later 1970s films that foreground the connections between class struggles and those of race and gender identity movements, I hope to show how the decade's broader investment in hard hats, rednecks, and macho men also made visible the liberatory possibilities of these cinematic acts of cross-class identification.

BLUE COLLAR'S "OREO GANG"

There are a few differing stories about the inspiration for *Blue Collar*, which are suggestive of the film's conflicted investments as well as some of its missed opportunities. According to Peter Biskind, Leonard Schrader, who co-wrote the screenplay with his brother Paul, claims that the idea was his:

> One day I came across the Lordstown, Ohio, strike, the Chevy Vega plant. All the autoworkers were under twenty-five, they were not interested in what the union had done for dad and grandpa. What it had done for them was nothing. They called their own strike, and the union told them they better get back to work. 'Yes, we hate management, but you know who we hate worse? Our union. It betrays us.' Never seen a movie about that before.[5]

The impulse behind *Blue Collar*, in this version, stems from an interest in a kind of generational rebellion that the initial youth-cult cycle took as its organizing principle. Interestingly, though, the story here focuses on a generational battle *within* the working class, which, as I argued in chapter 1, the youth-cult cycle found difficult to imagine, given its insistent depiction of blue-collar workers as aging and conservative.

Paul, however, described in interviews how he had come up with the idea for the film during conversations with Sydney A. Glass, a black screenwriter who had approached Schrader for advice:

> I asked [Glass] what he'd really like to write about and he said his father, an auto plant worker who'd committed suicide a day before his retirement. That's really interesting, I thought. Blacks in auto plants.

> I said that I wasn't particularly interested in his father, but that someone ought to make a movie about Blacks in auto plants.[6]

What is striking about this explanation (other than Paul's callous attitude toward the tragedy of Glass's father and his evident predilection for thinking of black characters only in sociological terms) is that it points to another social referent for the film's action: the troubled history of race relations within the auto industry. Again, this interest marks both a similarity to and departure from the youth-cult cycle that was Schrader's context of entry into Hollywood.[7] The politics of recent African American identity formations had been featured in several youth-cult films—consider, for example, the racial provocations of *Hi Mom!* and *Putney Swope* as well as the gentler comedy of Hal Ashby's directorial debut, *The Landlord* (all 1970). Yet these racial concerns were almost always subordinated to the cycle's focus on white, middle-class disaffiliation (*Swope* is the exception that proves the rule).

I am drawing attention to these concordances and divergences because *Blue Collar* betrays some of the same blind spots as the youth-cult cycle, even as its anomalous foregrounding of youthful worker rebellion and racial relations also incarnates some radical possibilities that were often left implicit in that cycle. These conflicting tendencies can be found in what is perhaps the most telling absence in *Blue Collar*: despite Leonard's interest in young rank-and-file insurgency and Paul's in the auto industry's racial conflicts, the film makes no mention of the League of Revolutionary Black Workers. This Detroit-based student-worker political group sprung from the African American wildcat strikes instigated by the area's various Revolutionary Union Movements (RUMs—such as DRUM, the Dodge Revolutionary Union Movement, FRUM, the Ford Revolutionary Union Movement, etc.) during the late 1960s and early 1970s.[8] Like the Lordstown strikers, these black, mostly youthful rank-and-file organizations challenged both the auto companies and their union (the United Auto Workers, or UAW), sometimes at considerable physical risk: during one 1973 work stoppage at a Chrysler plant, the UAW brought in 1,000 union officials from the surrounding area, some of whom arrived with baseball bats and other weapons, to force the wildcat strikers back to work.[9] Furthermore, the League of Revolutionary Black Workers, as their name suggests, followed an ideological and organizational program that focused on the specific concerns of African Americans within the auto industry.[10] Yet despite the ways in which the activities of black insurgents against both the auto companies and the UAW during this period speak to both Paul and Leonard's professed motivations for making *Blue Collar*, the League and its struggles are essentially absent from the film.

It is hardly a surprise that a major Hollywood film would fail to engage substantively and accurately with radical political movements. Furthermore, given the youth-cult cycle's inability to visualize an alliance between students and workers, it is perhaps to be expected that its cinematic descendant would ignore one of the most compelling examples of just such an alliance.[11] However, this group's absence from the film also suggests some of the utopian impulses and desires that fuelled the Schraders' imagination of the interracial working class. In other words, the disappearance of the League from *Blue Collar* illustrates not only what the Schraders chose not to see in their attempt to capture the contemporary state of race and class relations in Detroit but also what they projected in its place.

The issue of what *Blue Collar* endeavors to depict, and what it leaves outside the frame, is foregrounded by the mixed modes of its cinematic organization. During its opening half hour, *Blue Collar* strives to depict with an unsparing realism the conditions that would lead to radical resistance. The opening credits sequence emphasizes not just the punishing environment of the assembly line but also the relentless surveillance of the foreman and his constant badgering of the workers to keep the line moving. Furthermore, the following scene at a union meeting indicates the disregard the union has for the concerns of its members, especially its black members: when Zeke (Richard Pryor) complains, "The plant is just short for plantation," he echoes the rhetoric promulgated by the League of Revolutionary Black Workers.[12] In addition, Jerry (Harvey Keitel) often wears a cap reading "30 and Out," the name of a rank-and-file dissident group that joined the United National Caucus, which was also peopled with various RUM activists, in the early 1970s.[13] However, despite the presence of these textual markers of Detroit's recent radical past, the film's narrative ultimately concerns not a drama of rank-and-file insurgency but a heist gone wrong. When Zeke, Jerry, and Smokey (Yaphet Kotto) rob a safe from their local union's headquarters and find a record book of the union's illegal financial doings, they decide against using the information to expose its corruption and instead attempt to blackmail the union for monetary gain. The ensuing collapse of this plan—as the union has Smokey killed in an industrial "accident," co-opts Zeke by offering him a position within the union bureaucracy, and threatens Jerry and his family until he turns to the FBI for protection—signals the film's shift from social determinants to generic ones. As Nicolaus Mills observed, the "result is a movie in which the first half seems as if it were based on a script by Harvey Swados and the second half on one by Alfred Hitchcock."[14] The social referents of youthful rank-and-file rebellion and of race relations in the auto industry are mobilized primarily as a means to the film's genre-oriented end.

Despite this turn toward genre convention, *Blue Collar* was frequently praised as realistic by both critics and many Detroit workers. Richard Schickel asserted that "*Blue Collar* looks as if it might actually have been made by people who wear blue collars when they go to work, instead of turtlenecks, beads and suede jackets."[15] Vincent Canby observed that "everything in the characters' private lives looks right, from the pictures on the walls...to their color television sets, plastic slipcovers and bowling costumes," details that, Stanley Kauffman argued, gave the film "the smell of authenticity: of daili- ness dramatized as most documentaries cannot do it."[16] And even though many auto worker activists had criticisms of what they saw as the film's political pessimism, former League of Revolutionary Black Workers mem- ber Michele Russell admitted, "Well, it was real enough. No argument there. The daily grind, unsafe working conditions, backlogged grievances, rac- ist supervision, corrupt union officials, two jobs to meet the payments on whatever, downtime spent getting high in bars and with women."[17] Indeed, much of the disappointment in the film for many activists (and a number of film critics) was its failure to build upon its hard-won realism and offer something other than a genre exercise.

It is worth noting, though, a frequently remarked-upon break with the film's efforts at verisimilitude: the interracial friendships of the film's "Oreo Gang" (as they come to be called in the film). Detroit-based writer Dan Georgakas complained that Schrader "says the film operates out of the con- ceit that there are a lot of friendships between [blacks and whites in Detroit]. Well, it is a conceit, because basically there aren't a lot of friendships, and there are very few black and white bars of the type shown in the film."[18] Other commentators also critiqued this element of the film, as it ignores the profound segregation in and out of the auto industry and the resulting racial tension that had characterized Detroit for most of its history. Yet this conceit is central to the film's didactic conclusion, in which Jerry and Zeke, now bitterly divided by the fallout from the failed blackmail attempt, heatedly exchange racial insults before lunging at each other in what looks to be the beginning of a race riot on the shopfloor. This fight is halted in a dramatic closing freeze-frame (figure 6.1), over which we hear the now-dead Smokey repeat a line from earlier in the film: "They pit the lifers against the new boys; the young against the old; the black against the white. Everything they do is to keep us in our place." Schrader himself describes this scene as "a very specific Marxist conclusion," which Terry Curtis Fox unpacks as "the notion that race is used in place of class to keep workers on the line."[19] Indeed, much of the critical response to *Blue Collar* turned on how persuasive reviewers found this argument to be. Mills argued that the film's realism makes "what could be drug-store Marxism [appear] instead as an earned didacticism," whereas Pauline Kael (an early benefactor of Schrader's career) averred that "in all probability, the automotive industry wants to keep the assembly lines running, and doesn't want any dissension among the men which might slow the lines down," and blamed the film's "cynical" conclusion on its "jukebox Marxism."[20]

Figure 6.1. From *Blue Collar*. The quasi-Brechtian freeze frame concluding *Blue Collar*.

Of course, the largely unexamined premise of the film's argument about race and class is that, absent the malevolent intervention of "them" (which could, in the context of *Blue Collar*, denote either the bosses or the union), interracial friendships would develop naturally among the working class. In an insightful analysis of the film, Michael Omi points out that *Blue Collar* "leads us to believe that the material basis of racism (as reflected in people's location in the productive process of an auto assembly plant) has been obliterated," since the workforce is depicted as fully integrated. Thus, racism is treated by the film as "a form of *false consciousness*," which is imposed by the ruling powers to "hinder white workers from seeing that their objective interests are similar to those of racial minority workers."[21] Omi rightfully argues that such an analysis misapprehends the material causes of racism— that it does not acknowledge, for example, that the economic contractions of the period (and an absence of countervailing left economic policy) meant that newly integrated workers of color were often forced to compete with white workers who had seniority for fewer and fewer blue-collar jobs.[22] Omi concludes that "Hollywood may be rediscovering the working class, but it doesn't have an inkling about the conflicts and divisions within it. They extend beyond mere name-calling."[23]

Although Omi is not incorrect in his diagnosis of Hollywood's less than perspicacious grasp of working-class life, I would argue that it is precisely the film's depiction of a seemingly natural interracial solidarity that is its most noteworthy element. Omi himself observes how striking it is that "there isn't a hint of racial tension" in a party sequence where black men sleep with white women, and a white man with a black woman, despite the sexual anxieties about and taboos against interracial sex (particularly involving black men and white women) that have underwritten much of U.S. racism.[24] Similarly, the film never draws our attention to the casually interracial nature of the after-work bar the men frequent, nor the familiar camaraderie between their families as they spend an evening bowling together. In other words, the film never congratulates its characters, nor itself, for creating such seemingly uncomplicated interracial bonds. These bonds are treated as simple fact.

These ostensibly unremarkable interracial friendships might therefore explain the absence of the history of the League of Revolutionary Black Workers in the film, despite its thematic focus on race and class in the auto industry (and its self-described Marxist conclusion). The very existence of the League, of course, spoke precisely to the fact that the material location of black workers was in many ways different from that of white workers in Detroit, and that therefore such interracial working-class solidarity does not happen all by itself; it is the product of concerted political activism. What groups like the League saw as the eventual goal of their struggles[25] is what *Blue Collar* takes as a given.

As misguided as it is, this presumption—that the working-class is a space of natural interracial solidarity—is best understood as the film's utopian fantasy. The film's real political "message," then, is characterized not by Smokey's voice-over during the film's last freeze-framed clash but rather by its opening moments on the line, in the bar, and at the trio's sex- and drug-fuelled party, which ends with an anguished conversation about the endless cycle of alienated labor and unsatisfiable consumer desire. In these moments—which, it is important to remember, are those where the film works the hardest to establish its realism—*Blue Collar* posits the idea that the working class is automatically aligned due to their shared experience of economic oppression. And while Georgakas and Omi are right to argue that *Blue Collar*'s fantasy of natural interracial solidarity obscures the very real material and other barriers to said solidarity, the nature of this fantasy is nonetheless important to grasp. It imagines the ways in which working-class labor and experience, no matter how brutally exploitative, might produce not racialized (or gendered) resentment but rather its overcoming. This projected fantasy is all the more notable coming at the end of a decade in which the white working class was frequently depicted, in films from *Easy Rider* to *Saturday Night Fever*, as *inherently* racist—where racism was seen to be a product of working-class experience itself. *Blue Collar*'s projection of blacks and white united from their collective experience both on and off the line offers a way of imagining the working class that diverges significantly from this tradition—particularly that of the film's youth-cult predecessors.

As *Blue Collar* counters the youth-cult cycle's inability to depict a working class that is not just a bunch of aging, reactionary hard hats—to an important extent by recognizing that the class is in fact not only white—it also develops and sharpens that cycle's suspicion toward professional authority. *Blue Collar*'s central (and arguably only) PMC figure, John (Cliff De Young), introduces himself to the protagonists early in the film as an idealistic graduate student and college instructor who is writing his dissertation on Detroit unions and who encourages the workers to discuss their dissatisfaction with their union. Yet John is quickly revealed to be not a left-leaning academic but an FBI agent hoping to prosecute the union's leaders and, it is implied, break up the union. (One might say that, in Althusserian terms, he first appears as a professional representative of an Ideological State Apparatus, only to be revealed as a member of the Repressive State Apparatus.) In doing so, *Blue Collar*'s main representative of the PMC is shown to be one who speaks in the name of enlightened professional thought on behalf of workers' interests, yet whose own concealed agenda in fact works against those interests.

It is initially unclear how we are supposed to interpret John, and not just because he is an undercover agent. When he tells Smokey, Jerry, and Zeke, "The thing I don't understand is why you let the union rip you off as much as management. It's like you wanna get fucked over," he is essentially articulating Paul Schrader's own position. The filmmaker often argued in interviews that "the unions are no better [than the bosses]. They've become part of the larger power structure."[26] Yet the character who makes this claim within the diegesis is later uncovered as someone who is manipulating the workers for his own purposes.[27] By implicating himself in the deeply suspect motivations of the anti-union *faux* professor, Schrader may be engaged in a gesture of self-criticism—especially of his own professional position. This questioning of the filmmaker's own authority is subtly underlined in the opening credits sequence, which follows the movement of the assembly line and pauses at certain moments in freeze frames, over which the various credits appear. In doing so, *Blue Collar* mimics the contradictory visual strategies of the youth-cult cycle: as in *Five Easy Pieces*, a working-class space is depicted to establish authenticity, but it is shot in a way to emphasize the cultural capital of the director—more than one critic noted the allusions to Godard that structure this sequence's tracking shots of the assembly line.[28] Yet when the credit "Directed by Paul Schrader" comes up at the end of this sequence, it is superimposed next to the figure of "Dogshit" Miller, the foreman who is the embodiment of the factory's relentless pressure on the workers. In its understated way, this visual connection asks us to consider the other PMC authority figure—the one operating outside the frame—who is also directing the work of the film's blue-collar characters. While I do not want to overstate the influence of these minor elements of the film, their alignment of Schrader with those who manipulate and discipline workers suggests a more thorough interrogation of the auteur's position—and of professional authority in general—than we found in the youth-cult cycle.

Finally, *Blue Collar* also draws our attention to the racial investments behind the PMC interest in white, working-class men. When John (who is white) tries to press the workers to testify against their union, he concentrates his efforts on Jerry, the sole white protagonist. Schrader explained that one of the motivations behind the character of John was to emphasize that "the only difference between Harvey [Keitel, the actor playing Jerry] and Cliff [De Young, who played John] was money....When Harvey screams at him, 'When I was working on the line, you were trying to decide which suit to wear to your fucking sorority dance, man!'—that's really all it is, just class."[29] One could not say this about the difference between John and Smokey or Zeke. By having John serve as a representative of PMC forces who seek to undermine working-class institutions, the film suggests the key role whiteness can play in such endeavors. After all, when Jerry exchanges racist epithets with Zeke at the film's close, John is the character standing by his side. While critics are no doubt right to argue that the "they" invoked in Smokey's concluding voice-over could be either the bosses or the unions, we might also look to the film's sole PMC figure, who actually appears in the final freeze-frame, and who has persuaded the white protagonist that his material interests lie not with his black working-class friend (who has made a deal with the union), but rather with the state. Just as *Blue Collar* suggests that PMC authority that purports to speak on behalf of the working class is often hiding its own agenda, it also indicates the political dangers behind the racial belonging that white professionals seek to establish with white workers.

NORMA RAE'S UNIONIST FEMINISM

If *Blue Collar* offered an interracial, laborist revision of the youth-cult cycle's script, *Norma Rae* serves as a politicized recasting of the Southern's setting and narrative concerns. The critically acclaimed film, which won two Academy Awards, is about an organizing drive in a southern textile factory, a battle which, Vincent Canby argued in his review of the film, points to "the highly publicized industrial boom in the post-World War II South [which] was largely the result of the cheaper (nonunion) wages that lured manufacturers away from the Northeast and mid-Atlantic states."[30] In other words, the film directs our gaze toward the political economy of the Sunbelt. *Norma Rae* makes literal the class stakes of the Southern protagonist's defiance of redneck sheriffs and organized crime—especially since the film's textile manufacturer brazenly utilizes the racism and monopoly control that are the stock-in-trade of the usual antagonists found in the Southern cycle. But if *Norma Rae* makes manifest the latent content of its Southern predecessors, it also reverses their gender orientation—a reversal pointedly signalled by the presence of Sally Field as the titular protagonist, an actor who had appeared earlier in the Southern cycle as the love interest in *Smokey and the Bandit*. By focusing not on the fast-driving antics of a good ole boy but instead on the actions of a sexually promiscuous and fiercely determined good ole girl, *Norma Rae* displaces the Southern's interest in the reconstruction of southern white masculinity in order to explore the connections between unionist solidarity and feminist independence. Rather than offer the Southern cycle's standard pleasures of male homosocial bonding via automotive freedom, *Norma Rae* drew on the rebellious class energies of that cycle while also offering its PMC viewers a model of gendered liberation that followed a different kind of blue-collar self-determination.

It might be objected that the textile industry makes for a poor exemplar of the Sunbelt, since its long history in the region calls up associations with the Old South. As the *New York Times* observed in the 1973 article on union activist Crystal Lee Jordan that served as the inspiration for *Norma Rae*, the textile industry, despite its status as the region's largest employer, was "rarely...mentioned by the Southern economists, developers, newspapers and perennial 'New South' boosters who have marvelled over Dixie's boom times."[31] However, the actions of J. P. Stevens & Co., which served as the model for the film's O. P. Henley firm, fit the Sunbelt model in several keys aspects—especially the company's closure after World War II of all of its unionized, Northern plants in order to concentrate its activities in the right-to-work South. Yet *Norma Rae*'s depiction of the textile industry's resistance to unionization (which only scratched the surface of the industry's aggressively extralegal union-busting techniques) caused many reviewers to argue that the film seemed to hail from an earlier time. Canby, for example, begins his review by characterizing *Norma Rae*'s appeal as that of "stories about the early days of trade unionism," and only gets around to mentioning that the film "does not take place in the dim dark past of trade unionism ... [but instead] in today's rural South" in the fourth paragraph.[32] Similarly, Penelope Gilliatt initially described the film as "almost seem[ing] to go back to the thirties" before reminding herself that "it is actually 1978."[33] Granted, some of this rhetoric can be ascribed to the fact that, in U.S. political discourse, union-organizing stories signify "the '30s" much in the same way that antiwar demonstrations inevitably call up associations with "the '60s." However, *Norma Rae*'s shifting historical registers can also be seen as similar to those of *Deliverance*, in that the film seems to inhabit a past time and place even as it tells what turns out to be a very contemporary story.

In this case, the contemporary story was often interpreted to be that of feminism. Andrew Sarris argued that "*Norma Rae* combines contemporary feminism with antiquated working-class decency," while David Denby described the film as "formed by women's movement perceptions";[34] commenting on one particularly gender-oriented confrontation in the film,

Denby called director Martin Ritt "an old-time liberal" who "certainly knows when a new mood has ripened."[35] In accounts like these and others, *Norma Rae*'s union narrative is characterized as belonging to the past, while the film's depiction of its heroine's growing self-determination and self-possession is treated as its more contemporary element. Sarris's account makes this opposition explicit: he says that the filmmakers

> subscribe to a '30s and '40s ethos, according to which the 'people' and the 'folk' are supreme. To become 'human' and 'progressive' all one has to do is work on an assembly line....
>
> But there is nothing '30s or '40s about the eponymous heroine of *Norma Rae* played with '60s and '70s carnality by Sally Field.[36]

If the economic spaces of the film seemed to hail from another time, its female protagonist was rooted firmly in the present.

For many left and laborist critics of *Norma Rae*, though, the central problem with the film was that it scanted on the "antiquated" story of union organizing in order to devote more attention to the consciousness-raising of its protagonist. These critics argued that the film's narrative gives pride of place to Norma Rae's emerging feminist self-awareness through its focus on her complicated relationship with union organizer Reuben Warshovsky (Ron Leibman). Nicolaus Mills complained that

> the ultimate cost of the [unconsummated] romance between Reuben and Norma shows up ... in what happens to the original political concerns of the film....Crowded for time, Ritt ceases to make the union issues he began with an organic part of the film and instead reduces them to background material or sketches them quickly.[37]

Figure 6.2. From *Norma Rae*. Norma Rae (Sally Field) and Reuben (Ron Leibman) discuss their relationship while the class struggle passes by in the background (note the small, out-of-focus bodies behind the fence on the left).

One could argue that Mills's concerns are confirmed by the film's closing sequence, during which the results of the successful union certification vote are announced. Rather than follow the triumphant workers as they stream out of the mill, our attention is directed toward Norma Rae and Reuben, who are outside the mill's gates (as Norma Rae had been fired for her union activity earlier). The collective narrative of unionism quite literally serves as background material (figure 6.2) as the camera focuses on the individual relationship between Reuben and Norma Rae, with the class struggle passing by in an undifferentiated blur behind their backs.

This visual and narrative foregrounding of Norma Rae's feminist journey can be explained in large part by Ritt's adherence to many conventions of Hollywood filmmaking and marketing. Ritt described how he convinced Twentieth Century Fox to make the film by characterizing it as a story about not union organizing but "a girl who turns into a woman who can work, who can love, who can fight, who is as close to a complete woman of superior dimensions as any in film history."[38] Furthermore, in promoting the film, Ritt would occasionally claim that he did not mean for *Norma Rae* to be "a union or a labor film," and that he "wanted to make a film about that woman. I couldn't have cared less about labor unions."[39] Of course, in other contexts, the formerly blacklisted Ritt spoke of his long-standing interest in labor-oriented issues—testified to by such films as *The Molly Maguires* (1970)—which suggests that such comments were calculated to enable the successful production and marketing of *Norma Rae* despite its politically controversial plot. Still, when Crystal Lee Jordan, the initial model for Norma Rae, objected to the film's focus on the character's personal life and its lack of attention to the many other people involved in the union battles at J. P. Stevens, Ritt changed the name of the protagonist rather than alter the script (the film was initially entitled *Crystal Lee*).[40] Ritt's (perhaps strategic) decision to conform to the narrative principles of dominant Hollywood filmmaking by focusing on individuals rather than collectives made eminently available the (liberal) feminist readings of *Norma Rae*,[41] while the similarly protagonist-oriented promotional campaigns that sold the film to the public reinforced this interpretive strategy.

However, a funny thing happened amid this concerted narrative and promotional focus on Norma Rae's individual struggles: the film's reception persistently connected them to the larger battle for union recognition that Mills feared would only be seen as background. Here are a few of the headlines for the reviews and/or stories about *Norma Rae* during its initial release: "Strike Busting"; "Well-Organized Labor"; "Martin Ritt Focuses on Labor Strife"; "Heaven Praise the Working Girl"; "'Norma Rae,' Mill-Town Story"; "Good Ol' Girl Meets David Dubinsky."[42] Furthermore, more than one review related *Norma Rae* to other labor-oriented films such as

The Organizer (1963), *Union Maids* (1976), and especially Barbara Kopple's *Harlan County, U.S.A.* (1976).[43] The comparison with the latter two documentaries is particularly telling, since these films also focused the central role that women played in the labor struggles depicted. Gilliatt's final judgment of *Norma Rae* is representative in her claim that the film is "fascinating in what it tells us of the labor movement, and it does honor to a particular sort of involved character who will not be intimidated"—a sort of character that Gilliatt had just described as "a fighting woman."[44] Rather than forcing its viewers to focus on either a tale of collective union struggle or one of individual feminist uplift, *Norma Rae*, it would seem from its initial critical reception, made each the corollary of the other.

Even in the moments where *Norma Rae* seems most focused on what are commonly considered feminist issues—that is, those dealing with housework, marriage, and sexuality—their connection to those of class and labor is never far from the surface. Consider, for example, the scene that Denby cites as a sign of Ritt's deference to feminist principles: after Norma Rae's husband Sonny (Beau Bridges) complains about her union activities, which he claims have been causing her to neglect their family, she responds with an angry routine in which she bitterly mimics the household and conjugal "duties" that Sonny is demanding. Denby contrasts the power and energy of this sequence with those of the union battle, which he found wanting ("Some labor struggle!" he sneers), and argues that "what stays with the viewer is the image of the rueful angry woman."[45] But what is this sequence that Denby praises but another labor struggle? One need not be a scholar of socialist-feminist literature to recognize that Norma Rae's rejection of Sonny's presumption of free housework is of a piece with her refusal to accept the similarly patriarchal control she experiences at the textile mill (where her bosses are also all men). That what is "distracting" Norma Rae from her domestic labor (both physical and emotional) is her efforts to contest the organization of work at the factory only emphasizes the connection between these two shopfloors.

The film's treatment of Norma Rae's "promiscuity" also couches this topic in terms that are related to class politics as well as gender. Her sexual history—she has one child out of wedlock and is depicted as having a wide array of former lovers—is an issue not just for some characters in the film (Reuben's union bosses are wary of her involvement in the organization drive for precisely this reason) but also for a few critics: Aljean Harmetz described her character as "a undereducated young woman whose underarms stink of mill sweat and who will unzip her pants in return for a steak dinner" who becomes "transformed into a superior human being."[46] However, more common was Sarris's approving notice that "Norma Rae does not 'reform'; she simply finds a more satisfying outlet for her emotional energy."[47] Richard

Schickel concurred, positing that "Norma Rae's somewhat checkered sexual history, we come to understand, represents the only locally available outlet for a venturesome, restless but essentially very moral spirit."[48] Labor historian Robert Brent Toplin argues that the film's strategy of linking Norma Rae's sexuality with her rebelliousness and sense of social justice has precedents in actual labor battles in the South; he cites Jacquelyn Dowd Hall's research on the "lewd" and "disorderly women" who spearheaded a 1929 strike at a Tennessee nylon plant, and whose sexual freedom was both a threat to and target of their opponents.[49] Therefore, Norma Rae's twinning of unabashed sexuality and working-class rebellion not only bolsters the feminist argument of the film—in that it honors the protopolitical female agency behind her sexual escapades—but also signals the ways in which the protagonist's feminist self-realization and her class consciousness are mutually constitutive. Indeed, this connection is testified to by Harmetz's misguided put-down of the character, in that its classism and misogyny seem wholly of a piece.

While left-labor critics of Norma Rae are surely right that the film reduces a collective struggle to that of a few individuals, thus downplaying many of the complexities of union organizing (and also offering a feminism that is less the product of the women's movement's political institutions than a male Pygmalion's benevolent tutelage of a "naturally" feisty southern woman), the film nonetheless speaks to the imbrication of class and gender politics with a persuasive directness that few Hollywood films achieve. Indeed, this articulation of feminism via class politics is particularly important when one considers the other films to which Norma Rae was compared during its initial release. Edward Benson and Sharon Hartman Strom noted that most Hollywood films that attempted to address feminism in this period were those "pitched to the middle class" that "tend[ed] to explore either the anxieties of the repressed housewife or the frustrations of the upwardly mobile career woman," such as An Unmarried Woman (1978) and The Turning Point (1977).[50] Gilliatt agreed, stating that "we are used to films about middle-class neurotic women in America with nothing much that interests them."[51] Some of this dismissal of middle-class women's issues is no doubt the rhetorical PMC self-loathing that representations of working-class struggle sometimes engender; still, the implication that Norma Rae's feminism is more compelling because of its connection to wider struggles for social justice is striking. If the popular success of Norma Rae was due in part to the conventional nature of its individual-oriented narrative structure, its political resonance stemmed from the fact that its ensuing vision of female self-empowerment refused to stop at the level of the self.

In this way, Norma Rae encouraged another kind of cross-class identification for PMC viewers than the one found in the traditionally male form of the Southern. In contrast to the forms of middle-class feminism that tend to conceive of "women's issues" through the lens of the individual, *Norma Rae* offers a way of connecting a narrative of individual feminist self-development to larger movements for progressive change. By identifying with Norma Rae's unashamed sexuality and spirited refusal to submit to male authority (even, it should be noted, Reuben's), the female PMC viewer may also come to identify with her commitment to other battles for social equality. And this occurs not despite but because of the film's visual and narrative focus on its individual protagonist. If the Southern typically invited its male PMC viewers to side with its hell-raising, system-battling good ole boy—especially by (mis)recognizing his class rebellion as their own— *Norma Rae* spoke to its female PMC viewers by asking them to see their seemingly private, individual struggles for gender equality as cut from the same cloth as those for class justice.

9 TO 5'S PINK-COLLAR INSURRECTION

At the end of *Saturday Night Fever*, when Tony expresses a desire to move to Manhattan and get a different (and more upwardly mobile) job, Stephanie asks him what skills he has, explaining that she was able to find work because she could type. His nonplussed response reinforces the film's suggestion that, whatever the erotic charge of its display on the dance floor, Tony's physical labor is becoming less a valuable productive resource and more a performative image signalling its nostalgia-inducing disappearance. *Looking for Mr. Goodbar's* hardbodied blue-collar men appear similarly severed from any economic value creation, while its heroine is successful employed in one of the caring professions. If much of the appeal of the new nightlife films came from their spectacularization of the white, working-class male body, they also alluded to the forms of labor for which this body appeared increasingly ill-suited—a feminized work that quietly but persistently served as a counterpoint to the (absent) manual labor of its macho men.

9 to 5 addresses the gendered politics of these forms of labor by depicting the seemingly uncinematic work of typists and secretaries much like *Fever's* Stephanie. As in *Norma Rae*, both past and future are signalled by this chosen subject: typing, secretarial work, and other forms of clerical labor had been perceived as feminized since the end of the nineteenth century; thus the film's focus on female secretaries evokes a long-standing cultural type (as it were). Yet the explosion of positions in this field during the postwar period (clerical jobs in the United States tripled between 1940 and 1980, constituting 20 percent of the work force) points to the kinds of informational and interpersonal labor that were becoming increasingly central to the U.S. economy. These jobs, of course, were also emblematic of the massive influx of women into waged work during the postwar period, as the percentage of women in the U.S. paid labor force doubled between 1940 and 1975.[52] As a result, *9 to 5*'s subject matter places it at the intersection of the profound structural changes that transformed both class and gender during this period.

And in fact, the wildly successful *9 to 5*—it was second only to *The Empire Strikes Back* at the box office in the year it was released[53]—was conceived as an explicitly feminist commentary on these changes. As was often noted at the time of its release, *9 to 5*'s screenplay was shaped by a series of meetings that the filmmakers (including star Jane Fonda, screenwriter Patricia Resnick, and director and co-screenwriter Colin Higgins) had with members of a group called 9to5, an organization of female clerical workers that had formed in 1973 in the aftermath of a women's movement conference.[54] Karen Nussbaum, a founder of 9to5 and national director of its umbrella organization, Working Women, described how she saw these clerical worker organizations as providing the groundwork for unionization in what she called "the next big obvious sector" for organization.[55] Thus, many workers and activists had high hopes for *9 to 5*: as one member of Working Women told the *New York Times*, she went to the film "hoping for another *Norma Rae*."[56]

Yet even though she saw the film twice, this same office worker also said, "I'm afraid that this movie won't rally the workers the way *Norma Rae* did."[57] This disappointment was echoed, albeit for different reasons, in virtually all of the film's reviews. The general consensus was that *9 to 5*'s broad, slapstick comedy and convoluted, incredulity-courting plot—involving the attempted blackmailing and eventual kidnapping of sexist and exploitative boss Franklin Hart (Dabney Coleman Jr.) by three of his office workers, Judy Bernly (Fonda), Violet Newstead (Lily Tomlin), and Doralee Rhodes (Dolly Parton)—ultimately undercut whatever political critique the film might have tried to mount. As David Ansen put it, "It's not wild or dark enough to qualify as a truly disturbing farce and it's too fanciful and silly to succeed as realistic satire. Politically and esthetically, it's harmless."[58] Michael Sragow similarly complained that "Fonda and company get the raising of consciousness confused with the lowering of sensibility."[59] Yet other reviewers went beyond mere disappointment to vituperative denunciations of the film, calling it "progressively unpleasant" (Andrew Sarris), "disgusting" (Stanley Kauffman), and "a vile mess" (Richard Corliss).[60] What was it about *9 to 5* that angered critics even as they dismissed it as "harmless"? Part of this oddly mixed attitude, surely, stems from an ambivalence toward feminism—many of the critics who argued that the film shortchanged its gender critique also went out of their way to argue that Parton's character asks to be sexually harassed because of the tight-fitting clothing she wears.[61] Yet this critical unease also reveals some elements of the film that might actually serve to "rally the workers," albeit in a very un-*Norma Rae*-like visual and narrative idiom.

These elements begin to be articulated during the "pot party" that takes place between Judy, Violet, and Doralee after they have each been aggravated by the injustices of their workplace. Fuelled by marijuana (supplied by Violet's son),[62] each woman envisions killing the boss in a different, vividly cinematic scenario: Judy pictures herself as a big-game hunter who shoots Hart and mounts his head on the wall; Doralee imagines sexually harassing Hart in a Western-styled scenario that concludes with her lassoing, tying up, and roasting him on a spit; Violet's fantasy involves a Disneyesque sequence in which she, dressed as Snow White, poisons Hart's coffee and sends him flying out of his office window. Two of these scenarios, importantly, allude to the exploitation and revolt of their fellow office workers: Judy's fantasy begins with Hart being chased through the office by enraged workers bearing torches and weapons, while Violet's pictures an office filled with secretaries and typists chained and manacled to their desks—chains that are magically broken with the killing of Hart.

While many critics begrudgingly praised Tomlin's fantasy sequence, they largely critiqued these moments of the film as exemplifying its failed comic strategy. For example, Pauline Kael called Judy's and Doralee's dreams of murdering the boss "grimly unfunny," while David Denby complained of the "ugly clowning" of these sequences.[63] Yet what seems most problematic about these scenarios—in addition to the anger that motivates them—is that they all end up coming true, in one way or another. Violet accidentally puts rat poison in Hart's coffee (which he does not drink), which causes her to think that she killed him when he goes to the hospital after a minor injury. When Hart tries to use his knowledge of this accidental poisoning to pressure Doralee into an affair, she ties him up with a phone cord. Finally, when Judy unties him and he attempts to flee, she shoots at him with Doralee's gun (and misses), breaking the glass window of his office in a detail that echoes her fantasy. Kauffman identifies this last moment as that in which the film "goes very much stupider," arguing that "anyone who laughs at the humiliation of the man in this film is, I think, humiliating women, who are being exploited again in fake exposé of their business exploitation." Corliss complains that this turn in the film is one in which "it careers from cutsie-poo dream sequences to bondage-and-discipline revenge." Denby, finally, argues that this translation of the fantasy sequences' "mock sadism" into real violence and eventually kidnapping makes the film "a nastier *I Love Lucy*."[64]

What seems to be troubling these critics is the way *9 to 5* seems to indulge in broad comedy and an outlandish plot even as it traffics in feminist and laborist rage—although it is unclear whether some critics wish the rage were being spared the comedic presentation, or vice versa. The fact that the protagonists' cartoonish revenge fantasies materialize in almost equally silly actual episodes would serve to underline this complaint. However, there is something self-reflexive about the fact that the film's emphatically cinematic fantasies unexpectedly come to life. For *9 to 5* is itself a silly cinematic scenario in which the workers overthrow the boss and seize the means of production. After they kidnap Hart and sequester him in his home, the three protagonists transform their workplace according to feminist and progressive principles: a daycare center is added, health plans are expanded, family-friendly work schedules are introduced, the office is made accessible to workers with disabilities, and so on—a conclusion that offers a literal, realist rendering of the liberation of office workers imagined at the end of Violet's Disneyesque scenario. In other words, *9 to 5* operates by depicting filmic dreams of feminist insurrection that become realized in the "real" life of its characters. By extension, its final scenario of worker control might suggest a similar fantasy for the film's audience to enact in *their* real lives (and workplaces).[65]

Perhaps this explains why many critics who saw the film as overly silly also depicted it as overly militant, a complaint suggested by Sarris's description of the film as "a haphazard mixture of Sennett slapstick and Stalinist aesthetics."[66] As with *Norma Rae*, the line between feminist and laborist politics seems impossible to draw: calling its protagonists "office revolutionaries," Canby characterized the film's conclusion as one that "wav[es] the flag of feminism as earnestly as Russian farmers used to wave the hammer-and-sickle at the end of movies about collective farming."[67] Furthermore, Pauline Kael noted (with some dismay) that

> the Broadway audience I saw it with enjoyed it—men even cheered the militant feminist statements. When the black and Puerto Rican men in the Broadway audience applauded Goldie Hawn in the anti-male 'Private Benjamin,' I assumed that they identified with her misery in basic training; she was going through what they had gone through. And at 'Nine to Five' I assume that the men laughing are identifying with the underdog heroines in their fight against the boss."[68]

For all of its very real engagement with and promotion of the feminism that mobilized groups like 9to5 and Working Women, *9 to 5* also provided a powerful vision of worker solidarity and insurrection—a vision that hailed any number of audiences, perhaps even those who might feel otherwise targeted by its feminism. That this uprising comes dressed in pink collars—that gendered metonym that speaks to the widespread difficulty of distinguishing between the working and middle classes in the information economy—also suggests any number of possibilities for cross-class identification. If the new nightlife films largely dilated over their nostalgia for the white, working-class male body and its erotic labors, *9 to 5* imagined the radical potential of those sitting uncinematically at their desks, projecting filmic dreams about a workplace without bosses.

THE INTERSECTIONS OF SOLIDARITY

What is finally most striking about this set of films, which closed out the 1970s, is the way they make manifest the class stakes of their central conflicts—stakes that were implicit or otherwise veiled in the film cycles that I have surveyed in this study. Rather than obscure their class content, *Blue Collar, Norma Rae,* and *9 to 5*'s engagements with race and gender make their workplace antagonisms (and the multiple dimensions of these antagonisms) all the more visible. Indeed, the visions of working-class rebellion and solidarity placed front and center in these films are only gestured at vicariously in the middle-class slumming of the youth cult films, or displaced onto the open roads of the free-wheeling Southern films, or ogled at voyeuristically in the new nightlife films. This telling contrast suggests that the race and gender preoccupations of the white male body at the center of those films might have had some role in their avoidance of actual workplace conflict and their evasion of direct class politics. This tendency calls to mind David Roediger's persuasive argument concerning the dangers of the investments in whiteness for working-class struggles:

> We should focus on contrasting the bankruptcy of white politics with the possibilities of nonwhiteness. We should point out not just that whites and people of color often have common economic interests but that people of color act on those interests far more consistently—in politics, at the workplace, and increasingly in community-based environmental struggles—precisely because they are not burdened by whiteness.[69]

In other words, it is the desire to defend the privileges of whiteness—to assume common interests with whites from the middle and upper classes—that often hinders the class consciousness of white workers. A similar argument could be made about the politics of masculinity and its yearning for lost gender privileges. What *Blue Collar, Norma Rae,* and *9 to 5* illuminate, in different yet congruent ways, are the possibilities of working-class solidarity that are made available by an engagement with other, racial and gendered forms of solidarity. In doing so, these films also make clear the limits placed on a radical class imaginary by any vision of the working class that sees the white, blue-collar male as a synecdoche for the whole.

Yet if one of the attractions of these films is their ability to mobilize cross-class identification—as the middle-class viewer partakes in the apparently natural interracial camaraderie of *Blue Collar*, empathizes with the personal struggle embedded in Norma Rae's fight for the union, and sees their own office-based subordination in the opening sequences of *9 to 5*—then we need to recognize that such class desires are also at work in the 1970s films about hard hats, rednecks, and macho men. Since not all of the appeal of *Blue Collar*, *Norma Rae*, and *9 to 5* stems from their race and gender elements, neither does the PMC interest in *Five Easy Pieces*, *Walking Tall*, or *Saturday Night Fever* rely solely on the whiteness and maleness of their blue-collar protagonists. Instead, as the films I have discussed in this conclusion illustrate, what is often at the heart of the middle-class's fascination with representations of working-class life and experience is the forms of political association, resistance, and struggle these cinematic subjects bring to life—forms of political being that the middle class has trouble imagining itself inhabiting. As a result, the PMC frequently lives out their own contradictions, and fantasizes their resistance, through their working-class others—a collective act of projection that filled the cinema screens of the 1970s and continues to haunt the social and political life of our late capitalist present.

AFTERWORD

Hard Hats Revisited: The Labor of 9/11

My interest in the professional-managerial class's complicated relationship to representations of the working class during the 1970s was initially spurred by the many layers of complexity that attended the May 1970 hard hat riots. The main participants of those riots—at least, before the Wall Street office workers joined in—were men who were building the World Trade Center towers. It is perhaps fitting, then, to close with a brief consideration of how the working-class rescue and clean-up crews that labored in the ruins of those towers have come to be represented, cinematically and otherwise. For the representations of the 9/11 firefighters, policemen and women, and construction clean-up workers have been structured by many of the PMC fantasies of the working class that I have traced in the American cinema of the 1970s. These fantasies, then and now, are often informed by the notion that one kind of labor is simple, but also more "real" or "authentic," while another is more sophisticated, but also parasitic and maybe even gratuitous. My aim in tracing this (often heavily gendered) logic, and its persistence into our present situation, is to explode it. But another way of thinking about labor emanates from these accounts as well—one that socialists and others who wish to abolish class hierarchies must recognize and, in their (necessary) critical labors, nourish.

Just as the hard hat riots and related events led to a "discovery" of the working class, the terrorist attacks on the World Trade Center and Pentagon also disclosed a hitherto overlooked population. Describing, in the *New York Times Magazine*, the construction workers cleaning up the 9/11 site, Verlyn Klinkenborg suggested that a "city of unsoiled and unroughened hands has learned to love a class of laborers it once tried hard not to notice."[1] And, as with the earlier discovery, the working class was again taken to represent more traditional values that an implicitly middle-class nation has ignored or forgotten.

Bruce Nussbaum declared in *Business Week* that "big, beefy working-class guys became heroes once again" after the attacks, which "was, for a moment, an old America peeking out from behind the new, me-now America."[2] Nussbaum argued that this spoke to "America's quick return to family, community, church, and patriotism in the aftermath of the tragedy," something that Klinkenborg claimed New York was also doing, "tak[ing] its courageous note from the brawn of those workers, their material expertise, their reflexive patriotism."[3] This valorization of "brawn," and its apparent corollary, unthinking loyalty ("reflexive patriotism"), once more posits the working class as a body without a mind, or at least one resistant to critical, reflective thought. Such an articulation of the working-class male body, furthermore, offers it once again as a privileged form of masculinity. Camille Paglia remarked, "I can't help noticing how robustly, dreamily masculine the faces of the firefighters are. These are working-class men, stoical, patriotic. They're not on Prozac or questioning their gender."[4] That such accounts ignore, as Carol Gilligan has pointed out, the many women who have also performed these various labors during and after the terrorist attacks suggests the continuing investment in the idea of the working class as male (and, for that matter, white).[5]

This admiration for working-class men was most often articulated through a rejection of a previous set of class identifications. Nussbaum claimed that these "big, beefy, working-class guys" were "replacing the telegenic financial analysts and techno-billionaires who once had held the nation in thrall."[6] In a like manner, Patricia Leigh Brown, in her *New York Times* article on "The Return of Manly Men," argued that "the firefighter coated with ash and soot has provided a striking contrast to the now prehistoric-seeming male archetype of such a short time ago: the casually dressed dot-commer in khakis and a BMW."[7] This chastened sense of middle-class identity, and the concomitant movement of class dis- and reidentifications, points to the sorts of contradictions of the PMC's class location that it must address if it is to develop a coherent, progressive class politics. Chastising themselves for their association with finance capital and an avarice-motivated infatuation with dot-commerce, these PMC voices seemed to be expressing regret for having imagined themselves through a now-suspect set of class signifiers. To put it another way, after articulating its class identity through an unabashed affiliation with the forces of transnational, disembodied capital—an entity which underwent symbolic attack in the destruction of the World Trade Center[8]—the PMC's embrace of a fiercely national and eminently embodied form of labor suggests a desire to reorient its identity toward the other pole of its contradictory class location.

This logic informs Oliver Stone's 2006 film *World Trade Center*, a dramatized true story of two Port Authority police officers, Will Jemino and John McLoughlin, who were saved from the rubble of the Twin Towers. Much of the film's affective power comes from the fact that the men are injured doing a dangerous job, while their wives and children sit at home anguishing over their fate—the kind of traditional division of labor that writers such as Paglia find so praiseworthy about the working class. Furthermore, McLoughlin's (Nicolas Cage) connection to manual labor is reinforced during the flashback sequences, in which his wife recalls him working at his workbench, fixing the roof, and performing other "manly" household tasks. Importantly, *World Trade Center* also features a middle-class character who takes on the position of manual laborer: we first see accountant Dave Karnes (Michael Shannon) watching the 9/11 attacks at his Deloitte and Touche office in Wilton, Connecticut. Karnes leaves his office, gets a traditional military haircut, dons his old Marine uniform, and works his way into the World Trade Center site, where he and another Marine (in defiance of the ban on nighttime search and rescue work) discover Jemino and McLoughlin and direct help toward them. Karnes's reidentification from accountant to military laborer is emphasized when another rescue worker asks for his name, and he answers "Staff Sergeant Karnes." When asked for a shorter name, he replies "Staff Sergeant."[9] These details are in fact true, but it is of course necessary to remember that filmmakers can and do choose to include, alter, or omit such facts in the service of dramatic values; in a telling example, the other Marine that found Jimeno and McLoughlin, who is portrayed by a white actor in the film, was African American.[10] What *World Trade Center* emphasizes, then, in its selective reenactment of its true-life subject, is the heroism of a traditional working class—and those who would emulate this class.

In *World Trade Center*, Karnes admonishes his fellow accountants by remarking "I don't know if you guys know it yet, but this country's at war," and their stunned inaction, in contrast to his decision to trade in his suit and tie for Marine fatigues, suggests a subtle indictment of their middle-class powerlessness in the face of national tragedy. Indeed, the rediscovered value of working-class labor that attended 9/11 was often characterized through the implied lack of value in PMC labor. In his description of the construction workers' use of plastic buckets to carry the debris away from the World Trade Center ruins, Klinkenborg declared, "This is a kind of work as basic as the five-gallon plastic bucket itself, all hands, all back, all heart. It's the kind of work most New Yorkers believed no longer mattered in Manhattan." Even as "the white-collar trades resumed" their everyday work, the construction workers remained at the 9/11 site, where "manual labor was the only labor delicate enough to give hope." Klinkenborg's implicit criticism of those with "unsoiled and unroughened hands," who until recently thought that manual labor "no longer mattered in Manhattan" (a group he clearly numbers himself among), suggests a class self-loathing that longs for the authenticity of manual labor—a labor that, by definition, the PMC does not perform.[11]

But is the question about what *kind* of labor one does the most politically useful one? While these accounts of the blue-collar rescue and clean-up teams often focused on the brute physical nature of the teams' work, this labor was also admired and praised for its selflessness and social usefulness. Furthermore, the newly piqued suspicion and distrust of global capital seemed to be inspired as much by its aggressively antisocial actions—such as the airlines' demand for a publicly funded bailout even as they fired tens of thousands of employees—as by its seemingly disembodied and intangible methods of doing business. Rather than ask whether a particular kind of labor is good (or worthy, or admirable) in and of itself, perhaps the question should be, to what purposes is this labor being put?

If we talk about labor in this way, we can better understand how the intense approbation conferred upon these spectacles of working-class labor was generated by (among other things) an appreciation of the common good to which this labor was directed. Therefore, even though this labor was often fetishized through the kinds of class misrecognitions I have described throughout this project, the attempt to identify with these laboring bodies was also animated by the desire for work that has as its goal collective betterment, not just mere personal gain. As Nussbaum put it, "for Americans conditioned in the '90s to think of oneself first, to be rich above all else, to accumulate all the good material things," the "image of self-sacrifice by civil servants in uniform was simply breathtaking."[12] This image of labor deployed for the benefit of all, of course, is something any socialist would (and should) embrace—for here we find one of the central utopian impulses that have often motivated, and continue to motivate, the PMC's identifications with the working class.

This utopian desire is laid bare in a particularly revealing fashion in the little-seen 2002 film *The Guys*.[13] Like *World Trade Center*, its central motivation is to mourn the public servants who died in the 9/11 attacks: the film is about Joan (Sigourney Weaver), a female journalist (one who started out covering "the dirty wars" in Central America) who helps a fire captain, Nick (Anthony LaPaglia), write eulogies for the eight men who died from his company. To be sure, *The Guys*, like Oliver Stone's later film, testifies to the desire for an authentic masculinity from the working class. During one of their discussions, Nick tells Joan that he takes dance classes, explaining that the classes are sometimes "hard for these modern women. You know, they're professionals, they're educated; they're used to being in charge. But when you dance, you gotta be able to feel the lead you have to follow." In awe of her new acquaintance's selfless service to others, Joan agrees: "You gotta let go." He then leads her in a tango, during which she giddily follows his lead. However, in a marked difference from *World Trade Center*'s transparent narration, *The Guys* interrupts this dance with Joan's voiceover, and corresponding intertitles, that tell us, "Of course, that never happened"—neither the tango, nor the conversation about "modern women." The scene is revealed to be the product of a middle-class woman's imagination about a working-class man about whom she knows little, but with whom she wants to connect.

This self-aware acknowledgement of PMC fantasies about the working class underscores the film's central leitmotif, which is about middle-class anxiety over the alleged uselessness of their labor. When Joan is first told that the fire captain needs a writer to help him with his eulogies, she asks, "When was the last time I heard anyone say they needed a writer?" Later in the film, when Joan breaks down as she reads a draft aloud to Nick, she wails, "I wanna do something. But this is all I know how to do—words. This is all I have. I can't think of anything else." Nick reassures her that what she is doing is useful, that the ability to manipulate words is important: "They're your tools." The film reinforces this notion in its conclusion when Nick gives his last eulogy, which is also the first we see delivered at an actual funeral. As Joan stands in the back amid a crowd of uniformed men (and a few women), Nick talks about how Barney, the man being mourned that day, was particularly skilled at modifying and even inventing the devices they used for firefighting. As he meets Joan's gaze, he explains, "When you're answering an alarm, every tool counts. [Barney]...respected his tools and respected his job." The moment between them seems so heartfelt, as the firefighter implicitly lets the journalist know that her labor is as necessary as that of live-saving manual laborers, that one almost forgets that these are actually Joan's words that Nick is speaking.

One can (and perhaps should) be a little appalled at this scene, in which a national tragedy becomes yet another opportunity for the professional middle class to invent a working class that reinforces the value of its own position. Yet this scene is also salutary for how nakedly it testifies to a PMC desire for a way of understanding their labor as socially useful—as contributing to collective well-being in a manner as vital as that of the workers who attempted to save the victims of the 9/11 attacks. Further, what is remarkable about *The Guys* is that its middle-class protagonist, despite her evident desires to identify with her working-class interlocutor, does not attempt to evade the dilemmas of her laboring position by assuming that of another. Instead, the movie visualizes the regeneration of professional labor as serving the working class, not capital. A recurring visual trope of the film is the fire station's security tape, where we see the papers that floated from the World Trade Center drift onto the street in front of the station. In one key scene, the magnified image of these scattered papers dissolves onto that of the paper leaving Joan's printer as it prints out the eulogy she has just composed with Nick (figure 7.1). The implication of this dissolve, of course, is

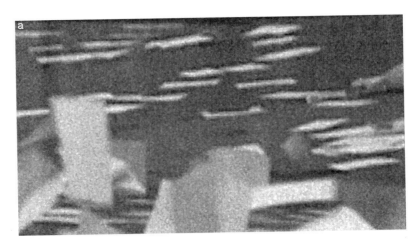

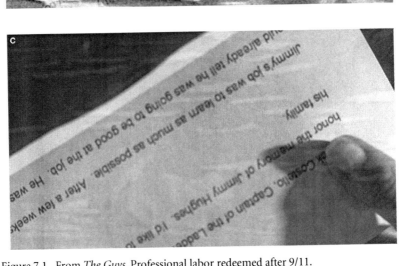

Figure 7.1. From *The Guys*. Professional labor redeemed after 9/11.

to counter the disarray of the blasted, blowing debris with the orderly procession of documents that will attempt to heal the wounds of that day. Yet we can also see in this image a contrast between the (most likely) financial papers generated by professional laborers on behalf of capital to benefit private interests and documents that perform an affective labor whose purpose is to serve the public servants—and thus the larger community of which they are both a part. *The Guys*, then, is in some ways less about the fallen men of 9/11 and more about the desire of that event's middle-class survivors to emulate their commitment to public service.

This desire for the transvaluation of professional work is, I would argue, the repressed content of a good deal of the PMC's fascination with the working class. In their tactile labor that seems to serve eminently visible needs, and in their frequent demonstrations of collective solidarity, the working class can offer the PMC a utopian vision of work performed with dignity and directed toward collective well-being. Yet while this willed identification with the working class is often motivated by such valuable desires, it also operates most frequently by evading the dilemma that generated them, which is the contradictory role of professional-managerial labor itself. The cross-class identifications I have examined in this book too often serve to enable PMCers to disown their own position and take up that of another class. And while this working-class location serves as a rebellion against a particular *form* of labor, it evades the issue of what would count as a good *use* of labor—manual or mental, working class or professional-managerial. That question—the central question of any attempt to construct an economic order that organizes its work for the public good, rather than private gain—cannot be answered by merely replacing one kind of labor with another. The potential role of the professional-managerial class in contributing to this alternative economic order, finally, can only be discerned through an engagement with its own class position, and its own forms of labor.

NOTES

PREFACE

1. David A. Cook, *History of the American Cinema, Vol. 9: Lost Illusions: American Cinema in the Shadow of Watergate and Vietnam, 1970–1979*, Charles Harpole, gen. ed. (New York: Scribner's, 2000).
2. For recent iterations of this line of argument, see Alexander Horwath, "The Impure Cinema: New Hollywood, 1967–1976," and Thomas Elsaesser, "American Auteur Cinema: The Last—or First—Picture Show?" in *The Last Great American Picture Show: New Hollywood Cinema in the 1970s*, eds. Thomas Elsaesser, Alexander Horwath, and Noel King (Amsterdam: Amsterdam University Press, 2004), 9–17, 37–69.
3. Scorsese himself discusses this aspect of his career in a 1990 interview with Anthony De Curtis ("Martin Scorsese," *Rolling Stone*, November 1, 1990, 58–65).

INTRODUCTION

1. Michael Storper and Susan Christopherson, "Flexible Specialization and Regional Industrial Agglomerations: The Case of the U.S. Motion Picture Industry," *Annals of the Association of American Geographers* 77.1 (March 1987): 104–117. "Flexible specialization" in this context refers to a mode by which the various aspects of filmmaking are no longer directed and executed by those under contract to a single studio but are instead subcontracted out to different, semi-independent firms and individuals.
2. Thomas Schatz, "The New Hollywood," in *Film Theory Goes to the Movies*, eds. Jim Collins, Hilary Radner, and Ava Preacher Collins (New York: Routledge, 1993), 8–36.
3. Peter Kramer offers a good overview of many of these accounts in "Post-Classical Hollywood," in *The Oxford Guide to Film Studies*, eds. John Hill and Pamela Church Gibson (New York: Oxford University Press, 1998), 289–309.

4. Thomas Elsaesser, "Notes on the Unmotivated Hero: The Pathos of Failure—American Film in the 70s," *Monogram* 6 (1975): 13; Warren Buckland, "A Close Encounter with *Raiders of the Lost Ark*: Notes on Narrative Aspects of the New Hollywood Blockbuster," in *Contemporary Hollywood Cinema*, eds. Steve Neale and Murray Smith (New York: Routledge, 1998), 167. It should be noted that Buckland ultimately argues against the above-quoted formulation of New Hollywood blockbuster narration.

5. Eric Hobsbawm, *The Age of Extremes: A History of the World, 1914–1991* (New York: Vintage, 1994).

6. Kim Moody, *An Injury to All: The Decline of American Unionism* (New York: Verso, 1988), 127–128.

7. Barry Bluestone and Bennett Harrison, *The Deindustrialization of America: Plant Closings, Community Abandonment, and the Dismantling of Basic Industry* (New York: Basic Books, 1982).

8. Mike Davis, *Prisoners of the American Dream: Politics and Economy in the History of the U.S. Working Class* (New York: Verso, 1986), 210, 145.

9. Davis, 213.

10. Peter Biskind and Barbara Ehrenreich, "Machismo and Hollywood's Working Class," in *American Media and Mass Culture: Left Perspectives*, ed. Donald Lazare (Berkeley: University of California Press, 1987), 201.

11. See, for example, David E. James, "Introduction: Is There Class in This Text?" in *The Hidden Foundation: Cinema and the Question of Class*, eds. David E. James and Rick Berg (Minneapolis: University of Minnesota Press, 1996), 1–25.

12. Quoted in Antony Easthope, "The Trajectory of *Screen*, 1971–79," in *The Politics of Theory: Proceedings of the Essex Conference on the Sociology of Literature, July 1982*, eds. Francis Barker et al. (Colchester, U.K.: University of Essex Press, 1983), 122.

13. Rosalind Coward, "Class, 'Culture,' and the Social Formation," *Screen* 18.1 (Spring 1977): 95.

14. See, for example, Colin MacCabe, "Realism and the Cinema: Notes on Some Brechtian Theses," *Screen* 15.2 (Autumn 1974): 7–27.

15. Easthope 127.

16. Ibid., emphasis in original.

17. This has been primarily accomplished through the adoption of reception-oriented models from television and cultural studies, which I discuss below.

18. These efforts have most often been focused on the question of race. See, for example, the essays in *Screen*'s "Last 'Special Issue' on Race" (*Screen* 29.4, Autumn 1988), especially Jane Gaines, "White Privilege and Looking Relations: Race and Gender in Feminist Film Theory," 12–27; Richard Dyer, "White," 44–65; and Manthia Diawara, "Black Spectatorship: Problems of Identification and Resistance," 66–76. See also Jacqueline Bobo, *Black Women as Cultural Readers* (New York: Columbia University Press, 1995).

19. For example, *Cineaste* asked activists in the Detroit labor movement to comment on the auto industry-based *Blue Collar* by answering the following questions: "Where is

the film most accurate in regard to present-day working-class life in Detroit? Where is the film most inaccurate? Is the film anti-union? [Is it] anti-working-class?" ("*Blue Collar*: Detroit Moviegoers Have Their Say," *Cineaste* 8:4 (Summer 1978): 28–31). As to the preference for false consciousness interpretations, see Peter Hoffman and Jim Purdy, "The Worker and Hollywood," *Cineaste* 9:1 (Fall 1978): 8–13. Some of the essays from *Jump Cut* are more sophisticated—they begin to investigate the cultural work done by representations of class, outside of any correspondence to the "real"—but too often tend toward reductive forms of analysis. For an introduction to the better 1970s and early 1980s work, see Peter Steven, ed., *Jump Cut: Hollywood, Politics, and Counter-Cinema* (New York: Praeger, 1985).

20. Stuart Hall's "Cultural Studies and the Centre: Some Problematics and Problems" is a particularly thorough introduction to the theoretical evolution of the Birmingham Centre for Contemporary Cultural Studies during the 1970s (*Culture, Media, Language: Working Papers in Cultural Studies, 1972–79*, eds. Stuart Hall et al. (London: Hutchinson, 1980), 15–47).

21. John Clarke, Stuart Hall, Tony Jefferson, and Brian Roberts, "Subcultures, Cultures and Class: A Theoretical Overview," in *Resistance Through Rituals: Youth Subcultures in Post-War Britain*, eds. Stuart Hall and Tony Jefferson (London: Hutchinson, 1976), 30–34. The Phil Cohen essay Clarke et al. discuss is reprinted in "Sub-Cultural Conflict and Working Class Community," in Hall et al. 78–87.

22. On these last two crucial determinants, see Dick Hebdige, *Subculture: The Meaning of Style* (New York: Routledge, 1988), and Angela McRobbie, "Settling Accounts with Subcultures: A Feminist Critique," *Screen Education* 34 (1980): 37–49.

23. Rita Felski, "Those Who Disdain Cultural Studies Don't Know What They're Talking About," *Chronicle of Higher Education*, July 23, 1999, B7.

24. John Fiske, *Understanding Popular Culture* (New York: Routledge, 1989), 105.

25. Meaghan Morris, "Banality in Cultural Studies," in *Logics of Television: Essays in Cultural Criticism*, ed. Patricia Mellencamp (Bloomington: Indiana University Press, 1990), 23.

26. These terms, of course, are those used by Stuart Hall in his "Notes on Deconstructing 'the Popular'" (*People's History and Socialist Theory*, ed. Raphael Samuel (London: Routledge, 1981), 227–240). While I agree with John Frow that Hall's emphasis, in this formulation, on the noncorrespondence between class position and cultural articulation creates "a real difficulty in understanding what it is that connects" the economic to the cultural and political, I do not think Hall can be held responsible for the subsequently sloppy use of this opposition. See John Frow's discussion of this Hall essay in *Cultural Studies and Cultural Value* (New York: Oxford University Press, 1995), 70–75.

27. Erik Olin Wright, "A General Framework for the Analysis of Class Structure," in *The Debate on Classes*, ed. Erik Olin Wright (New York: Verso, 1989), 3.

28. Barbara and John Ehrenreich, "The Professional-Managerial Class," in *Between Labor and Capital*, ed. Pat Walker (Boston: South End, 1979), 12.

29. See Erik Olin Wright, "The Biography of a Concept: Contradictory Class Locations," in *Classes* (London: Verso, 1985), 19–63.

30. Erik Olin Wright, "Rethinking, Once Again, the Concept of Class Structure," in *The Debate on Classes*, ed. Erik Olin Wright (New York: Verso, 1989), 303.

31. Ibid., 348.

32. Frow 121.

33. Ibid., 125, emphasis in original.

34. Ibid., 103, 104, emphasis in original.

35. Ibid., 111.

36. Steve Neale defines film cycles as "groups of films made within a specific and limited time-span, and founded, for the most part, on the characteristics of individual commercial successes" (*Genre and Hollywood* (New York: Routledge, 2000), 9).

37. "Race is thus, also, the modality in which class is 'lived,' the medium through which class relations are experienced, the form in which it is appropriated and 'fought through'" (Stuart Hall, "Race, Articulation, and Societies Structured in Dominance," in *Black British Cultural Studies: A Reader*, eds. Houston A. Baker Jr., Manthia Diawara, and Ruth H. Lindeborg (Chicago: University of Chicago Press, 1996), 55).

38. Jackie Stacey, *Star Gazing: Hollywood Cinema and Female Spectatorship* (New York: Routledge, 1994), 35–48.

39. Barbara Klinger, *Melodrama and Meaning: History, Culture, and the Films of Douglas Sirk* (Bloomington: Indiana University Press, 1994), 34, emphasis in original.

40. Klinger attributes the phrase "discursive surround" to Dana Polan (Barbara Klinger, "Film History Terminable and Interminable: Recovering the Past in Reception Studies," *Screen* 38.2 (Summer 1997): 107–128).

41. Robert C. Allen and Douglas Gomery, *Film History: Theory and Practice* (New York, Knopf, 1985), 90.

42. Klinger, "Film History," 119.

43. I use "lower class" here, a term I would normally eschew due to its derogatory thrust, to emphasize precisely that—the condescending implications of these reviewers' rhetoric. On the pursuit by journalistic publications of affluent readers in order to attract advertisers, see C. Edwin Baker, *Advertising and a Democratic Press* (Princeton, N.J.: Princeton University Press: 1994).

44. Tino Balio, "'A Major Presence in All of the World's Important Markets': The Globalization of Hollywood in the 1990s," in *Contemporary Hollywood Cinema*, eds. Steve Neale and Murray Smith (New York: Routledge, 1998), 61.

45. Yvonne Tasker, "Approaches to the New Hollywood," in *Cultural Studies and Communications*, eds. James Curran, David Morley, and Valerie Walkerdine (New York: Arnold, 1996), 219.

46. I should reiterate here that the postclassical, New Hollywood text Corrigan and Schatz describe is different from that of the "first" New Hollywood, which I address in chapter 1, whose films broke with classical Hollywood under the influence of European art cinema and through the deployment of non-goal-oriented protagonists.

47. Schatz 23.

48. Timothy Corrigan, *A Cinema Without Walls: Movies and Culture After Vietnam* (New Brunswick, N.J.: Rutgers University Press, 1991), 21–24.

49. See, for example, Murray Smith, "Theses on the Philosophy of Hollywood History," in Neale and Smith 3–20, and Elizabeth Cowie, "Storytelling: Classical Hollywood Cinema and Classical Narrative," in Neale and Smith 178–190.

50. Steven J. Ross, "Beyond the Screen: History, Class, and the Movies," in James and Berg 47.

51. Steven J. Ross, *Working-Class Hollywood: Silent Film and the Shaping of Class in America* (Princeton, N.J.: Princeton University Press, 1998). For other accounts of class dynamics and labor practices in the film industry, see Danae Clark, *Negotiating Hollywood: The Cultural Politics of Actors' Labor* (Minneapolis: University of Minnesota Press, 1995), and Mark Garrett Cooper, *Love Rules: Silent Hollywood and the Rise of the Managerial Class* (Minneapolis: University of Minnesota Press, 2003). On the film industry's mid-century labor history, see Gerald Horne, *Class Struggle in Hollywood, 1930–1950: Moguls, Mobsters, Stars, Reds, & Trade Unionists* (Austin: University of Texas Press, 2001).

52. See, for example, John Amman, "The Transformation of Industrial Relations in the Motion Picture and Television Industries: Craft and Production," in *Under the Stars: Essays on Labor Relations in Arts and Entertainment*, eds. Lois S. Gray and Ronald L. Seeber (Ithaca, N.Y.: Cornell University Press, 1996), 113–155.

CHAPTER 1

1. Barbara Ehrenreich, *Fear of Falling: the Inner Life of the Middle Class* (New York: HarperCollins, 1989), 97.

2. "Auteur" is the French word for author, and is usually used in the film world to refer to directors who exert authorial control over their films, thus expressing their personal vision. The term hails from François Truffaut's famous 1954 *Cahiers du Cinéma* essay "Une certaine tendance du cinéma français."

3. Peter Biskind, *Easy Riders and Raging Bulls: How the Sex-Drugs-and-Rock'n'Roll Generation Saved Hollywood* (New York: Simon & Schuster, 1998), 68.

4. Biskind notes that this expression is a paraphrase of Buck Henry's (75).

5. Ehrenreich, *Fear*, 101.

6. These debates are usually conducted in the terms set out in David Bordwell, Janet Staiger, and Kristin Thompson, *The Classical Hollywood Cinema: Film Style & Mode of Production to 1960* (New York: Columbia University Press, 1985).

7. For a good overview of these debates, see Yvonne Tasker, "Approaches to the New Hollywood," *Cultural Studies and Communications*, eds. James Curran, David Morley and Valerie Walkerdine (New York: Arnold, 1996), 213–228. As I explain in endnote 45 of the introduction, the postclassical "New Hollywood" explored in this chapter is a

precursor to the blockbuster-oriented New Hollywood described by Thomas Schatz and Timothy Corrigan (among others).

8. For a thorough consideration of this question, see Murray Smith, "Theses on the Philosophy of Hollywood History," *Contemporary Hollywood Cinema*, eds. Steve Neale and Murray Smith (New York: Routledge, 1998), 3–20.

9. Richard Maltby, "'Nobody Knows Everything': Post-classical historiographies and consolidated entertainment," in Neale and Smith 32; Robert Sklar, *Movie Made America: A Cultural History of American Movies*, rev. ed. (New York: Vintage, 1994), 323; "New kind of movie shakes Hollywood," *Business Week*, January 3, 1970, 40; John Izod, *Hollywood and the Box Office, 1895–1986* (New York: Columbia University Press, 1988), 171; Sklar 289.

10. Sklar 302; Peter Biskind 20; "The New Movies," *Newsweek*, December 7, 1970, 62.

11. "New Movies" 62; Richard F. Shepard, "Effect of TV on Moviegoing Is Examined," *New York Times*, November 24, 1971, late ed., 20; Richard Schickel, "The Movies Are Now High Art," *The New York Times Sunday Magazine*, January 5, 1969, 34; Shepard 20; Schickel, "High Art," 34.

12. See Maltby 33–34. Regarding classical era audiences, Robert Ray notes that "roughly ninety cents of every amusement dollar were spent at the movies" in 1946, a year during which weekly attendance figures represented three-fourths of the entire population which could be expected to have access to a movie theater (*A Certain Tendency of the Hollywood Cinema, 1930–1980* (Princeton, N.J.: Princeton University Press: 1985), 129).

13. Maltby 33; Fletcher Knebel, "Hollywood: Broke—and Getting Rich," *Look*, November 3, 1970, 52.

14. John Kenneth Galbraith, *The New Industrial State*, 2nd ed. (Boston: Houghton Mifflin, 1985), 74.

15. Barbara Ehrenreich, *Fear*, 12; "New kind of movie" 44; "New Movies" 71; quoted in "New Movies" 64. Sara Blair reminds me that Williams's reference to "aborigines" also bears more than a little relationship to the anti-Semitism that attended the popular understanding of the studio heads of the classical era, which points to the way that this shift in Hollywood's orientation was also thought of in ethnic terms as well as class ones.

16. The Ehrenreichs use the term "New Left" to "mean the consciously anti-racist and anti-imperialist (and later, anti-capitalist) white movement, centered initially in the universities but ultimately extending well beyond them." They add that the "New Left interacted with or was part of most of the other movements of the sixties, but it was not identical to them" (Ehrenreichs 33n50).

17. Ehrenreichs 31, 34; B. Ehrenreich 58.

18. See, for example, Tasker 220–221.

19. Michael Pye and Linda Myles, *The Movie Brats: How the Film Generation Took Over Hollywood* (New York: Holt, Rinehart and Winston, 1979), 32–37; Maltby 33–34. Furthermore, *Easy Rider* started out as an AIP production (Biskind 61).

20. "The Kids at Cannon," *Time*, August 31, 1970, 60.

21. David A. Cook, *History of the American Cinema, Vol. 9: Lost Illusions: American Cinema in the Shadow of Watergate and Vietnam, 1970–1979*, Charles Harpole, gen. ed. (New York: Scribner's, 2000), 171, 497–498. "Rentals" signifies the revenues returned to film distributors (most often major studios) after the print has been "rented" by exhibitors.

22. Ehrenreich, *Fear* 98–101; "Man and Woman of the Year: The Middle Americans," *Time*, January 5, 1970, 11; "The Troubled American: A Report on the White Majority," *Newsweek*, October 6, 1969, 29.

23. "Workers' Woodstock," *Time*, June 1, 1970, 12–13.

24. Ehrenreich 107; Peter B. Levy, *The New Left and Labor in the 1960s* (Chicago: University of Illinois Press, 1994), 61.

25. Len Levitt, "'Don't Get Me Wrong,'" *Time*, May 25, 1970, 21.

26. Homer Bigart, "War Foes Here Attacked by Construction Workers: City Hall is Stormed," *New York Times*, May 9, 1970, late ed., 10; italics mine.

27. Richard Rogin, "Joe Kelly Has Reached His Boiling Point," *A History of Our Time: Readings on Postwar America*, eds. William H. Chafe and Harvard Sitkoff (New York: Oxford University Press, 1983), 279, 285. Originally published in *New York Times Sunday Magazine*, June 28, 1970, 12–24.

28. "Almost overnight, 'hardhats' became synonymous with white working-class conservatives, already familiar among George Wallace's 1968 supporters" ("The Sudden Rising of the Hardhats," *Time*, May 25, 1970, 20–21).

    Of course, the "Wall Street and Broadway office workers" or "white-collar-and-tie man" to whom Joe Kelly refers could be clerical or "routine mental workers," and thus on some accounts of class position—including the Ehrenreichs'—would be considered members of the working-class and/or proletariat themselves. However, the journalistic accounts of the riots—unattuned as they are to Marxist debates concerning the new middle classes—do not specify the occupations of these nonconstruction workers. Yet the distinction between "blue" and "white" collar tends to serve as a crude mainstream tool for distinguishing between the working and middle classes. Therefore, according to the media's own class terminology, the riots were a cross-class affair—yet were not described as such. For a useful schematic diagram on the various Marxist positions regarding the taxonomy of the new middle classes, see Val Burris's chart in "Class Structure and Political Ideology," *The Insurgent Sociologist* 14.2 (Summer 1987): 33 (figure 1) (quoted in John Frow, *Cultural Studies and Cultural Value* (New York: Oxford University Press, 1995), 123).

29. J. Hoberman reports that "according to Susan Sarandon [who played Melissa], *Joe* was not only retitled but reconfigured in the wake of the Wall Street rumble: 'They saw that they had a godsend in Peter Boyle and the re-edited it to emphasize him.'" [*The Dream Life: Movies, Media, and the Mythology of the Sixties* (New York: The New Press, 2003), 283].

30. *Time* reviewer Mark Goodman describes how "Compton's harmless, homogenized ideas and civilized manners give way before the barbaric force of Joe's fury" ("Jonah in a Hard Hat," *Time*, July 27, 1970, 68).

31. *Contemporary Theatre, Film and Television, Vol. 10*, ed. Emily J. McMurray (Detroit: Gale Research: 1993); Pauline Kael, "Numbing the Audience," in *Film 70/71*, ed. David Denby (New York: Simon & Schuster, 1971), 295.

32. See, for example, Arnold 46; Kael 295.

33. "The Hard Hats," *Newsweek*, May 25, 1970, 34; Andy Logan, "Around City Hall," *New Yorker* June 6, 1970, 104; Leader editorial, *New York Times* May 9, 1970, late ed., 24.

34. Kim Moody, *An Injury to All: The Decline of American Unionism* (New York: Verso, 1988), 86.

35. Moody 17–40.

36. Ibid., 84, 86.

37. "The Blue Collar Worker's Lowdown Blues," *Time*, November 9, 1970, 69; Louise Kapp Howe, "Introduction," *The White Majority: Between Poverty and Affluence*, ed. Louise Kapp Howe (New York: Random House, 1970) 7, 4; on the 1970 postal workers strike, see Moody 86–88, and Stanley Aronowitz, *From the Ashes of the Old: American Labor and America's Future* (New York: Houghton Mifflin, 1998), 79–80; "Lowdown Blues" 68.

38. "Lowdown Blues" 68.

39. The only characters who could be said to be members of the counterculture are the two female hitchhikers Bobby and Rayette pick up in the middle of the film (who are caricatured), although their flight from society (toward Alaska, where it's "cleaner") *is* mirrored by Bobby's hitching a ride to either Canada or Alaska (the film leaves the destination ambiguous) in the film's final scene.

40. Penelope Gilliatt, "Study of an American Black Sheep," review of *Five Easy Pieces*, directed by Bob Rafelson, *New Yorker*, September 19, 1970, 101; Stefan Kanfer, "Supergypsy," review of *Five Easy Pieces*, directed by Bob Rafelson, *Time*, September 14, 1970, 89.

41. Shari Zeck has pointed out to me that there are a few hints as to Bobby's background that occur early in the film—particularly Rayette's reference to Bobby's musical knowledge, and Bobby's claim to Elton that he didn't know what he was getting into when joining an oil rig. However, I would contend that the import of these hints does not start to become legible until the piano-playing scene I describe above—a contention borne out by the contemporaneous reviews of the film.

42. Kanfer 89.

43. Stephen Farber noted in a later essay on director Bob Rafelson that he "eliminated a prologue from Carole Eastman's script which revealed Bobby Dupea's musical heritage," choosing instead "to begin Bobby's story in a more oblique fashion, involving us in Bobby's perplexing contradictions before disclosing the unconventional background of the hard hat in the oil fields" ("L.A. Journal," *Film Comment* May/June 1976: 3).

44. Peter Wollen, "Godard and Counter-Cinema: *Vent d'Est*," *Narrative, Apparatus, Ideology*, ed. Philip Rosen (New York: Columbia University Press, 1986), 121. On New Hollywood's narrative structures, see, for example, Thomas Elsaesser, "The Pathos

of Failure: American Films in the '70s," *Monogram* 6 (1975): 13–19, which discusses *Five Easy Pieces* in particular, and Steve Neale, "New Hollywood Cinema," *Screen* 17.2 (1976): 117.

45. Jacob Brackman, review of *Five Easy Pieces*, directed by Bob Rafelson, in Denby, *Film 70/71*, 34, 38.

46. Richard Schickel, "A Man's Journey Into His Past," review of *Five Easy Pieces*, directed by Bob Rafelson, *Life*, September 18, 1970, 16.

47. Ehrenreich, *Fear*, 75; Midge Decter, *Liberal Parents, Radical Children* (New York: Coward, McGann & Geoghegan, 1975), 16, 31, 27. In his otherwise positive review of the film, Jacob Brackman registers his disappointment over this class-specific denouement: "The piano? Is that all?" (38).

48. In more ways than one: as Gregg M. Campbell notes, the Tammy Wynette songs frequently "provide a Greek Chorus for all of Rayette Dipesto's hopes, aspirations and fears" ("Beethoven, Chopin, and Tammy Wynette: Heroines and Archetypes in *Five Easy Pieces*," *Film/Literature Quarterly* 2 (1974): 278).

49. Joseph Morgenstern, "Easy Piece, Hard Piece," *Newsweek*, December 21, 1970, 14.

50. As Janet Staiger reminds us, by 1970 such art cinema-influenced techniques had been consistently associated with "high-brow" culture for over a decade (178–195).

51. Stanley Kauffman, review of *Five Easy Pieces*, directed by Bob Rafelson, *New Republic*, September 26, 1970, 21.

52. John Simon, review of *Five Easy Pieces*, directed by Bob Rafelson, in Denby, *Film 70/71*, 42.

53. Simon 41.

54. A. D. Murphy, "Students: Stay Out of Hollywood," *New York Times*, August 18, 1968, late ed., sec. 2, 13.

55. Robert Gessner, "Youth Locked Out at the Film Gate," *Variety*, January 6, 1965, 25; John Gardiner, "The Below-the-Line Unions," *Television*, December 1967, 44; "The Things Workers Say About the IATSE," *Television*, December 1967, 49; Joseph Morgenstern, "Hollywood: Myth, Fact and Trouble," *Newsweek*, June 30, 1969, 86.

56. Murphy 13; "Film Unions and the Low-Budget Independent Film Production—An Exploratory Discussion," with Gideon Bachmann, Shirley Clarke, James Degangi, Adolfas Mekas, Jonas Mekas, Lew Clyde Stoumen, Willard Van Dyke, *Film Culture* 22–23 (Summer 1961): 136.

57. "The Entertainment Unions: A Progress Report," *Monthly Labor Review* 88.11 (Nov. 1965): 3–4; See Pye and Myles 60–61; Joseph Gelmis, *The Film Director as Superstar* (Garden City, N.Y.: Doubleday, 1970), 30; "Screen Actors Guild Moves for Withdrawals from Non-Union 'Swope,'" *Variety*, October 23, 1968, 16; "Actors Go 'Underground' At Own Peril," *Variety*, March 12, 1969, 5; "'Easy Rider' Biz Sparks NABET Use by Coast Indies," *Variety*, October 22, 1969, 6. The last practice—NABET's encroachment on IATSE's jurisdiction—resulted in a situation of "dual unionism," which, of course, tends to favor employers, who can then play the two unions against each other, and thus undermine the bargaining power of each union.

58. Dave Kaufman, "Coast Unemployment Gloom: Inventory High; O'seas a Factor," *Variety*, July 9, 1969, 7; "H'wood's Production Slump Sparks Record Drop in Craft Employment," *Variety*, January 21, 1970, 5; "Okay Half Wages, Under 50G Budget," *Variety*, August 20, 1969, 5; Dave Kaufman, "Creaky Rules & Featherbeds: Coast Crafts' Self-Appraisal," *Variety*, February 18, 1970, 24; "H'wood Craft Unions Dissatisfied With IATSE Concessions; Prod. Lags," *Variety*, June 24, 1970, 4; Ronald Gold, "Never-Be-The-Same IATSE: Close Votes and Wide Discontent," *Variety*, July 29, 1970, 7, 22.

59. "The Things Workers Say about the IATSE" 49; "Bob Altman Raps Studios' Overload of 'Non-Skilled,'" *Variety*, April 22, 1970, 5.

60. "Film Unions and Independent Film Production" 137, 150.

61. Gelmis 31; Dale Pollock, *Skywalking: The Life and Films of George Lucas* (New York: Harmony, 1983), 100 (quoted in Biskind 93); on PMC labor, see Ehrenreich, *Fear of Falling*, 260–263.

62. Whom we should perhaps designate, following the auteur theory, the other, now nonauthorial workers involved in filmmaking. For an excellent discussion on the ways in which capital would come to rearticulate autuerism as a marketing strategy, see Timothy Corrigan, "Auteurs and the New Hollywood," *The New American Cinema*, ed. Jon Lewis (Durham, N.C.: Duke University Press, 1998), 38–63.

63. Michael Everett, e-mail to the author, August 16, 1999; Axel Madsen, *The New Hollywood: American Movies in the '70s* (New York: Thomas Y. Crowell, 1975), 136, 6.

64. Levy 166.

65. "Even if they were not originally receptive to the counterculture, by 1971 white working-class youths adopted views more in line with their age cohorts than with their parents" (Levy 92); on Lordstown—and young worker rebellion at other plants—see Stanley Aronowitz, "Lordstown: Disruption on the Assembly Line," *False Promises: The Shaping of American Working Class Consciousness*, 2nd ed. (Durham, N.C.: Duke University Press, 1992), 21–50, and Bennett Kremen, "No Pride in this Dust: Young Workers in the Steel Mills," *The World of the Blue Collar Worker*, ed. Irving Howe (New York: Quadrangle, 1972), 11–22.

66. "Lowdown Blues" 68; Madsen 136.

67. Biskind 75.

68. See, for example, Eric Lott's treatment of this dynamic in *Love and Theft: Blackface Minstrelsy and the American Working Class* (New York: Oxford University Press, 1993), 147–152.

69. Elsaesser, "Pathos," 15, 14.

PART II

1. Thomas Schatz, "The Western," *Handbook of American Film Genres*, ed. Wes D. Gehring (New York: Greenwood, 1988), 33; David A. Cook, *History of the American Cinema, Vol. 9: Lost Illusions: American Cinema in the Shadow of Watergate and*

Vietnam, 1970–1979, Charles Harpole, gen. ed. (New York: Scribner's, 2000), 182; Schatz 31.

2. James Monaco, *American Film Now: The People, The Power, The Money, The Movies* (New York: New American, 1979), 64, 69; Warren French, "'The Southern': Another Lost Cause?" *The South and Film*, ed. Warren French (Jackson: University Press of Mississippi, 1981), 8–12; Richard Thompson, "What's Your 10–20?" *Film Comment* 16.4 (July/Aug. 1980): 36.

3. Thompson 37; Mike Davis, *Prisoners of the American Dream: Politics and Economy in the History of the U.S. Working Class* (New York: Verso, 1986), 177. On the New Right's racial and gender politics, see, for example, the "Race and Reaction" chapter in Michael Omi and Howard Winant, *Racial Formation in the United States: From the 1960s to the 1990s*, 2nd ed., (New York: Routledge, 1994), 113–136, and Alan Crawford, *Thunder on the Right: The "New Right" and the Politics of Resentment* (New York: Pantheon, 1980).

4. James C. Cobb, *The Selling of the South: The Southern Crusade for Industrial Development, 1936–1990* (Chicago: University of Illinois Press, 1993), 185.

5. "Right-to-work" refers to labor laws that give a worker the "right to work" in a unionized shop without having to join the union. Such laws, of course, have the (intended) effect of weakening unions already in place (as newly hired workers are able to gain the benefits of union contracts without supporting the union that fought for them) and making it more difficult for new unions to be established (since forming a union will seem less attractive, as the union's power will be more precarious as a result of this legal structure).

CHAPTER 2

1. Blaine A. Brownell, "Introduction," *Searching for the Sunbelt: Historical Perspectives on a Region*, ed. Raymond A. Mohl (Knoxville: University of Tennessee Press, 1990), 5. See also Raymond Arsenault, "The End of the Long Hot Summer: The Air Conditioner and Southern Culture," in Mohl 176–211.

2. Arsenault 191.

3. James B. Sterba, "Houston, as Energy Capital, Sets Pace in Sunbelt Boom," *New York Times*, February 9, 1976, late ed., 24.

4. Carl Abbott, "New West, New South, New Region: The Discovery of the Sunbelt," in Mohl 17.

5. Gurney Breckenfeld, "Business Loves the Sunbelt (And Vice Versa)," *Fortune*, June 1977, 133.

6. Jon Nordheimer, "Sunbelt Region Leads Nation in Growth of Population: Area Spans Southern Half of Country," *New York Times*, February 8, 1976, late ed., 42.

7. Here, I draw on the work of film historians such as Janet Staiger and Barbara Klinger, who argue that, in order to understand the cultural work any given film performs,

one must analyze not only the meanings suggested by a film's textual system but also various extracinematic contexts, such as industrial promotion, critical reception, and contemporaneous ideological discourses. See Barbara Klinger, *Melodrama and Meaning: History, Culture, and the Films of Douglas Sirk* (Bloomington: Indiana University Press, 1994), and Janet Staiger, *Interpreting Films: Studies in the Historical Reception of the American Cinema* (Princeton, N.J.: Princeton University Press, 1992).

8. This argument is motivated by more than the idea that an aesthetic production can tell us things about a historical moment that other documents cannot. It is also informed by John Frow's admonition to cultural studies critics that we not merely catalogue the uses to which a particular text is put in different interpretive communities; we must also signal the purposes *our* use of a text is meant to serve, and thus grapple with the question of what cultural value we assign that text in our own interpretive community. See John Frow, *Cultural Studies and Cultural Value* (New York: Oxford University Press, 1995).

9. Benjamin DeMott, "The 'More Life' School and James Dickey," review of *Deliverance*, by James Dickey, *Saturday Review*, March 28, 1970, 38.

10. "Oaters" is a shorthand term for Westerns. "Murf.," review of *Deliverance*, directed by John Boorman, *Variety*, July 19, 1972, 14.

11. James F. Beaton, "Dickey Down the River," *The Modern American Novel and the Movies*, eds. Gerald Peary and Roger Shatzkin (New York: Frederick Ungar, 1978), 296. Beaton too complains later in the essay about the film's violence and also associates it with Westerns, arguing that "it makes the most of the extreme discomforts of an ugly and perverse assault, precisely in the same way that Westerns used to revel in the taking of scalps by Indians" (301).

12. Clover 126–35.

13. In these passages, Lewis persuades the other men to go on the canoe trip, Ed returns to work at his office, and then, the next morning, has sex with his wife before preparing for the trip.

14. Robert F. Willson Jr., "*Deliverance* from Novel to Film: Where Is Our Hero?" *Literature/ Film Quarterly* 2 (Winter 1974): 54, 55.

15. Ernest Suarez, "*Deliverance*: Dickey's Original Screenplay," *The Southern Quarterly* 33.2–3 (Winter-Spring 1995): 161, 164. The quoted phrases are from James Dickey, *Deliverance (Screenplay)* (Carbondale: Southern Illinois University Press, 1982), 7–8.

16. Colin MacCabe, "Realism and the Cinema: Notes on Some Brechtian Theses," *Screen* 15.2 (Autumn 1974): 10. While I am in agreement with many of the critiques of MacCabe's position—especially those concerning its overbroad reach (i.e., its claims to describe all of classic Hollywood cinema)—his description of the invisible "metalanguage" of the visual, which seems to guarantee a nondiscursive "real," is apt for *Deliverance*. In addition to the film's emphasis on psychological and visual verisimilitude, *Deliverance*'s gestures toward a quasi-documentary realism were underscored by the many press accounts of both its on-location shooting and its relatively unique practice of shooting the film's scenes in chronological order.

17. "Saving the New," *Time*, September 27, 1976, 68–71.

18. John Egerton, *The Americanization of Dixie: The Southernization of America* (New York: Harper & Row, 1974), 58–74.

19. Paul D. Zimmerman, "Down the Rapids," review of *Deliverance*, directed John Boorman, *Newsweek*, August 7, 1972, 61 (emphasis mine).

20. Robert Armour, "*Deliverance*: Four Variations of the American Adam," *Literature/Film Quarterly* 1.3 (July 1973): 280, 282.

21. Stanley Kauffman, "Fair to Meddling," reviews of *The Candidate*, directed by Michael Ritchie, *Deliverance*, directed by John Boorman, and *Portnoy's Complaint*, directed by Ernest Lehman, *New Republic*, August 5 & 12, 1972, 24.

22. Jay Cocks, "Rites of Passage," review of *Deliverance*, directed by John Boorman, *Time*, August 7, 1972, 76; Richard Schickel, "White Water, Black Doings," review of *Deliverance*, directed by John Boorman, *Life*, August 8, 1972, 8; Penelope Gilliatt, review of *Deliverance*, directed by John Boorman, *New Yorker*, August 5, 1972, 52–53.

23. Stephen Farber, to take one example, described how both films center on "decent, rather fastidious men forced to confront the violence in nature and in themselves" ("*Deliverance*—How It Delivers," *New York Times*, August 1972, late ed., sec. 2, 9). Moira Walsh and Jay Cocks also compare *Straw Dogs* to *Deliverance* (Moira Walsh, review of *Fat City*, directed by John Huston, and *Deliverance*, directed by John Boorman, *America*, September 2, 1972, 127; Cocks, "Rites," 76).

24. Walsh 127.

25. Cocks, "Rites," 75; Farber also blurs the distinction between the hill people and their environment, remarking that "nature turns out to be threatening and destructive rather than regenerative…murder and violation, rather than mystical conversion, are at the end of the journey" (9); Walsh 127.

26. Fredric Jameson, "The Great American Hunter, or, Ideological Content in the Novel," *College English* 34.2 (Nov. 1972): 182.

27. Jameson 185–186.

28. James J. Griffith, "Damned If You Do and Damned If You Don't: James Dickey's *Deliverance*," *Post-Script: Essays in Film and the Humanities* 5.3 (Spring/Summer 1986): 51–52; James Dickey, *Deliverance* (New York: Bantam Doubleday Dell, 1970), 275–276; Beaton 306.

29. Suarez 169 (quoted passage is from Dickey, *Deliverance (Screenplay)* 150).

30. Dickey, *Deliverance*, 180.

31. Beaton, for example, complains that the film "overstat[es] the contrast between the intruders and the hillbillies" during the sequence in Oree, wherein the latter "appear to be impoverished, inscrutable, and literally degenerate." In this scene, Drew meets a local boy whom we are led to believe is a product of inbreeding (upon seeing him, Bobby comments, "Talk about genetic deficiencies. Isn't that pitiful?"). Drew begins trading riffs with him, and they play the now-notorious "Dueling Banjos." Yet when Drew tries to shake the boy's hand after being outplayed by him, the boy refuses,

turning quickly away. This representation of hostility and disconnection, Beaton insists, "disregard[s] the novel's attention to human probability and complexity"— and, by implication, the novel's interest in suggesting the connections, psychic and otherwise, between the hill people and the canoers (Beaton 298).

32. Jameson 185.

33. Margie Burns, "*Easy Rider* and *Deliverance*, or, the Death of the Sixties," *University of Hartford Studies in Literature* 22.2–3 (1990): 45.

Daylanne English has pointed out to me that the terms "redneck" and "hillbilly" (or "hill people") have historically marked out two distinct categories of poor rural whites: the former understood as properly working class in their economic location, while the latter signifying a more subsistence-based form of existence largely outside the relations of industrialized labor. Thus, to refer to *Deliverance's* hill people as rednecks is to confuse their class identity. This confusion, though, shows up repeatedly in the film's reception, in which there is a persistent slippage between the two terms—a slippage that suggests the ways in which *Deliverance's* hill people were made to stand in for a broader, more general form of southern working-class identity.

34. Cobb 122.

35. Numan V. Bartley, *The New South, 1945–1980* (Louisiana State University Press and The Littlefield Fund for Southern History: The University of Texas, 1995), 217.

36. Cobb 148.

37. Ibid., 128.

38. Bartley 260–61.

39. "New Day A'Coming in the South," *Time*, May 31, 1971, 16.

40. Lerone Bennett Jr., "Old Illusions and New Souths," *Ebony*, August 1971, 35, quoted in Bartley 400.

41. "The South Today," *Time*, September 27, 1976, 29.

42. Marshall Frady, "Gone With the Wind," *Newsweek*, July 28, 1975, 11.

43. *The South as the New America*, special issue of *Saturday Review*, September 4, 1976, 1–68.

44. Reg Murphy, "Not Since Jefferson and Madison..." *Saturday Review*, September 4, 1976, 8.

45. Bartley 199–206.

46. Cobb 148.

47. For example, in his survey of Boorman's *oeuvre*, Michael Ciment claims that the man Ed kills "was, in all likelihood, a stranger to the incident; and Drew, in any case, was not shot" [Michael Ciment, *John Boorman*, trans. Gilbert Adair (London: Faber and Faber, 1986), 126], while Richard Schickel describes Drew as being "murdered in revenge," and the man Ed kills as "the remaining assailant" (Schickel, "White Water, Black Doings," 8).

48. My discussion of this scene is indebted to Linda Ruth Williams's, although she derives different conclusions from the ones I suggest here. See "Blood Brothers," *Sight and Sound* 4.9 (Sept. 1994): 16–19.

CHAPTER 3

1. Richard Thompson, "What's Your 10–20?" *Film Comment* 16.4 (July/Aug. 1980): 35.

2. See, for example, Ed Guerrero's discussion of this dynamic in "The Rise and Fall of Blaxploitation" in his *Framing Blackness: The African American Image in Film* (Philadelphia: Temple University Press, 1993), 69–111.

3. Jon Kraszewski, "Recontextualizing the Historical Reception of Blaxploitation: Articulations of Class, Black Nationalism, and Anxiety in the Genre's Advertisements," *Velvet Light Trap* 50 (Fall 2002): 48–61.

4. Cook 499; Frank Segers, "*Walking Tall* Fresh Proof A Distrib Should Resist 'Drop-Dead' Psychology," *Variety*, August 1, 1973, 16; Paul D. Zimmerman, "Support Your Local Sheriff," *Newsweek*, October 8, 1973, 99.

5. Thomas Doherty, *Teenagers and Teenpics: The Juvenilization of American Movies in the 1950s* (Boston: Unwin Hyman, 1988), 10.

6. Doherty 7; Margo Jefferson, "Attack of the Killer B's," *Newsweek*, August 1, 1977, 52.

7. Jefferson 52.

8. Jane Stern, *Trucker: A Portrait of the Last American Cowboy* (New York: McGraw-Hill, 1975).

9. Vincent Canby, "Truckers and Women," review of *Convoy*, directed by Sam Peckinpah, *New York Times*, June 28, 1978, late ed., C17. Similarly, Stanley Kauffman observed in his review of *White Line Fever* that "there are suggestions of the Western updated, [with] the lone trucker instead of the lone rancher fighting the cattle syndicate" (Kauffman, review of *White Line Fever*, directed by John Kaplan, *New Republic*, September 27, 1975, 53).

10. "Payoff for Terror on the Road," *Time*, February 18, 1974, 36.

11. Harry Maurer, "Organizing the 'Gypsies,'" *Nation*, January 11, 1975, 14.

12. "The New Highway Guerrillas," *Time*, December 17, 1973, 33.

13. Industry observers often pointed out that the average owner-operator could make more money as a unionized company driver; instead, the perceived freedoms (and implied status) of ownership and self-directed employment accounted for the decision to be an owner-operator. See D. Daryll Wyckoff and David H. Maister, *The Owner-Operator: Independent Trucker* (Lexington, Mass.: D.C. Heath and Co., 1976).

14. Stuart Hall, "Encoding, Decoding," *The Cultural Studies Reader*, ed. Simon During (New York: Routledge, 1993), 98.

15. Jane Stern described the typical owner-operator as "the hard core of independent trucking…he truly is the last American cowboy—a man whose freedom to move has no bounds" (36).

16. Philip Shabecoff, "Explosion in Worker's Demands: Labor Sees Decline in 'Real' Wages as Trigger," *New York Times*, December 30, 1973, late ed., sec.3, 11; "The Energy Peril to Labor Peace," *Business Week*, December 8, 1973, 33; "Why Sacrifice?" *New York Times*, December 26, 1973, late ed., 38.

17. Charles Michener, "Keep on Truckin'," review of *White Line Fever*, directed by Jonathan Kaplan, *Newsweek*, September 1, 1975, 61; Kauffman, review of *White Line Fever* 53; Richard Eder, "Sometimes Violence is Called For," *New York Times*, September 7, 1975, late ed., sec. 2, 7; Vincent Canby, "Why *Smokey and the Bandit* Is Making A Killing," *New York Times*, December 18, 1977, late ed, sec. 2, 13; "Murf," review of *Deliverance*, directed by John Boorman, *Variety*, July 19, 1972, 14.

18. *Billy Jack*, another politically ambiguous film that celebrates antiwar, countercultural pacifism in some moments and karate-fueled self-defense in others, has a complex marketing history itself, best recounted in Justin Wyatt, "From Roadshowing to Saturation Release: Majors, Independents, and Marketing/Distribution Innovations," *The New American Cinema*, ed. Jon Lewis (Durham, N.C.: Duke University Press, 1999), 73–78.

19. Segers, "*Walking Tall*," 16. The quotes from the film's advertisement are taken from *Variety*, May 9, 1973, 16.

20. Zimmerman, "Support," 99.

21. I am using the term "populism" here in Ernesto Laclau's sense, as a discourse that does not have a necessary class belonging, nor a necessary political (i.e., left or right) affiliation, but instead organizes the ideological field around the opposed poles of "the people" and "the power bloc." See Ernesto Laclau, *Politics and Ideology in Marxist Theory: Capitalism, Fascism, Populism* (London: New Left Books, 1977).

22. Peter Biskind, "Vigilantes, Power, and Domesticity: Images of the Fifties in *Walking Tall*," *Journal of Popular Film* 3.3 (Summer 1974): 220.

23. Biskind, "Vigilantes," 220. Of course, this "racial brotherhood" is ultimately tempered by the power dynamics of the two men's relationship: Buford is the sheriff, Obra the deputy. Still, the film makes a point of Buford's rejection of his father's hostility to Obra's affiliation with Black Power.

24. Biskind, "Vigilantes," 220–221.

25. Judith Crist, "Hick, Hack, Hokum, Ho-Hum," review of *Walking Tall*, directed by Phil Karlson, *New York*, February 18, 1974, 74; Jay Cocks, review of *Walking Tall*, directed by Phil Karlson, *Time*, May 21, 1973, 72; Pauline Kael, "The Street Western," review of *Walking Tall*, directed by Phil Karlson, *New Yorker*, February 25, 1974, 101.

26. Paul Hendrickson, "Films Called Southerns: This Corn Makes Plenty of Bread," *National Observer*, October 25, 1975, 1; Canby, "Why," 13. In a like manner, Richard Schickel, in his review of the sequel to *White Lightning, Gator* (1976), describes it as the kind of film that "must be ranked as poor white trash" ("White Trash," review of *Gator*, directed by Burt Reynolds, *Time*, September 20, 1976, 80).

27. Canby, "Why," 13; Kael, "Western," 106, 102.

28. With respect to body types and class identity (and resistance), see Pierre Bourdieu, *Distinction: A Social Critique of the Judgment of Taste*, trans. Richard Nice (Cambridge, Mass.: Harvard University Press, 1984), 177–208.

29. Lawrence Van Gelder, review of *Smokey and the Bandit*, directed by Hal Needham, *New York Times*, May 20, 1977, late ed., C8.

30. On the division of labor into mental and manual categories, see Harry Braverman, *Labor and Monopoly Capital: The Degradation of Work in the Twentieth Century* (New York: Monthly Review, 1974). Jacquelyn Southern and others have argued that "mental and manual labor cannot be assigned to the blue and white collar, respectively, as most occupations have aspects of both" ("Blue Collar, White Collar: Deconstructing Classification," in *Class and its Others*, eds. J. K. Gibson-Graham, Stephen A. Resnick, Richard D. Wolff (Minneapolis: University of Minnesota Press, 2000), 197). Yet I agree with John Frow's argument that what the "development of new class relations" under advanced capitalism accomplished was a transformation "of what *counts* as knowledge. The ideology of rationalized, 'scientific' management was decisive in this respect in that it defined 'manual' workers as lacking in relevant knowledge" (119, emphasis in original).

31. Richard Schickel, "Fun on the Farm," review of *Smokey and the Bandit*, directed by Hal Needham, *Time*, June 20, 1977, 73. Richard Schickel, "Dirty Eleven," review of *The Longest Yard*, directed by Robert Aldrich, *Time*, September 23, 1974, S2.

32. Stanley Kauffman's review of *Walking Tall* evinces its appeal in a similar way: "*Walking Tall* is a smash hit because it makes Supermen out of all of us Clark Kents..." ("Three of a Kind, Sort of," reviews of *Conrack*, directed by Martin Ritt, *Walking Tall*, directed by Phil Karlson, and *Blazing Saddles*, directed by Mel Brooks, *New Republic*, March 16, 1974, 20). The success of certain Southerns outside their original demographic is discussed in "Dixie and Sunbelt Potential Notable, Per *Smokey and the Bandit*," *Variety*, September 7, 1977, 32.

33. "Nuisance—or a Boon? The Spread of Citizens' Radios," *U.S. News & World Report*, September 29, 1975, 26.

34. Kenneth L. Woodward, "The Trucker Mystique," *Newsweek*, January 26, 1976, 45.

35. "The Bodacious New World of C.B.," *Time*, May 10, 1976, 78–79.

36. Harry Crews, "The Trucker Militant," *Esquire*, August 1977, 148, emphasis in original; Bonnie Angelo, "Those Good Ole Boys," *Time*, September 27, 1976, 47.

37. Crews 148, emphasis mine.

38. Maurer 11.

39. Woodward 44.

40. For example, *Convoy* director Sam Peckinpah was criticized by Vincent Canby for mixing these modes, having "neither the guts to play the movie straight as melodrama nor the sense of humor to turn it into a kind of *Smokey and the Bandit* comedy" ("Truckers" C17). Yet *Smokey and the Bandit*'s comedy, Andrew Horton argued, was compromised by the "straight romance" and "serious confrontations...so that the general tone of the film becomes an ambiguous one. These moments puncture the comic spirit and leave us unconvinced by the 'happy' ending" ("Hot Car Films & Cool Individualism, or, 'What we have here is a lack of respect for the law,'" *Cineaste* 8.4 (Summer 1978): 15). Such ambiguity was also noted in nontrucker Southerns: *White Lightning*'s narrative is described by *Variety* as "most often...on the meller side, [but] comedy overtones frequently appear even in the midst of dramatic

moments to give nice balance" ("Whit.," review of *White Lightning*, directed by John Sargent, *Variety*, June 6, 1973, 18); *Gator*, on the other hand, is faulted by Richard Schickel for its "awkward mix of moods": "The picture's basic ambience is rather larkish, but there are melodramatic sequences of near-Victorian sentimentality" ("White Trash" 83).

41. Erik Olin Wright, *Classes* (London: Verso, 1985), 19–63. As I explain in the introduction, Wright's conception of the middle classes differs in some key ways from that of the Ehrenreichs'. However, the theoretical grounds for this disagreement are more or less irrelevant to my argument here.

42. Johanna Brenner, "Work Relations and the Formation of Class Consciousness," *The Debate on Classes*, ed. Erik Olin Wright (New York: Verso, 1989), 184–190.

43. "Murf.," review of *White Line Fever*, directed by Jonathan Kaplan, *Variety*, July 16, 1975, 21. Of course, this claim would seem to be due, in part, to the imprecision of U.S. class terminology. Yet it is precisely this kind of inability to make a distinction between the situation of the film's character, who is marked as blue collar (down to his sartorial presentation), and that of the "middle class" that is telling.

44. Cook 355, 395.

45. Rick Setlowe, "Flee Dixie's 'Intimidation': Find 'Ole South' in California," *Variety*, March 4, 1970, 3, 24. *Brother John* is discussed in the article under its working title, *Kane*.

46. For accounts of this conflict, see Henry Hart, *James Dickey: The World as a Lie* (New York: Picador, 2000), 513–514, and "He Shouted Loud, 'Hosanna, Deliverance Will Come,'" *Foxfire* 7.4 (Winter 1973): 297–312.

47. Christopher Dickey, *Summer of Deliverance* (New York: Simon & Schuster, 1998), 180, 183.

48. See Phil Garner, "The Deliverance Syndrome," *Atlanta Journal and Constitution Magazine*, November 18, 1973, 16–24; Jerry Bledsoe, "What Will Save Us From Boredom?" *Esquire*, December 1973, 227–233; and "'He Shouted Loud" 307–312.

49. Reg Murphy, "Is *Deliverance* Good for Atlanta?" *Atlanta Constitution*, April 29, 1972, 4A.

50. Phyllis Funke, "How You Gonna Keep 'em Down in Hollywood After They've Seen the Sticks?" *New York Times*, September 22, 1974, late ed., sec. 2, 15.

51. Aida A. Hozic, *Hollyworld: Space, Power, and Fantasy in the American Economy* (Ithaca, N.Y.: Cornell University Press, 2001), 115.

52. B. Drummond Ayres Jr., "'Good Ole Boy' Stars in Dixie Film-Making Boom," *New York Times*, November 1, 1975, late ed., 31.

53. Funke 30.

54. "Teamsters Hit 'Location Lure,'" *Variety*, January 2, 1974, 5.

55. "AFTRA, SAG In Texas Face Block By Right-To-Work," *Variety*, June 5, 1974, 26.

56. Dave Kaufman, "IATSE Sues on Non-Union Films Pickup," *Variety*, July 17, 1974, 5, 18; Frank Segers, "IATSE's Year of Challenges and Revisions," *Variety*, January 8, 1975, 7.

57. Thomas M. Pryor, "Hollywood's Muted 1975; U.S. Feature Statistics Hidden, In Part, By Non-Union Films," *Variety*, January 7, 1976, 14.

58. "Hunt Urges Ongoing Boss-Worker Détente in U.S. Films Crisis," *Variety*, August 14, 1974, 4.

59. "A Right to 'Stop' Work in Mid-Filming?" *Variety*, March 8, 1978, 7; "Pic Labor Loses 'Option' As To Over-Time," *Variety*, May 24, 1978, 7.

60. "Actor in Non-Union *Seabo*; Tells SAG Carolina Law Okays," *Variety*, July 27, 1977: 5; "North Carolina, Owensby Reject SAG's Dictate," *Variety*, September 28, 1977, 2.

61. Earl Owensby, "North Carolina's 'Hollywood'; Producer Acts As His Own Star; 11 Films To Date, None in Red," *Variety*, January 3, 1979, 36.

62. Sheriff Buford Pusser, on whose life *Walking Tall* is based, "extracted the promise from [producer-writer Mort] Briskin that the film not portray the South as 'a place where everybody walks around uneducated and in overalls,'" (Zimmerman, "Support," 99). See also the account of *Buster and Billie*'s production in Funke 30.

63. Moody 100–101.

64. Michael Storper and Susan Christopherson, "The Effects of Flexible Specialization on Industrial Politics and the Labor Market: The Motion Picture Industry," *Industrial and Labor Relations Review* 42.3 (April 1989): 331–347. See also their "The Transition to Flexible Specialization in the U.S. Film Industry: External Economies, the Division of Labor, and the Crossing of Industrial Divides," *Cambridge Journal of Economics* 13 (June 1989): 273–305. Storper and Christopherson's work treats Hollywood's decentralized organization of production in the postwar period as an exemplar of post-Fordist political economy. While many have quibbled with their understanding of the Fordist/post-Fordist divide, though (see Murray Smith's excellent discussion of this topic in "Theses on the Philosophy of Hollywood History"), their arguments concerning the effects these developments have had on film workers—developments I review above—have gone unchallenged.

65. The percentage of unionized nonfarm workers fell from 1945's high of 35.5 percent to 23 percent by 1980 (Davis 146–147). Amazingly, union density in the already weakly organized South also fell from 17.1 percent in 1953 to 12.8 percent in 1978, despite the disproportionate rise in employment experienced by the region during the period (Moody 121).

66. Davis 162–63, 169, emphases in original.

67. Ibid., 175–177.

68. Quoted in Crawford 168.

69. Davis 227, 178, 198.

70. J. K. Gibson-Graham, Stephen A. Resnick, and Richard D. Wolff, "Class in a Poststructuralist Frame," in *Class and Its Others* 5, 10.

   The move toward discussing "distributive flows" might seem to be a move from the terrain of Marxism to that of Weberian social theory. However, I agree with Val Burris's suggestion that much of recent Marxist theory has incorporated many of Weber's insights while still maintaining a focus on class antagonism and contradiction—and has become more nuanced and effective in the process (see Burris, "The Neo-Marxist Synthesis of Marx and Weber on Class," *The Marx-Weber Debate*, ed. Norbert Wiley (Beverly Hills, Calif.: Sage, 1987), 67–90).

71. Adam Przeworski, *Capitalism and Social Democracy* (New York: Cambridge University Press, 1985), 79.

72. "South Today" 39; Angelo 47.

73. Woodward 44.

74. Crawford 168; Paul M. Weyrich, "Blue Collar or Blue Blood? The New Right Compared with the Old Right," ed. Robert Whitaker, *The New Right Papers* (New York: St. Martin's, 1982), 52. See also Michael Kazin, "The Conservative Capture: From Nixon to Reagan," *The Populist Persuasion* (New York: BasicBooks, 1995), 245–266.

75. See Todd Gitlin, *The Twilight of Common Dreams: Why America Is Wracked By Culture Wars* (New York: Henry Holt, 1995), and Richard Rorty, *Achieving Our Country: Leftist Thought in Twentieth Century America* (Cambridge, Mass.: Harvard University Press, 2000) for two versions of this argument. Again, this is not to say that "cultural" issues were not influential in the New Right's rise—far from it. Instead, I am arguing that we need to recognize the influence of class discourses in these campaigns, and their imbrication with various discourses of race, gender, and sexuality.

PART III

1. Brian Henderson, "Romantic Comedy Today: Semi-Tough or Impossible?" *Film Quarterly* 31.4 (Summer 1978): 19; Molly Haskell, *From Reverence to Rape: The Treatment of Women in the Movies* (New York: Holt, Rinehart and Winston, 1974), 28; David Denby, "Men Without Women, Women Without Men," *Harper's*, September 1973, 51.

2. Denby, "Men," 54.

3. Haskell 323–324.

4. Henderson, aside from a reference to the gay liberation movement as another social change influencing the making and reception of romantic comedy, does not discuss this issue.

5. Denby, "Men," 52, emphasis in original.

6. Haskell 24, 28.

7. Frank Rose, "Travolta Puts Out," *Village Voice*, December 19, 1977, 50.

8. Peter Biskind and Barbara Ehrenreich, "Machismo and Hollywood's Working Class," in *American Media and Mass Culture: Left Perspectives*, ed. Donald Lazare (Berkeley: University of California Press, 1987), 202.

9. Biskind and Ehrenreich 206.

10. Ibid., 215.

11. Michael Hardt and Antonio Negri, *Empire* (Cambridge, Mass.: Harvard University Press, 2000), 290, emphasis in original.

CHAPTER 4

1. Eric Breitbart, "Lost in the Hustle: An Interview with John Badham," *Cineaste* 9:2 (Winter 1978/79): 2–5, 57; Richard Corliss, "Saturday Night Cleaver," review of *Saturday Night Fever*, directed by John Badham, *New Times*, January 23, 1978, 64.

2. Walter Hughes, "Feeling Mighty Real: Disco as Discourse and Discipline," *Village Voice Rock & Roll Quarterly*, July 20, 1993, 7.

3. Hughes 10.

4. Dennis Altman, *The Homosexualization of America, The Americanization of the Homosexual* (New York: St. Martin's, 1982), 19.

5. *Fever* ranked third on the list of top box-office rentals for 1977, behind only the record-breaking *Star Wars* and *Close Encounters of the Third Kind* (Cook 501). In addition, the soundtrack album became the best-selling soundtrack in history ("Disco Takes Over," *Newsweek*, April 2, 1979, 56).

6. Maureen Orth, "Get Up and Boogie!" *Newsweek*, November 8, 1976, 96.

7. Sally Helgesen, "Disco," *Harper's*, October 1977, 20–24; "Discomania," *Forbes*, June 1, 1976, 47–49.

8. "Disco Takes Over" 56, 63.

9. Orth 95.

10. Helgesen 20, 21.

11. Hughes 10.

12. Albert Goldman, "The Disco Style: Love Thyself," *Esquire*, June 20, 1978, 77–78.

13. Nik Cohn, "Tribal Rites of the New Saturday Night," *New York*, June 7, 1976, 31–43.

14. Cohn, "Tribal Rites," 31.

15. Nik Cohn, "Saturday Night's Big Bang," *New York*, December 8, 1997, 32–34, 96. Of course, the Bay Ridge disco itself, populated mostly by Italian-American straights, did exist—although Cohn explains that "the craze started in black gay clubs" ("Big Bang" 33).

16. Ehrenreich, *Fear* 120.

17. Both quoted in Altman 146.

18. Ibid., 166, 96.

19. Helgesen 21.

20. Ehrenreich, *Fear*, 50–51.

21. David Ansen, "The Boogie Man," review of *Saturday Night Fever*, directed by John Badham, *Newsweek*, December 19, 1977, 65; Pauline Kael, "Nirvana," review of *Saturday Night Fever*, directed by John Badham, *New Yorker*, December 26, 1977, 60.

22. Ehrenreich, *Hearts*, 24.

23. Ibid., 128–129.

24. Kael, "Nirvana," 60.

25. Martin P. Levine, *Gay Macho: The Life and Death of the Homosexual Clone*, ed. Michael S. Kimmel (New York: New York University Press, 1998).

26. Levine 60.

27. Richard Dyer, "Getting Over the Rainbow: Identity and Pleasure in Gay Cultural Politics," *Silver Linings: Some Strategies for the Eighties*, eds. George Bridges and Rosalind Brunt (London: Lawrence & Wishart, 1981), 61.

28. Levine 59.

29. Altman 13–14.

30. Interestingly, the Village People were assembled by gay producer Jacques Morali as "a protest against Anita Bryant," a prominent antigay activist ("Disco Takes Over" 64).

31. Judith Butler, *Gender Trouble: Feminism and the Subversion of Identity* (New York: Routledge, 1990), 151n6.

32. Kael, "Nirvana," 59.

33. Juan A. Suárez, *Bike Boys, Drag Queens, and Superstars: Avant-Garde, Mass Culture, and Gay Identities in the 1960s Underground Cinema* (Bloomington: Indiana University Press, 1996), 178.

34. Suárez 148.

35. "The film, in both a striking and mocking fashion, conveys Tony's narcissistic pre-disco ritual with images straight out of Kenneth Anger's underground, homosexual-cum-biker film, *Scorpio Rising*" (Al Auster and Leonard Quart, review of *Saturday Night Fever*, directed by John Badham, *Cineaste* 8.4 (Summer 1978): 36).

36. My critique of Butler here is informed by that of Susan Bordo (review of *Gender Trouble*, by Judith Butler, *Feminist Studies* 18.1 (Spring 1992): 159–176), and Leo Bersani's related critique of the more general "gender performance as subversion" argument ("Is the Rectum a Grave?" *AIDS: Cultural Analysis/ Cultural Activism*, ed. Douglas Crimp (Cambridge: MIT Press, 1988), 197–222).

37. Susan Bordo, *The Male Body: A New Look at Men in Public and Private* (New York: Farrar, Straus and Giroux, 1999), 198.

38. D. A. Miller, *Bringing Out Roland Barthes* (Berkeley: University of California Press, 1992), 30–31, emphasis in original.

39. Jeff Yanc, "'More Than A Woman': Music, Masculinity, and Male Spectacle in *Saturday Night Fever* and *Staying Alive*," *Velvet Light Trap* 38 (Fall 1996): 42.

40. Miller 28–29, emphasis in original.

41. Ibid., 31, emphasis in original.

42. It is not enough to point to the heterosexual plot of the film—both Denby and Haskell's discussions of the "decline of heterosexuality" included films with heterosexual interactions and relationships. The "problem," as they saw it, was that the relationships between men seemed to overshadow these heterosexual elements.

43. Yanc 43.

44. Ibid., 47.

45. In fact, what seems to link disco to nonnormative sexuality in Albert Goldman's anti-disco screed is its aura of narcissism: "Outside the entrance to every discotheque should be erected a statue to the presiding deity: Narcissus" (77).

46. Bordo 200.

47. Ansen, "Boogie Man," 65; Frank Rich, "Discomania," review of *Saturday Night Fever*, directed by John Badham, *Time*, December 19, 1977, 69. Stanley Kauffman, for his part, calls Tony a "flat-stomached, good-hearted, frustrated, vain and clever cockerel" ("Local Colors," review of *Saturday Night Fever*, directed by John Badham, and *Blue Collar*, directed by Paul Schrader, *New Republic*, February 11, 1978, 24). Note as well Auster and Quart's reference to Tony's narcissism cited in note 35.

48. Jenny Taylor and David Laing, "Disco-Pleasure-Discourse: On 'Rock and Sexuality'" *Screen Education* 31 (Summer 1979): 44.

49. Andrew Sarris, "Ethnic Fever," review of *Saturday Night Fever*, directed by John Badham, *Village Voice*, December 26, 1977, 41.

50. Levine 61. Levine notes that this strategy was often one of survival: "One might want to imitate that presentational style of masculinity, but one may not have wanted to confront it in real life. That might be dangerous" (62).

51. Kael, "Nirvana," 59, emphasis mine.

52. Corliss, "Cleaver," 64.

53. Molly Haskell, "High Travoltage," review of *Saturday Night Fever*, directed by John Badham, *New York*, January 9, 1978, 64; Corliss, "Cleaver," 64.

54. Corliss, "Cleaver," 64. In a similar if more negative vein, Philip Terzian asserted that "an archaeologist of the future will wonder how [the 1935 Astaire-Rogers film] *Top Hat* and *Saturday Night Fever* could have been made in the same century" ("Polyester Dreams," *Harper's*, May 1978, 89).

55. Haskell, "Travoltage," 64.

56. Laura Mulvey, "Visual Pleasure and Narrative Cinema," *Visual and Other Pleasures* (Bloomington: Indiana University Press, 1989), 14–26.

57. See my "The Gaze at Work: Knowledge Relations and Class Spectatorship" (forthcoming).

Chapter 5

1. Molly Haskell, "Exposing a Nerve," review of *Looking for Mr. Goodbar*, directed by Richard Brooks, *New York*, October 31, 1977, 116.

2. Roger Angell, "Mean Streets," review of *Cruising*, directed by William Friedkin, *New Yorker*, February 18, 1980, 127.

3. Robin Wood, "The Incoherent Text: Narrative in the 70s," *Hollywood from Vietnam to Reagan* (New York: Columbia University Pres: 1986), 47.

4. Rich, "Discomania," 69; Ansen, "Boogie Man," 65.

5. Haskell, "Nerve," 116.

6. Tracy Johnson notes that, since Quinn's parents and close friends would not talk to Fosburgh, "she had to piece her story together from bystanders, a bartender who was also her friend, and an old college roommate" ("Who Else Is Looking for Mr. Goodbar?" *Ms.*, February 1978, 24).

7. Haskell argued further that *Goodbar* "takes into account, as almost no other American film has, the necessarily antagonistic points of view in the sexual commodities exchange" ("Nerve" 119).

8. See, for example, E. Ann Kaplan, "Forms of Phallic Domination in the Contemporary Hollywood Film: Brooks's *Looking for Mr. Goodbar*," *Women & Film: Both Sides of the Camera* (New York: Routledge, 1983), 73–82, and Pauline Kael, "*Goodbar*, or How Nice Girls Go Wrong," review of *Looking for Mr. Goodbar*, directed by Richard Brooks, *New Yorker*, October 24, 1977, 147–150.

9. Richard Corliss, "A Morality Tale for Man-haters," review of *Looking for Mr. Goodbar*, directed by Richard Brooks, *New Times*, October 20, 1977, 74–75; Colin L. Westerbeck Jr., "Women of the Year," *Commonweal* 105, February 3, 1978, 82.

10. Virtually every review of the film noted how, as Betsy Erkkila put it, "Brooks accentuates the split between the daytime professional, Miss Dunn, and the nighttime hussy, Terry" (review of *Looking for Mr. Goodbar*, directed by Richard Brooks, *Cineaste* 8.3 (Winter 1977/78): 43).

11. See, for example, Mimi Abramovitz, *Regulating the Lives of Women: Social Welfare Policy from Colonial Times to the Present* (Boston: South End, 1988), particularly chapter 10, "Aid to Families With Dependent Children: Single Mothers in the Twentieth Century" (313–348).

12. Vincent Canby, "*Goodbar* Turns Sour," review of *Looking for Mr. Goodbar*, directed Richard Brooks, *New York Times*, October 20, 1977, C19; Erkkila 44.

13. Kaplan 79, emphasis in original. Kaplan admits later in the essay that James "has not really seemed to be 'the nice man' that the narrative requires" (81), but she fails to acknowledge the severity of James's pathologies, or the way they are analogous to Tony's.

14. Joan Mellen, "The Return of Women to Seventies Films" *Quarterly Review of Film Studies* 3.4 (Fall 1978): 536.

15. Frank Rich, "Diane in the Rough," review of *Looking for Mr. Goodbar*, directed by Richard Brooks, *Time*, October 24, 1977, 104.

16. John Simon, "Double Whammy," review of *Looking for Mr. Goodbar*, directed by Richard Brooks, *National Review*, December 9, 1977, 1443.

17. Corliss, "Man-haters," 74–75, emphasis in original.

18. Wood 57; Haskell, "Nerve," 118. John Simon notes that "even people who haven't read the book know that this girl gets killed," so the film seems to "make a guessing game out of which one of her outlandish men will do her in" ("Double Whammy" 1443).

19. Of course, those who read Rossner's novel would also know that she is actually killed by Gary. Yet the significant differences between James's character in the novel and the film make it at least plausible that, in the filmed version of the narrative, he (James) might be the murderer—especially since Richard Brooks hinted at making significant changes in the film from the novel, which he confessed to disliking; see Aljean Harmetz, "Will *Mr. Goodbar* Make Voyeurs of Us All?" *New York Times*, July 24,

1977, late ed., sec. 2, 1, and "Dialogue on Film: Richard Brooks," *American Film* (Oct. 1977): 33–48.

20. Erkkila 44.

21. Kael, "*Goodbar*," 150, 147.

22. Ibid., 150.

23. The anguished panic that registers in Gary when Theresa asks him to have sex with her—and his dialogue while he tries to give himself an erection ("In my neighborhood, if you didn't fight, you were a fruit. In prison, if you didn't fight, you spread ass")—underlines both his sexual orientation and his panicked relationship to it. He eventually does achieve an erection, but only after beating Theresa; he then rapes her, and finally stabs her to death.

24. Kaplan 81.

25. Kael, "*Goodbar*," 147.

26. Bryan Bruce, "Madness, Pleasure, & Transgression: *Looking for Mr. Goodbar*," *CineAction!* 2 (Fall 1985): 13.

27. Wood 58.

28. Jack Kroll, "Nightcrawl," review of *Looking for Mr. Goodbar*, directed by Richard Brooks, *Newsweek*, October 24, 1977, 126.

29. Geoffrey Nowell-Smith, "Minnelli and Melodrama," *Home Is Where the Heart Is: Studies in Melodrama and the Woman's Film*, ed. Christine Gledhill (London: British Film Institute, 1987), 70–74.

30. I am indebted to Bruce's article for pointing this scene out. And while we had seen Gary and his lover earlier in the film in the gay bar scene, they were not yet marked as important characters, and thus the sequence in which they argue is the first time they appear as characters who are apparently necessary to the plot.

31. Nowell-Smith notes that "often the 'hysterical' moment of the text can be identified as the point at which the realist representative convention breaks down" (74). This scene, of course, does adhere to the conventions of realism, but as I note, it does violate the more particular representational conventions of the film.

32. Cohn, "Tribal Rights," 31–32.

33. Rich, "Discomania," 69. In a similar vein, Haskell, after declaring the dancing sequences of the film "dazzling," asked "if the highly disciplined patterns of dance and uniform and hierarchical bonding don't satisfy some primitive need once filled by the army, even down to the ritualized expressions of violence, honorable and otherwise" ("Travoltage" 64).

34. Rita Felski has rightly pointed out to me that the pleasure PMC observers may take in spectacles of violent working-class masculinity can be quite different for men and women. While I largely agree with this, I also point out, in my analysis of *Cruising* in particular, moments in which male observers may partake in the masochistic desire with respect to violent working-class men that seems at times to motivate *Goodbar*'s Theresa, in addition to their presumed identification with such figures.

35. Simon Watney, "Hollywood's Homosexual World," *Screen* 23.3–4 (Sept./Oct. 1982): 110–11.
36. In a way, the scene seems to echo the opening sequence of director William Friedkin's 1970 film, *The Boys in the Band* (a notorious example of pre-Stonewall representations of gay experience), in which Michael, one of the main characters, races around Fifth Avenue in preparation for a party. The contrast between the self-hating, effeminate characters of that film and the swaggering, hypermasculine gay men of *Cruising* is a telling indication of the transformation of gay male identity after Stonewall.
37. Indeed, a shot from earlier in the film is interpolated into this sequence—a shot of an earlier murder victim lying naked on his stomach, and looking over his shoulder at the killer.
38. Watney 111. It should be noted that Watney's argument against *Cruising* is more theoretically sophisticated than most, but his complaints echo those of the film's many detractors.
39. Vito Russo, "*Cruising*: The Controversy Continues," *New York*, August 13–20, 1979, 46.
40. Janet Maslin, "Friedkin Defends His *Cruising*," *New York Times*, September 18, 1979, late ed., C12.
41. Russo 46; Maslin C12.
42. Daniel Harris, *The Rise and Fall of Gay Culture* (New York: Hyperion, 1997), 180–81. Harris's work tends to be uneven—it is often laced with overly broad, undersupported, and tendentiously argued claims—but his account of the early stages of gay male S/M culture is consonant with other, less concisely written descriptions of this history.
43. Quoted in Elizabeth Cowie, "Fantasia," *Representing the Woman: Cinema and Psychoanalysis* (Minneapolis: University of Minnesota Press, 1997), 125.
44. Leo Bersani, *Homos* (Cambridge, Mass.: Harvard University Press, 1995), 89. I should note that Bersani himself is somewhat suspicious of the liberatory claims for S/M, but he does acknowledge the parodic power of its practices.
45. Pat Califia, "A Secret Side of Lesbian Sexuality," *S and M: Studies in Sadomasochism*, eds. Thomas Weinberg and G. W. Levi Kamel (Buffalo, N.Y.: Prometheus, 1983), 135.
46. Wood 63.
47. David Savran, *Taking It Like a Man: White Masculinity, Masochism, and Contemporary American Culture* (Princeton, N.J.: Princeton University Press, 1998), 216.
48. Bersani, *Homos*, 84. Friedkin, in a 1998 interview, described one entire sequence excised by censors, which he claimed "remains my favorite scene I've ever shot," involving two cops playing Liars Poker, in which one cop tells the other that the winner gets to paddle the loser with his nightstick. The cop who suggests this deal is then seen trying to lose; when he does, he demands to be paddled, pulling down his pants and spreading his legs while leaning against a patrol car. While being paddled, he exhorts his fellow cop to "Do it harder!" Friedkin argues that the scene was cut because it was "a direct attack on authority" (Mark Kermode, "Cruise Control," *Sight and Sound* 8.11 (Nov. 1998): 23).

49. David Ansen, "Hell Bent for Leather," review of *Cruising*, directed by William Friedkin, *Newsweek*, February 18, 1980, 92.

50. David Denby, "Flesh for Fantasy," review of *Cruising*, directed by William Friedkin, *New York*, March 3, 1980, 72.

51. Vincent Canby, "Pacino Stars in Friedkin's *Cruising*," review of *Cruising*, directed by William Friedkin, *New York Times*, February 15, 1980, late ed., C6.

52. Robert Hatch, review of *Cruising*, directed by William Friedkin, *Nation*, February 23, 1980, 218. It should be noted that Hatch attributes the "obscenely infantile messing around" to Friedkin's attempt "to offend almost anyone, whatever his or her erotic inclination"—which, to my mind, is more about Hatch's desire to universalize his disgust than anything else.

53. Denby, "Flesh," 72.

54. Frank Rich, "Cop-Out in a Dark Demimonde," review of *Cruising*, directed by William Friedkin, *Time*, February 18, 1980, 67.

55. Canby, "Pacino," C6.

56. Angell 126.

57. In yet another allusion to the intense homosocial energy of the police force, Edelson responds, "I need you. You're my partner and you can't let me down. We're up to our ass in this."

58. In this way, the film utilizes the same "genre bending" strategy that Friedkin deployed in making the more successful (in virtually every sense of the term) *The French Connection* (1971). As Todd Berliner explains, in contrast to a "genre breaking" film, which "loudly broadcasts its violation of tradition, inviting audiences to join in the film's efforts to expose, and often mock, genre conventions," a "genre bending" film "relies on the viewers' habitual responses to generic codes, thereby misleading them to expect a conventional outcome. The film seems true to form at first, then, like a booby trap, it catches the spectator off guard" (Todd Berliner, "The Genre Film as Booby Trap: 1970s Genre Bending and *The French Connection*," *Cinema Journal* 40.3 (Spring 2001): 25).

59. See Jean-Louis Baudry, "Ideological Effects of the Basic Cinematographic Apparatus," in *Narrative, Apparatus, Ideology*, ed. Philip Rosen (New York: Columbia University Press, 1986), 286–298.

60. Bersani, "Rectum," 212.

61. Friedkin explained that these frames were added in the editing process "mainly as a snub to the censors who kept telling us we had to cut down the number of stab wounds. I thought they were fools, so as we were carrying out the cuts I got Bud Smith [the editor] to drop in a couple of frames from a hardcore pornographic film each time a knife enters flesh" (Kermode 24).

62. Rather than conceive of fantasy as merely the wish for a desired object, "fantasy involves, is characterized by, not the achievement of desired objects, but the arranging of, a setting out of, desire; a veritable mise en scène of desire" (Cowie 133). As Laplanche and Pontalis argue, "in fantasy, the subject does not pursue its object or its

sign: he appears caught up in the sequence of images....The subject, although always present in fantasy, may be so in desubjectivised form, that is to say, in the very syntax of the sequence in question" (quoted in Cowie 133). Cowie illustrates this point by discussing Freud's "A Child is Being Beaten," in which, during the various renditions of the fantasy, the subject identifies with the father beating a child, the child being beaten by the father, and an observer watching the beating scene. (Cowie 135).

63. Cowie 134.

64. Donald Symons, *The Evolution of Human Sexuality* (New York: Oxford University Press, 1979), 304, 301.

65. "The Gay World's Leather Fringe," *Time*, March 24, 1980, 74–75.

66. John Stoltenberg, "Sadomasochism: Eroticized Violence, Eroticized Powerlessness," *Against Sadomasochism: A Radical Feminist Analysis*, ed. Robin Ruth Linden, Darlene R. Pagano, Diana E. H. Russell, Susan Leigh Star (East Palo Alto, Calif.: Frog in the Well, 1982), 124–125.

67. Levine 63–65. An episode of *The Simpsons* makes a witty reference to this practice: When Homer wishes to ensure his son Bart's heterosexuality, he takes him to a steel mill. The butch, muscular male employees are soon discovered to be gay, and as the whistle blows signaling the end of the workday, the mill becomes a nightclub (with a sign reading "The Anvil"), and the steelworkers begin dancing with each other.

68. Ansen, "Hell Bent," 92.

69. Angell 126.

70. Canby, "Pacino," C6.

71. On *Fever*'s location work, see Tom Burke, "Struttin' His Stuff," *Rolling Stone*, 15 June 1978, 72–77; on *Goodbar*'s, see Corliss, "Man-haters," "Dialogue on Film: Richard Brooks," and John Mariani, "Richard Brooks Directs *Looking for Mr. Goodbar*," *Millimeter* July/Aug. 1977: 24–30; on *Cruising*'s, see Nat Segaloff, *Hurricane Billy: The Stormy Life and Films of William Friedkin* (New York: William Morrow, 1990).

72. Burke 77.

73. Kelly Hankin, "Lesbian Locations: The Production of Lesbian Bar Space in *The Killing of Sister George*," *Cinema Journal* 41.1 (Fall 2001): 3–27.

74. See Michael Hardt and Antonio Negri, *Empire* (Cambridge, Mass.: Harvard University Press, 2000), 280–300.

75. Hardt and Negri 285–286.

76. Michael Hardt, "Affective Labor," *Boundary 2* 26.2 (Summer 1999): 97.

77. Ibid., 89, 95.

78. Matthew Tinkcom, *Working Like a Homosexual: Camp, Capital, Cinema* (Durham, N.C.: Duke University Press, 2002), 10, 11, 12; for Tinkcom's discussion of the Garland number, see 57–59.

79. Eve Kosofsky Sedgwick, *The Epistemology of the Closet* (Berkeley: University of California Press, 1990), 154, quoted in Tinkcom 46.

80. Arthur Bell noted that "whistles and noisemakers" had been used to disrupt "filming of *Cotton Comes to Harlem* [1970] on Harlem streets. Protesters claimed that *Cotton*

depicted blacks in a stereotypical and negative manner" ("The Hollywood Hassle," *Village Voice*, September 3, 1979, 32).

81. Arthur Bell, "Bell Tells" column, *Village Voice*, July 16, 1979, 36.
82. Richard Goldstein, "Why the Village Went Wild," *Village Voice*, August 6, 1979, 1, 16, 18.
83. Segaloff 200.
84. Arthur Bell, "Bells Tells" column, *Village Voice*, July 30, 1979, 36.
85. Segaloff 209.
86. Goldstein wrote that about twenty extras quit during filming (16).
87. Alexander Wilson, "Friedkin's *Cruising*, Ghetto Politics, and Gay Sexuality," *Social Text* 4 (Fall 1981): 103.
88. Johnson then said, "I remember thinking, 'Give me back your voucher, pal, you expect me to pay for that?'" (quoted in Segaloff 201). Vito Russo also reported on the actual, nonsimulated sexual activity on the set (46, 49).
89. Edward Guthmann, "The *Cruising* Controversy: William Friedkin vs. the Gay Community," *Cineaste* 10.3 (Summer 1980): 6.
90. Lee Smith, "Hard Times Come to Steeltown," *Fortune*, December 1977, 87.
91. Bill Nichols, "*Strike* and the Question of Class," in *The Hidden Foundation: Cinema and the Question of Class*, eds. David E. James and Rick Berg (Minneapolis: University of Minnesota Press, 1996), 82. Nichols's account of Eisenstein's depiction of the utopian possibilities of workers, and their homoerotic figurations, has significantly informed my discussion of *Cruising*'s extras.
92. Biskind and Ehrenreich 215.
93. Bersani, "Rectum," 209, emphasis in original.

CONCLUSION

1. Sally Robinson, *Marked Med: White Masculinity in Crisis* (New York: Columbia University Press, 2000), 6.
2. Robinson 190, 9.
3. In fact, Creed even denigrates his own status as a boxer in favor of professional labor. During an interview, he addresses the camera and says, "Stay in school and use your brain. Be a doctor, be a lawyer, carry a leather briefcase. Forget about sports as a profession. Sports make you grunt and smell. See, be a thinker, not a stinker."
4. David Denby, "Good Ol' Girl Meets David Dubinsky," review of *Norma Rae*, directed by Martin Ritt, *New York*, March 12, 1979, 72–73.
5. Biskind, *Easy Riders*, 348.
6. Mark Patrick Carducci, "Interview with Paul Schrader," *Millimeter* February 1979: 71. The capitalization of "Blacks" is in the original.
7. Schrader's early success as a screenwriter—he was twenty-seven when he sold the screenplay for *The Yakuza* (1974), for $300,000—caused him to be identified as one of

the Film Generation's rising talents (Richard Thompson, "Screenwriter: *Taxi Driver's* Paul Schrader," *Film Comment* 12.2 (Mar./Apr. 1976): 6).

8. See James A. Geschwender, *Class, Race, and Worker Insurgency: The League of Revolutionary Black Workers* (New York: Cambridge University Press, 1977) for a thoughtful and thorough history of this organization.

9. Moody 98. See also Geschwender 190–98. Both authors note that many of the wildcatters were physically assaulted by the UAW officials during the confrontation.

10. Geschwender 127–152.

11. On the student-worker makeup of the group, see Geschwender 87–102.

12. Geschwender 138, 216–218.

13. Geschwender 199–205; Moody 88–92. "30 and Out" sought the right to retirement and a pension after thirty years of labor, no matter the worker's age.

14. Nicolaus Mills, "The Unions and the Mobs," *Dissent* 26.1 (Winter 1979): 98. Harvey Swados was a socialist and author of, among other things, *On the Line* (1957), a short story collection about auto workers.

15. Richard Schickel, "Union Dues," review of *Blue Collar*, directed by Paul Schrader, *Time*, February 13, 1978, 66.

16. Vincent Canby, "On the Auto Front," review of *Blue Collar*, directed by Paul Schrader, *New York Times*, February 10, 1978, C5; Stanley Kauffman, "Local Colors," reviews of *Saturday Night Fever*, directed by John Badham, and *Blue Collar*, directed by Paul Schrader, *New Republic*, February 11, 1978, 25.

17. Quoted in "*Blue Collar*: Detroit Moviegoers Have Their Say." *Cineaste* 8.4 (Summer 1978): 28.

18. "Hollywood and the Working Class: A Discussion," with Al Auster, Lynn Garafola, Dan Georgakas, Leonard Quart, and Fred Siegel, *Socialist Review* 9.4 (July/Aug. 1979): 111.

19. Gary Crowdus and Dan Georgakas, "*Blue Collar*: An Interview with Paul Schrader," *Cineaste* 8.3 (Winter 1977/78): 34; Terry Curtis Fox, "The Shameless Cinema of Paul Schrader," *Village Voice*, February 27, 1978, 31.

20. Mills 99; Pauline Kael, "The Cotton Mather of the Movies," review of *Blue Collar*, directed by Paul Schrader, *New Yorker*, Feb. 27, 1978, 84.

21. Michael Omi, "Race Relations in *Blue Collar*," *Jump Cut* 26 (Dec. 1981): 7–8, emphasis in original.

22. See, for example, Judith Stein's analysis of this dilemma in the steel industry during the 1970s and 1980s in *Running Steel, Running America* (Chapel Hill: University of North Carolina Press, 1998).

23. Omi 8.

24. Ibid., 7.

25. See Geschwender 128–29, 138–139.

26. Charles Higham, "When I Do It, It's Not Gore, Says Writer Paul Schrader," *New York Times*, February 5, 1978, D15.

27. One might argue that this turn in the narrative also speaks to a more conflicted position regarding organized labor on Schrader's part: he told *Cineaste* that he thought

of the Oreo Gang's robbery as "a wonderfully self-hating kind of act" because it was an "attack [on] the organization that's supposed to help them," which implies that he nonetheless sees unions as institutions which protect and defend working-class interests. (Crowdus and Georgakas, "*Blue Collar*," 34).

28. Kauffman, "Local Colors," 25; Andrew Sarris, "Off the Assembly Line: One Lemon, One Authentic Model," reviews of *The Betsy*, directed by Daniel Petrie, and *Blue Collar*, directed by Paul Schrader, *Village Voice*, February 27, 1978, 32.

29. Crowdus and Georgakas, "*Blue Collar*," 37.

30. Vincent Canby, "'Norma Rae': Mill-Town Story," review of *Norma Rae*, directed by Martin Ritt, *New York Times*, March 2, 1979, C10.

31. Henry P. Leifermann, "Trouble in the South's First Industry: The Unions are Coming," *New York Times Magazine*, August 5, 1973, 10.

32. Canby, "'Norma Rae,'" C10.

33. Penelope Gilliatt, review of *Norma Rae*, directed by Martin Ritt, *New Yorker*, March 19, 1979, 128.

34. Andrew Sarris, "Heaven Praise the Working Girl," review of *Norma Rae*, directed Martin Ritt, *Village Voice*, March 5, 1979, 39; Denby, "Good Ol' Girl," 73.

35. Denby, "Good Ol' Girl," 73.

36. Sarris, "Working Girl," 39.

37. Nicolaus Mills, "Engaging Norma Rae: A Journal," *Dissent* 26 (Fall 1979): 481–82. For a similar set of concerns, see Jackie Wolf, "*Crystal Lee Jordan, Testimony, The Inheritance*: Filmmakers Take On J. P. Stevens," *Jump Cut* 22 (May 1980): 8, 24, 37.

38. Quoted in Aljean Harmetz, "Martin Ritt Focuses on Labor Strife," *New York Times*, February 25, 1979, D1.

39. Quoted in Robert Brent Toplin, "*Norma Rae*: Unionism in an Age of Feminism," *Labor History* 36.2 (Spring 1995): 287; quoted in Pat Aufderheide, review of *Norma Rae*, directed Martin Ritt, *Cineaste* 9.3 (Spring 1979): 43.

40. Toplin 288–290, 296–98. See also Elizabeth Stone, "'Norma Rae': The Story They Could Have Told," *Ms.*, May 1979, 28–33.

41. Both Aufderheide and Stone note that the feminism of Norma Rae's character is qualified by the fact that it develops under the Pygmalion-like guidance of Reuben. Furthermore, it cannot go unmentioned that the film features almost no signs of solidarity between women—that Norma Rae's feminist self-determination is in no way realized through an alliance with the other, similarly situated female characters.

42. Richard Schickel, "Strike Busting," review of *Norma Rae*, directed by Martin Ritt, *Time*, March 12, 1979, 76; Stanley Kauffman, "Well-Organized Labor," review of *Norma Rae*, directed by Martin Ritt, *New Republic*, March 17, 1979, 24–25; Harmetz, "Labor Strife"; Sarris, "Working Girl"; Canby, "'Norma Rae'"; Denby, "Good Ol' Girl" (David Dubinsky was the longtime leader of the International Ladies' Garment Workers' Union (ILGWU)).

43. See Kauffman "Labor," and Denby "Good Ol' Girl."

44. Gilliatt, review of *Norma Rae*, 128.

45. Denby, "Good Ol' Girl," 73.

46. Harmetz, "Labor Strife," D1.

47. Sarris, "Working Girl," 39.

48. Schickel, "Strike Busting," 76.

49. Toplin 284.

50. Edward Benson and Sharon Hartman Strom, "Crystal Lee, Norma Rae, and All Their Sisters," *Film Library Quarterly* 12 (1979): 18, 22.

51. Gilliatt, review of *Norma Rae*, 128. Marcy Rein, writing in the feminist newspaper *off our backs*, also praised the film for avoiding "the bourgeois angst that's passed off as sophistication" in its depiction of the protagonist (review of *Norma Rae*, directed by Martin Ritt, *off our backs*, April 30, 1979, 23).

52. Sharlene Hagy Hesse-Biber and Gregg Lee Carter, *Working Women in America: Split Dreams* (New York: Oxford University Press, 2005), 141–46, 21.

53. David A. Cook, *History of the American Cinema, Vol. 9: Lost Illusions: American Cinema in the Shadow of Watergate and Vietnam, 1970–1979*, Charles Harpole, gen. ed. (New York: Scribner's, 2000), 502.

54. See, for example, Elaine Attias and Mimi White, "How Patricia Resnick Came to Write the Script of '9 to 5,'" *Ms.*, January 1981, 44–46. For a brief history of 9to5, see Karen Nussbaum, "Working Women's Insurgent Consciousness," *The Sex of Class: Women Transforming American Labor*, ed. Dorothy Sue Cobble (Ithaca, N.Y.: Cornell University Press, 2007), 159–76. It is unclear if the film's title was meant as an explicit reference to the activist group's name.

55. Karen Nussbaum, Interview, "Women Clerical Workers and Trade Unionism," *Socialist Review* 10.1 (Jan.–Feb. 1980): 157.

56. Georgia Dullea, "Secretaries See Parallels in 'Nine to Five,'" *New York Times*, January 2, 1981, A14.

57. Dullea A14. It should be noted that *Norma Rae* did indeed "rally the workers": Crystal Lee Jordan took advantage of her newfound fame as the "real" Norma Rae to promote the Amalgamated Clothing and Textile Workers Union's boycott of J. P. Stevens, and in fact Stevens signed an agreement with the union in 1980—a year after *Norma Rae*'s release—that recognized the ACTWU as the union representative of the employees in many Stevens plants (Toplin 290–291).

58. David Ansen, "Get the Boss," review of *9 to 5*, directed by Colin Higgins, *Newsweek*, December 22, 1980, 72–73.

59. Michael Sragow, "Small Triumphs Over the Formula," reviews of *9 to 5*, directed by Colin Higgins, *Inside Moves*, directed by Richard Donner, *Altered States*, directed by Ken Russell, and *The Idolmaker*, directed by Taylor Hackford, *Rolling Stone*, February 5, 1981, 37.

60. Andrew Sarris, "The Silly Season," reviews of *9 to 5*, directed by Colin Higgins, and *The Mirror Crack'd*, directed by Guy Hamilton, *Village Voice*, December 24, 1980, 41; Stanley Kauffman, "Old But New, New But Old," reviews of *Let There Be Light*, directed by John Huston, and *9 to 5*, directed by Colin Higgins, *New Republic*, January 31, 1981, 21;

Richard Corliss, "Stenos, Anyone?" review of *9 to 5*, directed by Colin Higgins, *Time*, December 22, 1980, 73.

61. Kauffman argues that "Parton would have had to be mentally defective to wear dresses like that on the job" ("Old but New" 21), while Sarris refers to her as the "not-completely innocent office tease" ('Silly Season" 41), and Canby mocks her for wearing "sweaters two sizes too small and pretends to be utterly surprised when men make passes at her" ("'Nine to Five': Office Comedy," *New York Times*, December 19, 1980, C20).

62. One of the subtlely transgressive elements of the film is the fact that a son sharing illegal drugs with his mother is presented as a sign of their healthy relationship.

63. Pauline Kael, "Tramont's Mirror, Women à la Mode," reviews of *All Night Long*, directed by Jean-Claude Tramont, *Caddie*, directed by Donald Crombie, *The Incredible Shrinking Woman*, directed by Joel Schumacher, and *9 to 5*, directed by Colin Higgins, *New Yorker*, March 9, 1981, 113; David Denby, "Blissed Out," reviews of *Altered States*, directed by Ken Russell, *9 to 5*, directed by Colin Higgins, *Tess*, directed by Roman Polanski, and *The Formula*, directed by John G. Avildsen, *New York*, December 22, 1980, 62.

64. Kauffman, "Old But New," 21; Corliss, "Stenos," 73; Denby "Blissed Out," 62.

65. Of course, the workers here are not *fully* in control: the company's CEO, Russell Tinsworthy (Sterling Hayden), is still in charge. Interestingly, he approves of almost of the women's changes, but he resists their plan for an "equal pay" policy—a central feminist demand of the period.

66. Sarris, "Silly Season," 41.

67. Canby, "'Nine to Five,'" C20.

68. Kael, "Women à la Mode," 112.

69. David Roediger, *Towards the Abolition of Whiteness* (New York: Verso, 1994), 17.

Afterword

1. Verlyn Klinkenborg, "The Roughneck," *New York Times Magazine*, September 30, 2001, 24.

2. Bruce Nussbaum, "Real Masters of the Universe," *Business Week*, October 1, 2001, 55.

3. Klinkenborg 24; Nussbaum 55.

4. Quoted in Patricia Leigh Brown, "Heavy Lifting Required: The Return of Manly Men," *New York Times*, October 28, 2001, late ed., sec. 4, 5.

5. Brown 5. One wonders if the coverage of the Fire Department of New York tended to outpace that of the Police Department (who also lost many members of their force on September 11) because of the fact that the FDNY is 93 percent white and has only thirty-three female firefighters on a force of 11,000, as opposed to the NYPD, which is 65 percent white with 6,200 women among its 39,000 members. See Jessica Seigel, "Firefighter Chic," *Village Voice*, November 6, 2001, 49–51.

6. Nussbaum 55.

7. Brown 5.

8. I hasten to note that I do not take, as some ultraleft commentators do, the September 11 attacks to be something that socialist critics of U.S. hegemony and global capitalism should find salutary in any way. There are many reasons to oppose U.S. hegemony and global capitalism, but those cited by the al-Qaeda terrorists are, for the most part, elements of political and cultural modernity that any socialist would want to support.

9. Of course, staff sergeant is not, strictly speaking, as proletarianized a position within the Marine Corps as, say, private; however, this position in the military is usually represented cinematically as embodying a working-class ethos, since the sergeants are noncommissioned officers who serve as a link between the common soldier and the officers.

10. Rebecca Liss, "Oliver Stone's *World Trade Center* Fiction: How the Rescue Really Happened," *Slate*, August 9, 2006, http://www.slate.com/id/2147350/.

11. Klinkenborg 24.

12. Nussbaum 55.

13. *The Guys* was released on only fifteen screens in the United States, http://www .boxofficemojo.com/movies/?id=guys.htm.

WORKS CITED

Abbott, Carl. "New West, New South, New Region: The Discovery of the Sunbelt." In *Searching for the Sunbelt: Historical Perspectives on a Region*. Edited by Raymond A. Mohl, 7–24. Knoxville: University of Tennessee Press, 1990.

Abramovitz, Mimi. *Regulating the Lives of Women: Social Welfare Policy from Colonial Times to the Present*. Boston: South End, 1988.

"Actor in Non-Union *Seabo*; Tells SAG Carolina Law Okays." *Variety*, Jul. 27, 1977, 5.

"Actors Go 'Underground' At Own Peril." *Variety*, March 12, 1969, 5.

"AFTRA, SAG In Texas Face Block By Right-To-Work." *Variety*, June 5, 1974, 26.

Allen, Robert C., and Douglas Gomery. *Film History: Theory and Practice*. New York: Knopf, 1985.

Altman, Dennis. *The Homosexualization of America: The Americanization of the Homosexual*. New York: St. Martin's, 1982.

Amman, John. "The Transformation of Industrial Relations in the Motion Picture and Television Industries: Craft and Production." In *Under the Stars: Essays on Labor Relations in Arts and Entertainment*. Edited by Lois S. Gray and Ronald L. Seeber, 113–155. Ithaca, N.Y.: Cornell University Press, 1996.

Angell, Roger. "Mean Streets." Review of *Cruising*, directed by William Friedkin. *New Yorker*, February 18, 1980, 126–28.

Angelo, Bonnie. "Those Good Ole Boys." *Time*, September 27, 1976, 47.

Ansen, David. "The Boogie Man." Review of *Saturday Night Fever*, directed by John Badham. *Newsweek*, December 19, 1977, 65.

———. "Get the Boss." Review of *9 to 5*, directed by Colin Higgins. *Newsweek* December 22, 1980, 72–73.

———. "Hell Bent for Leather." Review of *Cruising*, directed William Friedkin. *Newsweek*, February 18, 1980, 92.

Armour, Robert. "*Deliverance*: Four Variations of the American Adam." *Literature/Film Quarterly* 1.3 (July 1973): 280–85.

Arnold, Gary. Review of *Joe*, directed by John G. Avildsen. In Denby, *Film 70/71*, 43–49.

Aronowitz, Stanley. *False Promises: The Shaping of American Working Class Consciousness*, 2nd ed. Durham, N.C.: Duke University Press, 1992.

———. *From the Ashes of the Old: American Labor and America's Future*. New York: Houghton Mifflin, 1998.

Arsenault, Raymond. "The End of the Long Hot Summer: The Air Conditioner and Southern Culture." In *Searching for the Sunbelt: Historical Perspectives on a Region*. Edited by Raymond A. Mohl, 176–211. Knoxville: University of Tennessee Press, 1990.

Attias, Elaine, and Mimi White. "How Patricia Resnick Came to Write the Script of '9 to 5.'" *Ms.*, January 1981, 44–46.

Aufderheide, Pat. Review of *Norma Rae*, directed Martin Ritt. *Cineaste* 9.3 (Spring 1979): 42–43.

Auster, Al, and Leonard Quart. Review of *Saturday Night Fever*, directed by John Badham. *Cineaste* 8.4 (Summer 1978): 36–37.

Ayres, B. Drummond, Jr. "'Good Ole Boy' Stars in Dixie Film-Making Boom." *New York Times*, November 1, 1975, 31.

Bachmann, Gideon, Shirley Clarke, James Degangi, Adolfas Mekas, Jonas Mekas, Lew Clyde Stoumen, and Willard Van Dyke. Round-table Discussion. "Film Unions and the Low-Budget Independent Film Production—An Exploratory Discussion." *Film Culture* 22–23 (Summer 1961): 134–150.

Baker, C. Edwin. *Advertising and a Democratic Press*. Princeton, N.J.: Princeton University Press, 1994.

Balio, Tino. "'A Major Presence in All of the World's Important Markets': The Globalization of Hollywood in the 1990s." In *Contemporary Hollywood Cinema*. Edited by Steve Neale and Murray Smith, 58–73. New York: Routledge, 1998.

———. "Retrenchment, Reappraisal, and Reorganization, 1948—." In *The American Film Industry*, rev. ed. Edited by Tino Balio, 401–447. Madison: University of Wisconsin Press, 1985.

Bartley, Numan V. *The New South, 1945–1980*. Louisiana State University Press and The Littlefield Fund for Southern History: The University of Texas, 1995.

Baudry, Jean-Louis. "Ideological Effects of the Basic Cinematographic Apparatus." In *Narrative, Apparatus, Ideology*, by Philip Rosen, 286–298. New York: Columbia University Press, 1986.

Beaton, James F. "Dickey Down the River." In *The Modern American Novel and the Movies*. Edited by Gerald Peary and Roger Shatzkin, 293–306. New York, Frederick Ungar: 1978.

Bell, Arthur. "Bell Tells" column. *Village Voice*, July 16, 1979, 36.

———. "Bells Tells" column. *Village Voice*, July 30, 1979, 36.

———. "The Hollywood Hassle." *Village Voice*, September 3, 1979, 30–33.

Bennett, Lerone, Jr. "Old Illusions and New Souths." *Ebony*, August 1971, 35–40.

Benson, Edward, and Sharon Hartman Strom. "Crystal Lee, Norma Rae, and All Their Sisters." *Film Library Quarterly* 12 (1979): 18–23.

Berliner, Todd. "The Genre Film as Booby Trap: 1970s Genre Bending and *The French Connection*." *Cinema Journal* 40.3 (Spring 2001): 25–46.

Bersani, Leo. *Homos*. Cambridge, Mass.: Harvard University Press, 1995.

———. "Is the Rectum a Grave?" In *AIDS: Cultural Analysis/ Cultural Activism*. Edited by Douglas Crimp, 197–222. Cambridge, Mass.: MIT Press, 1988.

Bigart, Homer. "War Foes Here Attacked by Construction Workers: City Hall is Stormed." *New York Times*, May 9, 1970, late ed., 1.

Biskind, Peter. *Easy Riders and Raging Bulls: How the Sex-Drugs-and-Rock'n'Roll Generation Saved Hollywood*. New York: Simon & Schuster, 1998.

———. "Vigilantes, Power, and Domesticity: Images of the Fifties in *Walking Tall*." *Journal of Popular Film* 3.3 (Summer 1974): 219–229.

Biskind, Peter, and Barbara Ehrenreich. "Machismo and Hollywood's Working Class." In *American Media and Mass Culture: Left Perspectives*. Edited by Donald Lazare, 210–215. Berkeley: University of California Press, 1987.

Bledsoe, Jerry. "What Will Save Us From Boredom?" *Esquire*, December 1973, 227–233.

"*Blue Collar*: Detroit Moviegoers Have Their Say." *Cineaste* 8.4 (Summer 1978): 28–31.

Blue Collar. Directed by Paul Schrader. Universal, 1978.

"The Blue Collar Worker's Lowdown Blues." *Time*, November 9, 1970, 68–76.

Bluestone, Barry, and Bennett Harrison. The Deindustrialization of America: Plant Closings, Community Abandonment, and the Dismantling of Basic Industry. New York: Basic Books, 1982.

"Bob Altman Raps Studios' Overload of 'Non-Skilled.'" *Variety*, April 22, 1970, 5.

Bobo, Jacqueline. *Black Women as Cultural Readers*. New York: Columbia University Press, 1995.

"The Bodacious New World of C.B." *Time*, May 10, 1976, 78–79.

Bordo, Susan. Review of *Gender Trouble*, by Judith Butler. *Feminist Studies* 18.1 (Spring 1992): 159–176.

———. *The Male Body: A New Look at Men in Public and Private*. New York: Farrar, Straus and Giroux, 1999.

Bordwell, David, Janet Staiger, and Kristin Thompson. *The Classical Hollywood Cinema: Film Style & Mode of Production to 1960*. New York: Columbia University Press, 1985.

Bourdieu, Pierre. *Distinction: A Social Critique of the Judgment of Taste*. Trans. Richard Nice. Cambridge, Mass.: Harvard University Press, 1984.

Box Office Mojo. The Guys. Accessed February 1, 2008, http://www.boxofficemojo.com/movies/?id=guys.htm.

The Boys in the Band. Directed by William Friedkin. National General Pictures, 1970.

Brackman, Jacob. Review of *Five Easy Pieces*, directed by Bob Rafelson. In Denby, *Film 70/71*, 33–39.

Braverman, Harry. *Labor and Monopoly Capital: The Degradation of Work in the Twentieth Century*. New York: Monthly Review, 1974.

Breaker! Breaker! Directed by Don Hulette. Worldwide/AIP. 1977.

Breckenfeld, Gurney. "Business Loves the Sunbelt (And Vice Versa)." *Fortune*, June 1977, 132–146.

Breitbart, Eric. "Lost in the Hustle: An Interview with John Badham." *Cineaste* 9.2 (Winter 1978/79): 2–5.

Brenner, Johanna. "Work Relations and the Formation of Class Consciousness." In *The Debate on Classes*. Edited by Erik Olin Wright, 184–190. New York: Verso, 1989.

Brooks, Tim and Earle Marsh. *The Complete Directory to Prime Time Network TV Shows: 1946-Present*, rev. ed. New York: Ballantine, 1981.

Brown, Patricia Leigh. "Heavy Lifting Required: The Return of Manly Men." *New York Times*, October 28, 2001, late ed., sec. 4, 5.

Brownell, Blaine A. "Introduction." In *Searching for the Sunbelt: Historical Perspectives on a Region*. Edited by Raymond A. Mohl, 1–6. Knoxville: University of Tennessee Press, 1990.

Bruce, Bryan. "Madness, Pleasure, & Transgression: *Looking for Mr. Goodbar*." *CineAction!* 2 (Fall 1985): 7–13.

Buckland, Warren. "A Close Encounter with *Raiders of the Lost Ark*: Notes on Narrative Aspects of the New Hollywood Blockbuster." In *Contemporary Hollywood Cinema*. Edited by Steve Neale and Murray Smith, 166–177. New York: Routledge, 1998.

Burns, Margie. "*Easy Rider* and *Deliverance*, or, the Death of the Sixties." *University of Hartford Studies in Literature* 22.2–3 (1990): 44–58.

Burris, Val. "Class Structure and Political Ideology." *The Insurgent Sociologist* 14.2 (Summer 1987): 5–46.

——. "The Neo-Marxist Synthesis of Marx and Weber on Class." In *The Marx-Weber Debate*. Edited by Norbert Wiley, 67–90. Beverly Hills, Calif.: Sage, 1987.

Butler, Judith. Gender Trouble: Feminism and the Subversion of Identity. New York: Routledge, 1990.

Califia, Pat. "A Secret Side of Lesbian Sexuality." *S and M: Studies in Sadomasochism*. Edited by Thomas Weinberg and G. W. Levi Kamel, 129–136. Buffalo, N.Y.: Prometheus, 1983.

Campbell, Gregg M. "Beethoven, Chopin, and Tammy Wynette: Heroines and Archetypes in *Five Easy Pieces*." *Film/Literature Quarterly* 2 (1974): 275–283.

Canby, Vincent. "*Goodbar* Turns Sour." Review of *Looking for Mr. Goodbar*, directed by Richard Brooks. *New York Times*, October 20, 1977, late ed., C19.

——. "'Nine to Five': Office Comedy." *New York Times*, December 19, 1980, late ed., C20.

——. "'Norma Rae': Mill-Town Story." Review of *Norma Rae*, directed by Martin Ritt. *New York Times*, March 2, 1979, C10.

——. "On the Auto Front." Review of *Blue Collar*, directed by Paul Schrader. *New York Times*, February 10, 1978, late ed., C5.

——. "Pacino Stars in Friedkin's *Cruising*." Review of *Cruising*, directed by William Friedkin. *New York Times*, February 15, 1980, late ed., C6.

——. "Playing On Our Prejudices." Review of *Joe*, directed by John G. Avildsen. *New York Times*, August 2, 1970, late ed., sec. 2, 1.

———. "Truckers and Women." Review of *Convoy*, directed by Sam Peckinpah. *New York Times*, June 28, 1978, late ed., C17.

———. "Why *Smokey and the Bandit* Is Making A Killing." *New York Times*, December 18, 1977, late ed., sec. 2, 13.

Carducci, Mark Patrick. "Interview with Paul Schrader." *Millimeter* (Feb. 1979): 60–72.

Ciment, Michael. *John Boorman*. Translated by Gilbert Adair. London: Faber and Faber, 1986.

Clark, Danae. *Negotiating Hollywood: The Cultural Politics of Actors' Labor*. Minneapolis: University of Minnesota Press, 1995.

Clarke, John, Stuart Hall, Tony Jefferson, and Brian Roberts. "Subcultures, Cultures and Class: A Theoretical Overview." In *Resistance Through Rituals: Youth Subcultures in Post-War Britain*. Edited by Stuart Hall and Tony Jefferson, 9–74. London: Hutchinson, 1976.

Clover, Carol. *Men, Women, and Chainsaws: Gender in the Modern Horror Film*. Princeton, N.J.: Princeton University Press, 1992.

Cobb, James C. *The Selling of the South: The Southern Crusade for Industrial Development, 1936–1990*. Chicago: University of Illinois Press, 1993.

Cocks, Jay. "Rites of Passage." Review of *Deliverance*, directed by John Boorman. *Time*, August 7, 1972, 75–76.

———. Review of *Walking Tall*, directed by Phil Karlson. *Time*, May 21, 1973, 72.

Cohen, Phil. "Sub-Cultural Conflict and Working Class Community." In *Culture, Media, Language: Working Papers in Cultural Studies, 1972–79*. Edited by Stuart Hall et al., 78–87. London: Hutchinson, 1980.

Cohn, Nik. "Saturday Night's Big Bang." *New York*, December 8, 1997, 32–34.

———. "Tribal Rites of the New Saturday Night." *New York*, June 7, 1976, 31–43.

Convoy. Directed by Sam Peckinpah. United Artists, 1978.

Cook, David A. *History of the American Cinema, Vol. 9: Lost Illusions: American Cinema in the Shadow of Watergate and Vietnam, 1970–1979*, gen. ed. Charles Harpole. New York: Scribner's, 2000.

Cooper, Mark Garrett. *Love Rules: Silent Hollywood and the Rise of the Managerial Class*. Minneapolis: University of Minnesota Press, 2003.

Corliss, Richard. "A Morality Tale for Man-haters." Review of *Looking for Mr. Goodbar*, directed by Richard Brooks. *New Times*, October 28, 1977, 74–75.

———. "Saturday Night Cleaver." Review of *Saturday Night Fever*, directed by John Badham. *New Times*, January 23, 1978, 64–65.

———. "Stenos, Anyone?" Review of *9 to 5*, directed by Colin Higgins. *Time*, December 22, 1980, 73.

Corrigan, Timothy. "Auteurs and the New Hollywood." In *The New American Cinema*. Edited by Jon Lewis, 38–63. Durham, N.C.: Duke University Press, 1998.

———. *A Cinema Without Walls: Movies and Culture After Vietnam*. New Brunswick, N.J.: Rutgers University Press, 1991.

Coward, Rosalind. "Class, 'Culture,' and the Social Formation." *Screen* 18.1 (Spring 1977): 75–105.

Cowie, Elizabeth. "Fantasia." In *Representing the Woman: Cinema and Psychoanalysis*, 123–165. Minneapolis: University of Minnesota Press, 1997.

———. "Storytelling: Classical Hollywood Cinema and Classical Narrative." In *Contemporary Hollywood Cinema*. Edited by Steve Neale and Murray Smith, 178–190. New York: Routledge, 1998.

Crawford, Alan. *Thunder on the Right: The "New Right" and the Politics of Resentment*. New York: Pantheon, 1980.

Crews, Harry. "The Trucker Militant." *Esquire*, August 1977, 82–84.

Crist, Judith. "Hick, Hack, Hokum, Ho-Hum." Review of *Walking Tall*, directed by Phil Karlson. *New York*, February 18, 1974, 74–75.

Crowdus, Gary, and Dan Georgakas. "*Blue Collar*: An Interview with Paul Schrader." *Cineaste* 8.3 (Winter 1977/78): 34–37.

Cruising. Directed by William Friedkin. Lorimar/UA, 1980.

Davis, Mike. *Prisoners of the American Dream: Politics and Economy in the History of the U.S. Working Class*. New York: Verso, 1986.

Decter, Midge. *Liberal Parents, Radical Children*. New York: Coward, McGann & Geoghegan, 1975.

De Curtis, Anthony. "Martin Scorsese." *Rolling Stone*, November 1, 1990, 58–65.

Deliverance. Directed by John Boorman. Warner Bros., 1972.

DeMott, Benjamin. "The 'More Life' School and James Dickey." Review of *Deliverance*, directed by James Dickey. *Saturday Review*, March 28, 1970: 25–26.

Denby, David. "Blissed Out." Reviews of *Altered States*, directed by Ken Russell, *9 to 5*, directed by Colin Higgins, *Tess*, directed Roman Polanski, and *The Formula*, directed by John G. Avildsen. *NewYork*, December 22, 1980, 60–62.

———, ed. *Film 70/71*. New York: Simon & Schuster, 1971.

———. "Flesh for Fantasy." Review of *Cruising*, directed by William Friedkin. *New York*, March 3, 1980, 72–73.

———. "Good Ol' Girl Meets David Dubinsky." Review of *Norma Rae*, directed by Martin Ritt. *NewYork*, March 12, 1979, 72–73.

———. "Men Without Women, Women Without Men." *Harper's*, September 1973, 51–54.

———. "New York Blues." Reviews of *Joe*, directed by John G. Avildsen, and *Diary of a Mad Housewife*, directed by Frank Perry. *Atlantic*, November 1970, 104–8.

"Dialogue on Film: Richard Brooks." *American Film*, October 1977, 33–48.

Diawara, Manthia. "Black Spectatorship: Problems of Identification and Resistance." *Screen* 29.4 (Autumn 1988): 66–76.

Dickey, Christopher. *Summer of Deliverance*. New York: Simon & Schuster, 1998.

Dickey, James. *Deliverance*. New York: Bantam Doubleday Dell, 1970.

———. *Deliverance (Screenplay)*. Carbondale: Southern Illinois University Press, 1982.

Dimock, Wai Chee, and Michael T. Gilmore. "Introduction." In *Rethinking Class: Literary Studies and Social Formations*. Edited by Wai Chee Dimock and Michael T. Gilmore, 1–11. New York: Columbia University Press, 1994.

"Discomania." *Forbes*, June 1, 1976, 47–49.

"Disco Takes Over." *Newsweek*, April 2, 1979, 56–64.

"Dixie and Sunbelt Potential Notable, Per *Smokey and the Bandit*." *Variety*, September 7, 1977, 32.

Doherty, Thomas. *Teenagers and Teenpics: The Juvenilization of American Movies in the 1950s*. Boston: Unwin Hyman, 1988.

Dullea, Georgia. "Secretaries See Parallels in 'Nine to Five.'" *New York Times*, January 2, 1981, late ed., A14.

Dyer, Richard. "Getting Over the Rainbow: Identity and Pleasure in Gay Cultural Politics." In *Silver Linings: Some Strategies for the Eighties*. Edited by George Bridges and Rosalind Brunt, 53–67. London: Lawrence & Wishart, 1981.

——. "White." *Screen* 29.4 (Autumn 1988): 44–65.

Easthope, Antony. "The Trajectory of *Screen*, 1971–79." In *The Politics of Theory: Proceedings of the Essex Conference on the Sociology of Literature, July 1982*. Edited by Francis Barker et al., 121–133. Colchester, U.K.: University of Essex Press, 1983.

Easy Rider. Directed by Dennis Hopper. BBS/Columbia, 1969.

"'Easy Rider' Biz Sparks NABET Use by Coast Indies." *Variety*, October 22, 1969, 6.

Eder, Richard. "Sometimes Violence is Called For." *New York Times*, September 7, 1975, late ed., sec. 2, 7.

Egerton, John. *The Americanization of Dixie: The Southernization of America*. New York: Harper & Row, 1974.

Ehrenreich, Barbara. *Fear of Falling: the Inner Life of the Middle Class*. New York: HarperCollins, 1989.

——. *The Hearts of Men: American Dreams and the Flight from Commitment*. New York: Doubleday, 1983.

Ehrenreich, Barbara and John Ehrenreich. "The Professional-Managerial Class." In *Between Labor and Capital*. Edited by Pat Walker, 5–45. Boston: South End, 1979.

Elsaesser, Thomas. "American Auteur Cinema: The Last—or First—Picture Show?" In *The Last Great American Picture Show: New Hollywood Cinema in the 1970s*. Edited by Thomas Elsaesser, Noel King, and Alexander Horwath, 37–69. Amsterdam: Amsterdam University Press, 2004.

——. "The Pathos of Failure: American Films in the '70s." *Monogram* 6 (1975): 13–19.

"The Energy Peril to Labor Peace." *Business Week*, December 8, 1973, 33–34.

"The Entertainment Unions: A Progress Report." *Monthly Labor Review* 88:11 (Nov. 1965): 3–4.

Erkkila, Betsy. Review of *Looking for Mr. Goodbar*, directed by Richard Brooks. *Cineaste* 8.3 (Winter 1977/78): 43–45.

Everett, Michael. E-mail to the Author. August 16, 1999.

Farber, Stephen. "*Deliverance*—How It Delivers." *New York Times*, August 20, 1972, late ed., sec. 2, 9.

——. "L.A. Journal." *Film Comment* (May/June 1976): 2–3.

Felski, Rita. "Those Who Disdain Cultural Studies Don't Know What They're Talking About." *Chronicle of Higher Education*, July 23, 1999, B6–7.

Fiske, John. *Understanding Popular Culture*. New York: Routledge, 1989.

Five Easy Pieces. Directed by Bob Rafelson. BBS/Columbia, 1970.

Fox, Terry Curtis. "The Shameless Cinema of Paul Schrader." *Village Voice*, February 27, 1978, 29–32.

Frady, Marshall. "Gone With the Wind." *Newsweek*, July 28, 1975, 11.

French, Warren. "'The Southern': Another Lost Cause?" In *The South and Film*. Edited by Warren French, 3–13. Jackson: University Press of Mississippi, 1981.

Frow, John. *Cultural Studies and Cultural Value*. New York: Oxford University Press, 1995.

Funke, Phyllis. "How You Gonna Keep 'em Down in Hollywood After They've Seen the Sticks?" *New York Times*, September 22, 1974, late ed., sec. 2, 15.

Gaines, Jane. "White Privilege and Looking Relations: Race and Gender in Feminist Film Theory." *Screen* 29.4 (Autumn 1988): 12–27.

Galbraith, John Kenneth. *The New Industrial State*, 2nd ed. Boston: Houghton, 1985.

Gardiner, John. "The Below-the-Line Unions." *Television*, December 1967, 44–47.

Garner, Phil. "The Deliverance Syndrome." *Atlanta Journal and Constitution Magazine*, November 18, 1973, 16–24.

"The Gay World's Leather Fringe." *Time*, March 24, 1980, 74–75.

Gelmis, Joseph. *The Film Director as Superstar*. Garden City, N.Y.: Doubleday, 1970.

Geschwender, James A. *Class, Race, and Worker Insurgency: The League of Revolutionary Black Workers*. New York: Cambridge University Press, 1977.

Gessner, Robert. "Youth Locked Out at the Film Gate." *Variety*, January 6, 1965, 25.

Getting Straight. Directed by Richard Rush. Columbia, 1970.

Gibson-Graham, J. K., Stephen A. Resnick, and Richard D. Wolff, eds. *Class and Its Others*. Minneapolis: University of Minnesota Press, 2000.

——. "Introduction: Class in a Poststructuralist Frame." In *Class and Its Others*. Edited by J. K. Gibson-Graham, Stephen A. Resnick, and Richard D. Wolff, 1–22. Minneapolis: University of Minnesota Press, 2000.

Gilliatt, Penelope. Review of *Deliverance*, directed by John Boorman. *New Yorker*, August 5, 1972: 52–53.

——. Review of *Norma Rae*, directed by Martin Ritt, *New Yorker*, March 19, 1979, 128.

——. "Study of an American Black Sheep." Review of *Five Easy Pieces*, directed by Bob Rafelson. *New Yorker*, September 19,1970, 101–103.

Gitlin, Todd. *The Twilight of Common Dreams: Why America Is Wracked By Culture Wars*. New York: Henry Holt, 1995.

Gold, Ronald. "Never-Be-The-Same IATSE: Close Votes and Wide Discontent." *Variety*, July 29, 1970, 7.

Goldman, Albert. "The Disco Style: Love Thyself." *Esquire*, June 20, 1978, 76–78.

Goldstein, Richard. "Why the Village Went Wild." *Village Voice*, August 6, 1979, 1.

Goodman, Mark. "Jonah in a Hard Hat." Review of *Joe*, directed by John G. Avildsen. *Time*, July 27, 1970, 68.

The Graduate. Directed by Mike Nichols. Embassy Pictures, 1967.

Griffith, James J. "Damned If You Do and Damned If You Don't: James Dickey's *Deliverance.*" *Post-Script: Essays in Film and the Humanities* 5.3 (Spring/Summer 1986): 47–59.

Guerrero, Ed. "The Rise and Fall of Blaxploitation." *Framing Blackness: The African American Image in Film*, 69–111. Philadelphia: Temple University Press, 1993.

Guthmann, Edward. "The *Cruising* Controversy: William Friedkin vs. the Gay Community." *Cineaste* 10.3 (Summer 1980): 2–8.

The Guys. Directed by Jim Simpson. Focus Features, 2002.

Hall, Stuart. "Cultural Studies and the Centre: Some Problematics and Problems." In *Culture, Media, Language: Working Papers in Cultural Studies, 1972–79.* Edited by Stuart Hall et al., 15–47. London: Hutchinson, 1980.

———. "Encoding, Decoding." In *The Cultural Studies Reader.* Edited by Simon During, 90–103. New York: Routledge, 1993.

———. "Notes on Deconstructing 'the Popular.'" In *People's History and Socialist Theory.* Edited by Raphael Samuel, 227–240. London: Routledge, 1981.

———. "Race, Articulation, and Societies Structured in Dominance." In *Black British Cultural Studies: A Reader.* Edited by Houston A. Baker Jr., Manthia Diawara, and Ruth H, Lindeborg, 16–60. Chicago: University of Chicago Press, 1996.

Hall, Stuart et al., eds. *Culture, Media, Language: Working Papers in Cultural Studies, 1972–79.* London: Hutchinson, 1980.

Halle, David. *America's Working Man: Work, Home, and Politics among Blue-Collar Property Owners.* Chicago: University of Chicago Press, 1984.

Hankin, Kelly. "Lesbian Locations: The Production of Lesbian Bar Space in *The Killing of Sister George.*" *Cinema Journal* 41.1 (Fall 2001): 3–27.

"The Hard Hats." *Newsweek*, May 25, 1970, 34–35.

Hardt, Michael. "Affective Labor." *Boundary 2* 26.2 (Summer 1999): 89–100.

Hardt, Michael, and Antonio Negri. *Empire.* Cambridge, Mass.: Harvard University Press, 2000.

Harmetz, Aljean. "Martin Ritt Focuses on Labor Strife." *New York Times*, February 25, 1979, late ed., D1.

———. "Will *Mr. Goodbar* Make Voyeurs of Us All?" *New York Times*, July 24, 1977, late ed., sec. 2, 1.

Harris, Daniel. *The Rise and Fall of Gay Culture.* New York: Hyperion, 1997.

Hart, Henry. *James Dickey: The World as a Lie.* New York: Picador, 2000.

Haskell, Molly. "Exposing a Nerve." Review of *Looking for Mr. Goodbar*, directed by Richard Brooks. *New York*, October 31, 1977, 116–19.

———. *From Reverence to Rape: The Treatment of Women in the Movies.* New York: Holt, Rinehart and Winston, 1974.

———. "High Travoltage." Review of *Saturday Night Fever*, directed by John Badham. *New York*, January 9, 1978, 64–65.

Hatch, Robert. Review of *Cruising*, directed by William Friedkin. *Nation*, February 23, 1980, 218.

Hebdige, Dick. *Subculture: The Meaning of Style.* New York: Routledge, 1988.

Helgesen, Sally. "Disco." *Harper's,* October 1977, 20–24.

Henderson, Brian. "Romantic Comedy Today: Semi-Tough or Impossible?" *Film Quarterly* 31.4 (Summer 1978): 11–23.

Hendrickson, Paul. "Films Called Southerns: This Corn Makes Plenty of Bread." *National Observer,* October 25, 1975, 1.

"He Shouted Loud, 'Hosanna, Deliverance Will Come.'" *Foxfire* 7:4 (Winter 1973): 297–312.

Hesse-Biber, Sharlene Hagy, and Gregg Lee Carter. *Working Women in America: Split Dreams.* New York: Oxford University Press, 2005.

Higham, Charles. "When I Do It, It's Not Gore, Says Writer Paul Schrader." *New York Times,* February 5, 1978, D15.

Hoberman, J. *The Dream Life: Movies, Media, and the Mythology of the Sixties.* New York: New Press, 2003.

Hobsbawm, Eric. *The Age of Extremes: A History of the World, 1914–1991.* New York: Vintage, 1994.

Hoffman, Peter, and Jim Purdy. "The Worker and Hollywood." *Cineaste* 9.1 (Fall 1978): 8–13.

"Hollywood and the Working Class: A Discussion." With Al Auster, Lynn Garafola, Dan Georgakas, Leonard Quart and Fred Siegel, *Socialist Review* 9.4 (July/Aug. 1979): 109–121.

Horne, Gerald. *Class Struggle in Hollywood, 1930–1950: Moguls, Mobsters, Stars, Reds, & Trade Unionists.* Austin: University of Texas Press, 2001.

Horton, Andrew. "Hot Car Films & Cool Individualism, or, 'What we have here is a lack of respect for the law.'" *Cineaste* 8.4 (Summer 1978): 12–15.

Horwath, Alexander. "The Impure Cinema: New Hollywood, 1967–1976." In *The Last Great American Picture Show: New Hollywood Cinema in the 1970s.* Edited by Thomas Elsaesser, Noel King, and Alexander Horwath, 9–17. Amsterdam: Amsterdam University Press, 2004.

Howe, Louise Kapp. "Introduction." In *The White Majority: Between Poverty and Affluence.* Edited by Louise Kapp Howe, 3–9. New York: Random House, 1970.

Hozic, Aida A. *Hollyworld: Space, Power, and Fantasy in the American Economy.* Ithaca, N.Y.: Cornell University Press, 2001.

Hughes, Walter. "Feeling Mighty Real: Disco as Discourse and Discipline." *Village Voice Rock & Roll Quarterly,* July 20, 1993, 7–11.

"Hunt Urges Ongoing Boss-Worker Détente in U.S. Films Crisis." *Variety,* August 14, 1974, 4.

"H'wood Craft Unions Dissatisfied With IATSE Concessions; Prod. Lags." *Variety,* June 24, 1970, 4.

"H'wood's Production Slump Sparks Record Drop in Craft Employment." *Variety,* January 21, 1970, 5.

Izod, John. *Hollywood and the Box Office, 1895–1986.* New York: Columbia University Press, 1988.

James, David E., and Rick Berg, eds. *The Hidden Foundation: Cinema and the Question of Class*. Minneapolis: University of Minnesota Press, 1996.

James, David E. "Introduction: Is There Class in This Text?" In *The Hidden Foundation: Cinema and the Question of Class*. Edited by David E. James and Rick Berg, 1–25. Minneapolis: University of Minnesota Press, 1996.

Jameson, Fredric. "The Great American Hunter, or, Ideological Content in the Novel." *College English* 34.2 (Nov. 1972): 180–199.

Jefferson, Margo. "Attack of the Killer B's." *Newsweek*, August 1, 1977, 52.

Joe. Directed by John G. Avildsen. Cannon, 1970.

Johnson, Tracy. "Who Else is Looking for Mr. Goodbar?" *Ms.*, February 1978, 24–26.

Kael, Pauline. "The Cotton Mather of the Movies." Review of *Blue Collar*, directed by Paul Schrader. *New Yorker*, February 27, 1978, 84–87.

———. "*Goodbar*, or How Nice Girls Go Wrong." Review of *Looking for Mr. Goodbar*, directed by Richard Brooks. *New Yorker*, October 24, 1977, 147–150.

———. "Nirvana." Review of *Saturday Night Fever*, directed by John Badham. *New Yorker*, December 26, 1977, 59–60.

———. "Numbing the Audience." In Denby, *Film 70/71*, 286–295.

———. "The Street Western." Review of *Walking Tall*, directed by Phil Karlson. *New Yorker*, February 25, 1974, 100–106.

———. "Tramont's Mirror, Women à la Mode." Reviews of *All Night Long*, directed by Jean-Claude Tramont, *Caddie*, directed by Donald Crombie, *The Incredible Shrinking Woman*, directed by Joel Schumacher, and *9 to 5*, directed by Colin Higgins, *New Yorker*, March 9, 1981, 104–113.

Kanfer, Stefan. "Supergypsy." Review of *Five Easy Pieces*, directed by Bob Rafelson. *Time*, September 14, 1970, 89.

Kaplan, E. Ann. "Forms of Phallic Domination in the Contemporary Hollywood Film: Brooks's *Looking for Mr. Goodbar*." In *Women & Film: Both Sides of the Camera*, 73–82. New York: Routledge, 1983.

Kauffman, Stanley. "Fair to Meddling." Review of *The Candidate*, directed by Michael Ritchie, *Deliverance*, directed by John Boorman, and *Portnoy's Complaint*, directed by Ernest Lehman. *New Republic*, August 5 & 12, 1972, 24.

———. Review of *Five Easy Pieces*, directed by Bob Rafelson. *New Republic*, September 26, 1970, 21.

———. "Local Colors." Reviews of *Saturday Night Fever*, directed by John Badham, and *Blue Collar*, directed by Paul Schrader. *New Republic*, February 11, 1978, 24–25.

———. "Old But New, New But Old." Reviews of *Let There Be Light*, directed by John Huston, and *9 to 5*, directed by Colin Higgins. *New Republic*, January 31, 1981, 20–21.

———. "Three of a Kind, Sort of." Reviews of *Conrack*, directed by Martin Ritt, *Walking Tall*, directed by Phil Karlson, and *Blazing Saddles*, directed by Mel Brooks. *New Republic*, March 16, 1974, 20.

———. "Well-Organized Labor." Review of *Norma Rae*, directed by Martin Ritt, *New Republic*, March 17, 1979, 24–25.

———. Review of *White Line Fever*, directed by Jonathan Kaplan. *New Republic*, September 27, 1975, 52–53.

Kaufman, Dave. "Coast Unemployment Gloom: Inventory High; O'seas a Factor." *Variety*, July 9, 1969, 7.

———. "Creaky Rules & Featherbeds: Coast Crafts' Self-Appraisal." *Variety*, February 18, 1970, 3.

———. "IATSE Sues on Non-Union Films Pickup." *Variety*, July 17, 1974, 5.

Kazin, Michael. *The Populist Persuasion*. New York: BasicBooks, 1995.

Kermode, Mark. "Cruise Control." *Sight and Sound* 8.11 (Nov. 1998): 22–24.

"The Kids at Cannon." *Time*, August 31, 1970, 60.

Klemesrud, Judy. "His Happiness is a Thing Called *Joe*." *New York Times*, Aug. 2, 1970, late ed., sec. 2, 9.

Klinger, Barbara. "Film History Terminable and Interminable: Recovering the Past in Reception Studies." *Screen* 38.2 (Summer 1997): 107–128.

———. *Melodrama and Meaning: History, Culture, and the Films of Douglas Sirk*. Bloomington: Indiana University Press, 1994.

Klinkenborg, Verlyn. "The Roughneck." *New York Times Magazine*, September 30, 2001, 24.

Knebel, Fletcher. "Hollywood: Broke—and Getting Rich." *Look*, November 3, 1970, 50–52.

Kramer, Peter. "Post-Classical Hollywood." In *The Oxford Guide to Film Studies*. Edited by John Hill and Pamela Church Gibson, 289–309. New York: Oxford University Press, 1998.

Kraszewski, Jon. "Recontextualizing the Historical Reception of Blaxploitation: Articulations of Class, Black Nationalism, and Anxiety in the Genre's Advertisements." *Velvet Light Trap* 50 (Fall 2002): 48–61.

Kremen, Bennett. "No Pride in this Dust: Young Workers in the Steel Mills." In *The World of the Blue-Collar Worker*. Edited by Irving Howe, 11–22. New York: Quadrangle, 1972.

Kroll, Jack. "Nightcrawl." Review of *Looking for Mr. Goodbar*, directed by Richard Brooks. *Newsweek*, October 24, 1977, 126.

Laclau, Ernesto. *Politics and Ideology in Marxist Theory: Capitalism, Fascism, Populism*. London: New Left Books, 1977.

Leader editorial. *New York Times*, May 9, 1970, late ed., 24.

Leifermann, Henry P. "Trouble in the South's First Industry: The Unions are Coming." *New York Times Magazine*, August 5, 1973, 10–11.

Levine, Martin P. *Gay Macho: The Life and Death of the Homosexual Clone*. Edited by Michael S. Kimmel. New York: New York University Press, 1998.

Levitt, Len. "'Don't Get Me Wrong.'" *Time*, May 25, 1970, 21.

Levy, Peter B. *The New Left and Labor in the 1960s*. Chicago: University of Illinois Press, 1994.

Lewis, Jon, ed. *The New American Cinema*. Durham, N.C.: Duke University Press, 1998.

Liss, Rebecca. "Oliver Stone's *World Trade Center* Fiction: How the Rescue Really Happened." *Slate*, August 9, 2006. Accessed September 1, 2007, http://www.slate.com/id/2147350/.

Logan, Andy. "Around City Hall." *New Yorker*, June 6, 1970, 104–108.

Looking for Mr. Goodbar. Directed by Richard Brooks. Paramount, 1977.

Lott, Eric. *Love and Theft: Blackface Minstrelsy and the American Working Class*. New York: Oxford University Press, 1993.

MacCabe, Colin. "Realism and the Cinema: Notes on Some Brechtian Theses." *Screen* 15:2 (Autumn 1974): 7–27.

Madsen, Axel. *The New Hollywood: American Movies in the '70s*. New York: Thomas Y. Crowell, 1975.

Maltby, Richard. "'Nobody Knows Everything': Post-classical Historiographies and Consolidated Entertainment." In *Contemporary Hollywood Cinema*. Edited by Steve Neale and Murray Smith, 21–44. New York: Routledge, 1998.

"Man and Woman of the Year: The Middle Americans." *Time*, January 5, 1970, 10–17.

Mariani, John. "Richard Brooks Directs *Looking for Mr. Goodbar*." *Millimeter* July/Aug. 1977: 24–30.

Maslin, Janet. "Friedkin Defends His *Cruising*." *New York Times*, September 18, 1979, late ed., C12.

Maurer, Harry. "Organizing the 'Gypsies.'" *Nation*, January 11, 1975, 10–15.

McMurray, Emily J., ed. *Contemporary Theatre, Film and Television*. Vol. 10. Detroit: Gale Research, 1993.

McRobbie, Angela. "Settling Accounts with Subcultures: A Feminist Critique." *Screen Education* 34 (1980): 37–49.

Mellen, Joan. "The Return of Women to Seventies Films." *Quarterly Review of Film Studies* 3.4 (Fall 1978): 525–543.

Michener, Charles. "Keep on Truckin'." Review of *White Line Fever*, directed by Jonathan Kaplan. *Newsweek*, September 1, 1975, 61.

Miller, D. A. *Bringing Out Roland Barthes*. Berkeley: University of California Press, 1992.

Mills, Nicolaus. "Engaging Norma Rae: A Journal." *Dissent* 26 (Fall 1979): 480–83.

——. "The Unions and the Mobs." *Dissent* 26.1 (Winter 1979): 97–100.

Mohl, Raymond A., ed. *Searching for the Sunbelt: Historical Perspectives on a Region*. Knoxville: University of Tennessee Press, 1990.

Monaco, James. *American Film Now: The People, The Power, The Money, The Movies*. New York: New American, 1979.

Moody, Kim. *An Injury to All: The Decline of American Unionism*. New York: Verso, 1988.

Morgenstern, Joseph. "Easy Piece, Hard Piece." *Newsweek*, December 21, 1970, 14.

——. "Hollywood: Myth, Fact and Trouble." *Newsweek*, June 30, 1969, 82–87.

Morris, Meaghan. "Banality in Cultural Studies." In *Logics of Television: Essays in Cultural Criticism*. Edited by Patricia Mellencamp, 14–43. Bloomington: Indiana University Press, 1990.

Mulvey, Laura. "Visual Pleasure and Narrative Cinema." In *Visual and Other Pleasures*, 14–26. Bloomington: Indiana University Press, 1989.

"Murf." Review of *Deliverance*, directed by John Boorman. *Variety*, July 19, 1972, 14.

———. Review of *White Line Fever*, directed by Jonathan Kaplan. *Variety*, July 16, 1975, 21.

Murphy, A. D. "Students: Stay Out of Hollywood." *New York Times*, August 18, 1968, late ed., sec.2, 13.

Murphy, Reg. "Is *Deliverance* Good for Atlanta?" *Atlanta Constitution*, April 29, 1972, 4A.

———. "Not Since Jefferson and Madison…" *Saturday Review*, September 4, 1976, 8–11.

Neale, Steve. *Genre and Hollywood*. New York: Routledge, 2000.

———. "New Hollywood Cinema." *Screen* 17.2 (1976): 117–122.

Neale, Steve, and Murray Smith, eds. *Contemporary Hollywood Cinema*. New York: Routledge, 1998.

"New Day A'Coming in the South." *Time*, May 31, 1971, 14–20.

"The New Highway Guerrillas." *Time*, December 17, 1973, 33.

"New Kind of Movie Shakes Hollywood." *Business Week*, January 3, 1970, 40–45.

"The New Movies." *Newsweek*, December 7, 1970, 62–64.

Nichols, Bill. "*Strike* and the Question of Class." In *The Hidden Foundation: Cinema and the Question of Class*. Edited by David E. James and Rick Berg, 72–89. Minneapolis: University of Minnesota Press, 1996.

9 to 5. Directed by Colin Higgins. Twentieth Century Fox, 1980.

Nordheimer, Jon. "Sunbelt Region Leads Nation in Growth of Population: Area Spans Southern Half of Country." *New York Times*, February 8, 1976, late ed., 1.

Norma Rae. Directed by Martin Ritt. Twentieth Century Fox, 1979.

"North Carolina, Owensby Reject SAG's Dictate." *Variety*, September 28, 1977, 2.

Nowell-Smith, Geoffrey. "Minnelli and Melodrama." In *Home is Where the Heart is: Studies in Melodrama and the Woman's Film*. Edited by Christine Gledhill, 70–74. London: British Film Institute, 1987.

"Nuisance—or a Boon? The Spread of Citizens' Radios." *U.S. News & World Report*, September 29, 1975, 26–28.

Nussbaum, Bruce. "Real Masters of the Universe." *Business Week*, October 1, 2001, 55.

Nussbaum, Karen. Interview, "Women Clerical Workers and Trade Unionism." *Socialist Review* 10.1 (Jan.–Feb. 1980): 157.

———. "Working Women's Insurgent Consciousness." In *The Sex of Class: Women Transforming American Labor*. Edited by Dorothy Sue Cobble, 159–176. Ithaca, N.Y.: Cornell University Press, 2007.

"Okay Half Wages, Under 50G Budget." *Variety*, August 20, 1969, 5.

Omi, Michael. "Race Relations in *Blue Collar*." *Jump Cut* 26 (Dec. 1981): 7–8.

Omi, Michael, and Howard Winant. *Racial Formation in the United States: From the 1960s to the 1990s*, 2nd ed. New York: Routledge, 1994.

Orth, Maureen. "Get Up and Boogie!" *Newsweek*, November 8, 1976, 94–98.

Owensby, Earl. "North Carolina's 'Hollywood'; Producer Acts As His Own Star; 11 Films To Date, None in Red." *Variety*, January 3, 1979, 36.

"Payoff for Terror on the Road." *Time*, February 18, 1974, 36.

Pechter, William S. "Three Easy Pieces." Reviews of *Five Easy Pieces*, directed by Bob Rafelson, *WUSA*, directed by Stuart Rosenberg, and *Joe*, directed by John G. Avildsen. *Commentary*, January 1971, 92–94.

"Pic Labor Loses 'Option' As To Over-Time." *Variety*, May 24, 1978, 7.

Pollock, Dale. *Skywalking: The Life and Films of George Lucas*. New York: Harmony, 1983.

Pryor, Thomas M. "Hollywood's Muted 1975; U.S. Feature Statistics Hidden, In Part, By Non-Union Films." *Variety*, January 7, 1976, 14.

Przeworski, Adam. *Capitalism and Social Democracy*. New York: Cambridge University Press, 1985.

Pye, Michael, and Linda Myles. *The Movie Brats: How the Film Generation Took Over Hollywood*. New York: Holt, Rinehart and Winston, 1979.

Ray, Robert. *A Certain Tendency of the Hollywood Cinema, 1930–1980*. Princeton, N.J.: Princeton University Press: 1985.

Rein, Marcy. Review of *Norma Rae*, directed by Martin Ritt. *off our backs*, April 30, 1979, 23.

Rich, Frank. "Cop-Out in a Dark Demimonde." Review of *Cruising*, directed by William Friedkin. *Time*, February 18, 1980, 67.

——. "Diane in the Rough." Review of *Looking for Mr. Goodbar*, directed by Richard Brooks. *Time*, October 24, 1977, 104.

——. "Discomania." Review of *Saturday Night Fever*, directed by John Badham. *Time*, December 19, 1977, 69–70.

"A Right to 'Stop' Work in Mid-Filming?" *Variety*, March 8, 1978, 7.

Robinson, Sally. *Marked Med: White Masculinity in Crisis*. New York: Columbia University Press, 2000.

Rocky. Directed by John G. Avildsen. United Artists, 1976.

Roediger, David. *Towards the Abolition of Whiteness*. New York: Verso, 1994.

Rogin, Richard. "Joe Kelly Has Reached His Boiling Point." *New York Times Magazine*, June 28, 1970, 12–24.

Rorty, Richard. *Achieving Our Country: Leftist Thought in Twentieth Century America*. Cambridge, Mass.: Harvard University Press, 2000.

Rose, Frank. "Travolta Puts Out." *Village Voice*, December 19, 1977, 49–50.

Rosen, Philip, ed. *Narrative, Apparatus, Ideology*. New York: Columbia University Press, 1986.

Ross, Steven J. "Beyond the Screen: History, Class, and the Movies." In *The Hidden Foundation: Cinema and the Question of Class*. Edited by David E. James and Rick Berg, 26–55. Minneapolis: University of Minnesota Press, 1996.

——. *Working-Class Hollywood: Silent Film and the Shaping of Class in America*. Princeton, N.J.: Princeton University Press, 1998.

Russo, Vito. "*Cruising*: The Controversy Continues." *New York*, August 13–20, 1979, 46–49.

Sale, Kirkpatrick. *Power Shift: The Rise of the Southern Rim and Its Challenge to the Eastern Establishment*. New York, Random House: 1975.

Sarris, Andrew. "Ethnic Fever." Review of *Saturday Night Fever*, directed by John Badham. *Village Voice*, December 26, 1977, 41.

———. "Heaven Praise the Working Girl." Review of *Norma Rae*, directed by Martin Ritt. *Village Voice*, March 5, 1979, 39.

———. "Off the Assembly Line: One Lemon, One Authentic Model." Reviews of *The Betsy*, directed by Daniel Petrie, and *Blue Collar*, directed by Paul Schrader. *Village Voice*, February 27, 1978, 32–33.

———. "The Silly Season." Reviews of *9 to 5*, directed by Colin Higgins, and *The Mirror Crack'd*, directed by Guy Hamilton. *Village Voice*, December 24, 1980, 41.

Saturday Night Fever. Directed by John Badham. Paramount, 1977.

"Saving the New." *Time*, September 27, 1976, 68–71.

Savran, David. *Taking It Like a Man: White Masculinity, Masochism, and Contemporary American Culture*. Princeton, N.J.: Princeton University Press, 1998.

Schatz, Thomas. "The New Hollywood." In *Film Theory Goes to the Movies*. Edited Jim Collins, Hilary Radner, and Ava Preacher Collins, 8–36. New York: Routledge, 1993.

———. "The Western." In *Handbook of American Film Genres*. Edited by Wes D. Gehring, 25–46. New York: Greenwood, 1988.

Schickel, Richard. "Dirty Eleven." Review of *The Longest Yard*, directed by Robert Aldrich. *Time*, September 23, 1974, 6.

———. "Fun on the Farm." Review of *Smokey and the Bandit*, directed by Hal Needham. *Time*, June 20, 1977, 73.

———. "A Man's Journey Into His Past." Review of *Five Easy Pieces*, directed by Bob Rafelson. *Life*, September 18, 1970, 16.

———. "The Movies Are Now High Art." *New York Times Magazine*, January 5, 1969, 32–44.

———. "Strike Busting." Review of *Norma Rae*, directed by Martin Ritt. *Time*, March 12, 1979, 76.

———. "Union Dues." Review of *Blue Collar*, directed by Paul Schrader. *Time*, February 13, 1978, 66.

———. "White Trash." Review of *Gator*, directed by Burt Reynolds. *Time*, September 20, 1976, 80–83.

———. "White Water, Black Doings." Review of *Deliverance*, directed by John Boorman. *Life*, August 8, 1972, 8.

"Screen Actors Guild Moves for Withdrawals from Non-Union 'Swope.'" *Variety*, October 23, 1968, 16.

Sedgwick, Eve Kosofsky. *The Epistemology of the Closet*. Berkeley: University of California Press, 1990.

Segaloff, Nat. *Hurricane Billy: The Stormy Life and Films of William Friedkin*. New York: William Morrow and Co., 1990.

Segers, Frank. "IATSE's Year of Challenges and Revisions." *Variety*, January 8, 1975, 7.

———. "*Walking Tall* Fresh Proof A Distrib Should Resist 'Drop-Dead' Psychology." *Variety*, August 1, 1973, 16.

Seigel, Jessica. "Firefighter Chic." *Village Voice*, November 6, 2001, 49–51.

Setlowe, Rick. "Flee Dixie's 'Intimidation': Find 'Ole South' in California." *Variety*, March 4, 1970, 3.

Shabecoff, Philip. "Explosion in Worker's Demands: Labor Sees Decline in 'Real' Wages as Trigger." *New York Times*, December 30, 1973, late ed., sec. 3, 11.

Shepard, Richard F. "Effect of TV on Moviegoing Is Examined." *New York Times*, November 24, 1971, late ed., 20.

Simon, John. "Double Whammy." Review of *Looking for Mr. Goodbar*, directed by Richard Brooks. *National Review*, December 9, 1977, 1443–44.

——. Review of *Five Easy Pieces*, directed by Bob Rafelson. In Denby, *Film 70/71*, 40–43.

Sklar, Robert. *Movie-Made America: A Cultural History of American Movies*, rev. ed. New York: Vintage, 1994.

Smith, Lee. "Hard Times Come to Steeltown." *Fortune*, December 1977, 87–93.

Smith, Murray. "Theses on the Philosophy of Hollywood History." In *Contemporary Hollywood Cinema*, edited by Steve Neale and Murray Smith, 3–20. New York: Routledge, 1998.

Smokey and the Bandit. Directed by Hal Needham. Universal, 1977.

The South as the New America. Spec. issue of *Saturday Review*, September 4, 1976, 1–68.

"The South Today." *Time*, September 27, 1976, 29.

Southern, Jacquelyn. "Blue Collar, White Collar: Deconstructing Classification." In *Class and Its Others*. Edited by J. K. Gibson-Graham, Stephen A. Resnick, and Richard D. Wolff, 191–224. Minneapolis: University of Minnesota Press, 2000.

Sragow, Michael. "Small Triumphs Over the Formula." Reviews of *9 to 5*, directed by Colin Higgins, *Inside Moves*, directed by Richard Donner, *Altered States*, directed by Ken Russell, and *The Idolmaker*, directed by Taylor Hackford. *Rolling Stone*, February 5, 1981, 37.

Stacey, Jackie. *Star Gazing: Hollywood Cinema and Female Spectatorship*. New York: Routledge, 1994.

Staiger, Janet. *Interpreting Films: Studies in the Historical Reception of the American Cinema*. Princeton, N.J.: Princeton University Press, 1992.

Stallybrass, Peter, and Allon White. *The Politics and Poetics of Transgression*. Ithaca, N.Y.: Cornell University Press, 1986.

Stein, Judith. *Running Steel, Running America*. Chapel Hill, N.C.: University of North Carolina Press, 1998.

Sterba, James B. "Houston, as Energy Capital, Sets Pace in Sunbelt Boom." *New York Times*, February 9, 1976, late ed., 24.

Stern, Jane. *Trucker: A Portrait of the Last American Cowboy*. New York: McGraw-Hill, 1975.

Steven, Peter, ed. *Jump Cut: Hollywood, Politics, and Counter-Cinema*. New York: Praeger, 1985.

Stoltenberg, John. "Sadomasochism: Eroticized Violence, Eroticized Powerlessness." In *Against Sadomasochism: A Radical Feminist Analysis*. Edited by Robin Ruth Linden et al., 124–130. East Palo Alto, Calif.: Frog in the Well, 1982.

Stone, Elizabeth. "'Norma Rae': The Story They Could Have Told." *Ms.*, May 1979, 28–33.

Storper, Michael, and Susan Christopherson. "The Effects of Flexible Specialization on Industrial Politics and the Labor Market: The Motion Picture Industry." *Industrial and Labor Relations Review* 42.3 (April 1989): 331–347.

———. "Flexible Specialization and Regional Industrial Agglomerations: The Case of the U.S. Motion Picture Industry." *Annals of the Association of American Geographers* 77.1 (Mar. 1987): 104–117.

———. "The Transition to Flexible Specialization in the U.S. Film Industry: External Economies, the Division of Labor, and the Crossing of Industrial Divides." *Cambridge Journal of Economics* 13 (June 1989): 273–305.

Suarez, Ernest. "*Deliverance*: Dickey's Original Screenplay." *The Southern Quarterly* 33.2–3 (Winter/Spring 1995): 161–69.

Suárez, Juan A. *Bike Boys, Drag Queens, and Superstars: Avant-Garde, Mass Culture, and Gay Identities in the 1960s Underground Cinema.* Bloomington: Indiana University Press, 1996.

"The Sudden Rising of the Hardhats." *Time*, May 25, 1970, 20–21.

Symons, Donald. *The Evolution of Human Sexuality.* New York: Oxford University Press, 1979.

Tasker, Yvonne. "Approaches to the New Hollywood." In *Cultural Studies and Communications.* Edited by James Curran, David Morley, and Valerie Walkerdine, 213–228. New York: Arnold, 1996.

Taxi Driver. Directed by Martin Scorsese. Columbia, 1976.

Taylor, Jenny and David Laing. "Disco-Pleasure-Discourse: On 'Rock and Sexuality.'" *Screen Education* 31 (Summer 1979): 43–48.

"Teamsters Hit 'Location Lure.'" *Variety*, January 2, 1974, 5.

Terzian, Philip. "Polyester Dreams." *Harper's*, May 1978, 88–89.

"The Things Workers Say About the IATSE." *Television*, December 1967, 49.

Thompson, Richard. "Screenwriter: *Taxi Driver*'s Paul Schrader." *Film Comment* 12.2 (Mar./Apr. 1976): 6–19.

———. "What's Your 10–20?" *Film Comment* 16.4 (July/Aug. 1980): 34–42.

Thompson, Thomas. "The Crapshoot for Half a Billion." *Life*, September 10, 1971, 47–58.

Tinkcom, Matthew. *Working Like a Homosexual: Camp, Capital, Cinema.* Durham, N.C.: Duke University Press, 2002.

Toplin, Robert Brent. "*Norma Rae*: Unionism in an Age of Feminism." *Labor History* 36.2 (Spring 1995): 282–298.

"The Troubled American: A Report on the White Majority." *Newsweek*, October 6, 1969, 29–36.

Van Gelder, Lawrence. Review of *Smokey and the Bandit*, directed by Hal Needham. *New York Times*, May 20, 1977, C8.

Walking Tall. Advertisement. *Variety*, May 9, 1973, 16.

Walking Tall. Directed by Phil Karlson. Cinerama, 1973.

Walsh, Moira. Reviews of *Fat City*, directed by John Huston, and *Deliverance*, directed by John Boorman. *America*, September 2, 1972, 126–27.

Watney, Simon. "Hollywood's Homosexual World." *Screen* 23.3–4 (Sept./Oct. 1982): 107–121.

Westerbeck, Colin L., Jr., "Women of the Year." *Commonweal*, February 3, 1978, 82–83.

Weyrich, Paul M. "Blue Collar or Blue Blood? The New Right Compared with the Old Right." In *The New Right Papers*. Edited by Robert Whitaker, 48–62. New York: St. Martin's, 1982.

"Whit." Reverend of *White Lightning*, directed by Joseph Sargent. *Variety*, June 6, 1973, 18.

White Lightning. Directed by Joseph Sargent. United Artists, 1973.

White Line Fever. Directed by Jonathan Kaplan. Columbia, 1975.

"Why Sacrifice?" *New York Times*, December 26, 1973, late ed., 38.

Williams, Linda Ruth. "Blood Brothers." *Sight and Sound* 4.9 (September 1994): 16–19.

Willson, Robert F., Jr. "*Deliverance* from Novel to Film: Where Is Our Hero?" *Literature/Film Quarterly* 2 (Winter 1974): 52–58.

Wilson, Alexander. "Friedkin's *Cruising*, Ghetto Politics, and Gay Sexuality." *Social Text* 4 (Fall 1981): 98–109.

Wolf, Jackie. "*Crystal Lee Jordan, Testimony, The Inheritance*: Filmmakers Take On J. P. Stevens." *Jump Cut* 22 (May 1980): 8.

Wollen, Peter. "Godard and Counter-Cinema: *Vent d'Est*." In *Narrative, Apparatus, Ideology*. Edited by Philip Rosen, 120–29. New York: Columbia University Press, 1986.

Wood, Robin. "The Incoherent Text: Narrative in the 70s." In *Hollywood from Vietnam to Reagan*, 46–69. New York: Columbia University Press, 1986.

Woodward, Kenneth L. "The Trucker Mystique." *Newsweek*, January 26, 1976, 44–45.

"Workers' Woodstock." *Time*, June 1, 1970, 12–13.

World Trade Center. Directed by Oliver Stone. Paramount, 2006.

Wright, Erik Olin. *Classes*. London: Verso, 1985.

———, ed. *The Debate on Classes*. New York: Verso, 1989.

———. "A General Framework for the Analysis of Class Structure." In *The Debate on Classes*. Edited by Erik Olin Wright, 3–43. New York: Verso, 1989.

———. "Rethinking, Once Again, the Concept of Class Structure." In *The Debate on Classes*. Edited by Erik Olin Wright, 269–348. New York: Verso, 1989.

Wyatt, Justin. "From Roadshowing to Saturation Release: Majors, Independents, and Marketing/Distribution Innovations." In *The New American Cinema*. Edited by Jon Lewis, 64–86. Durham, N.C.: Duke University Press, 1998.

Wyckoff, D. Daryll, and David H. Maister. *The Owner-Operator: Independent Trucker*. Lexington, Mass.: D.C. Heath and Co., 1976.

Yanc, Jeff. "'More Than A Woman': Music, Masculinity, and Male Spectacle in *Saturday Night Fever* and *Staying Alive*." *Velvet Light Trap* 38 (Fall 1996): 39–50.

Zimmerman, Paul D. "Down the Rapids." Review of *Deliverance*, directed by John Boorman. *Newsweek*, August 7, 1972, 61.

———. "Support Your Local Sheriff." *Newsweek*, October 8, 1973, 99–100.

INDEX

DATE DUE

GAYLORD   PRINTED IN U.S.A.

LaVergne, TN USA
02 September 2010
195527LV00002B/5/P

9 780195 336771